The Role of Economic Theory

RECENT ECONOMIC THOUGHT SERIES

Editor:

Warren G. Samuels
Michigan State University
East Lansing, Michigan, U.S.A.

Other books in the series:

Mercuro, N.: LAW AND ECONOMICS
Hennings, K. and Samuels, W.:
  NEOCLASSICAL ECONOMIC THEORY,
  1870 to 1930
Samuels, W.: ECONOMICS AS DISCOURSE
Lutz, M.: SOCIAL ECONOMICS
Weimer, D.: POLICY ANALYSIS AND
  ECONOMICS
Bromley, D. and Segerson, K.: THE SOCIAL
  RESPONSE TO ENVIRONMENTAL RISK
Roberts, B. and Feiner, S.: RADICAL
  ECONOMICS
Mercuro, N.: TAKING PROPERTY AND JUST
  COMPENSATION
de Marchi, N.: POST-POPPERIAN
  METHODOLOGY OF ECONOMICS
Gapinski, J.: THE ECONOMICS OF SAVING
Darity, W.: LABOR ECONOMICS: PROBLEMS
  IN ANALYZING LABOR MARKETS
Caldwell, B. and Boehm, S.: AUSTRIAN
  ECONOMICS: TENSIONS AND
  DIRECTIONS
Tool, Marc R.: INSTITUTIONAL ECONOMICS:
  THEORY, METHOD, POLICY
Babe, Robert E.: INFORMATION AND
  COMMUNICATION IN ECONOMICS
Magnusson, Lars: MERCANTILIST
  ECONOMICS
Garston, Neil: BUREAUCRACY: THREE
  PARADIGMS
Friedman, James W.: PROBLEMS OF
  COORDINATION IN ECONOMIC ACTIVITY

This series is devoted to works that present divergent views on the development, prospects, and tensions within some important research areas of international economic thought. Among the fields covered are macromonetary policy, public finance, labor and political economy. The emphasis of the series is on providing a critical, constructive view of each of these fields, as well as a forum through which leading scholars of international reputation may voice their perspectives on important related issues. Each volume in the series will be self-contained; together these volumes will provide dramatic evidence of the variety of economic thought within the scholarly community.

The Role of Economic Theory

edited by
Philip A. Klein
The Pennsylvania State University

Kluwer Academic Publishers
Boston/Dordrecht/London

Distributors for North America:
Kluwer Academic Publishers
101 Philip Drive
Assinippi Park
Norwell, Massachusetts 02061 USA

Distributors for all other countries:
Kluwer Academic Publishers Group
Distribution Centre
Post Office Box 322
3300 AH Dordrecht, THE NETHERLANDS

Library of Congress Cataloging-in-Publication Data
The Role of economic theory/edited by Philip A. Klein.
        p. cm. — (Recent economic thought series)
    ISBN 0-7923-9452-6
    1. Economics. 2. Economics—Philosophy. I. Klein, Philip A.
  II. Series.
  HB71.R63   1994
  330—dc20   93-47645
                                                              CIP

Printed on acid-free paper.

Printed in the United States of America

Contents

Contributing Authors   vii

Preface   ix

1
Introduction   1
Philip A. Klein

2
The Roles of Theory in Economics   21
Warren J. Samuels, Eclectic Institutionalist

3
Economic Theory In the Postrevolutionary Moment of the 1990s   47
James M. Buchanan, Public-Choice Economist

4
The Role of Economic Theory: Keynesian Macroeconomics   61
Lawrence R. Klein, Keynesian Economist

5
Methodology of Critical Marxian Economic Theory   77
Howard J. Sherman, Critical Marxist Economist

6
Does Economics Need Theories?   97
John F. Muth, Rational Expectations and Production Economist

7
The Multifarious Role of Theories in Economics: The Case of
Different Keynesianisms   121
Andrea Boitani and Andrea Salanti, New Post-Keynesian Economists

8
Monetarism and Its Rhetoric   159
Thomas Mayer, An Eclectic Who Has Monetarist Sympathies

9
Conceptual Economic Theory   187
Eric S. Maskin, Game Theorist

10
An Institutionalist Mode of Inquiry: Limitations of Orthodoxy   197
Marc R. Tool, Neoinstitutionalist

11
An Assessment   229
Philip A. Klein

About the Authors   249

Index   253

Contributing Authors

Andrea Boitani
Università degli Studi di Bergamo
Via Salvecchio, 19
I–24100 BERGAMO Italy

James M. Buchanan
George Mason University
4400 University Drive
Fairfax, VA 22020

Lawrence R. Klein
Wharton School
University of Pennsylvania
Philadelphia, PA 19104

Philip A. Klein
Department of Economics
Pennsylvania State University
University Park, PA 16802

Eric S. Maskin
Department of Economics
Littauer Center—Room 308
Harvard University
Cambridge, MA 02138

Thomas Mayer
3054 Buena Vista Way
Berkeley, California 94708

John F. Muth
School of Business 670
Indiana University
Tenth Street and Fee Lane
Bloomington, IN 47405

Andrea Salanti
Università degli Studi di Bergamo
Via Salvecchio, 19
I–24100 BERGAMO Italy

Warren J. Samuels
Department of Economics
Michigan State University
East Lansing, MI 48824

Howard J. Sherman
Department of Economics
University of California
Riverside, CA 92521

Marc R. Tool
Professor Emeritus of Economics
5708 McAdoo Avenue
Sacramento, CA 95819

Preface

What is the role of economic theory? Is there any common ground among economists of different schools concerning the role or roles to be played by theory? These were the basic questions in my mind when I undertook to edit a book on the subject. I thought it might prove insightful to examine the views of distinguished economists of very different persuasions and perspectives on the discipline in general. Accordingly, I invited economists from many of the major schools or groups in contemporary economics to contribute essays. Some were uninterested; some were too busy; but many were more than willing to participate in the exercise. The results make up this book.

I knew (or thought I knew) what economists who believe in interventionist policy were going to say, but I was unsure what other economists would say. I found the diversity in the replies, as well as some unexpected agreement, to be thought-provoking. I learned from all the participants.

I wish to thank Warren Samuels, who originally invited me to edit a book in his series for Kluwer, and Marc Tool, who gave much needed advice and counsel along the way. They both have my thanks for their assistance to me. I thank my colleague, Michael Baye, for his help.

My greatest debt, of course, is to the ten economists who produced the nine essays that comprise this book. All have my gratitude for producing views that I would expect the profession at large will find interesting and challenging. I thank, too, their secretaries, for their unfailingly prompt assistance in processing the papers. At Penn State the work on the volume was handled first by Mrs. Elizabeth Reeser and then by Mrs. Nancy Cole. They both have my thanks.

Philip A. Klein

University Park, PA

1 INTRODUCTION: THE ROLE OF ECONOMIC THEORY

Philip A. Klein

The contributors to this volume all received the same assignment: to define *economic theory* in a way that is meaningful to the economist producing the definition and then to consider the role of theory, so viewed.

The replies are remarkable in their diversity. Several chose to consider the question in the broadest possible way: what range can be given for definitions of economic theory, within that range, how can economic theory definitions be classified? The approach to theory employed in organizing this book had to do primarily with the basic economic theories developed by the major schools of thought, and the level of generality chosen by contributors has been at this fairly fundamental level.

Design of the Book

One of our objectives initially was to gather as disparate a group of economists as possible. In a recent volume Edmund S. Phelps (1990) considers seven schools of macroeconomic thought alone. We cannot here cover all schools of modern economic thought in that degree of detail, but we are satisfied that enough are included to consider the basic question, "What are the possible roles each sees for theory?" We also consider, insofar as possible, the factors that influence the way economists view the role of theory.

Economists representing different schools of thought would be expected to define *economic theory* in different ways. Of initial interest was the question of how these differences would manifest themselves in the role that each assigned to economic theory.

A useful perspective from which to assesses the analyses in this book is to divide economists broadly into those who believe that government intervention can improve economic performance and those who believe that in general "leaving it to the market" is the prudent course both for the macroeconomy and the microeconomy. One might expect the interventionists to find the role for theory to lie in improving public policy. An interesting aspect of these essays is how many roles for economic theory are delineated by noninterventionists.

Another initial question that is relevant to interventionists and possibly to noninterventionists involves the distinction between basic theory and applied theory. For interventionists, the question becomes, "How indirectly may theory find policy applications before it is declared too abstract to be useful?" For noninterventionists the same question may be, "How far removed from economic reality may pure theory be and still be useful in understanding the economy?"

Ultimately we wrestle with the age-old question of whether economic theory is normative, positive, or something else. We need to ask in some cases whether a given economist's policy views are the result of positive theory or part of a value structure that affects both theory and policy views. Did the conviction that economic theory is positive finally put to rest the old debate about whether economic theory could be value free? This concern led to the notion that if the same question concerning the role of economic theory were put in open-ended fashion to representatives drawn from these—and related—schools of modern economic thought, the results might be illuminating. We sought out neoclassical economists, institutionalists, radical economists, monetarists, believers in rational expectations, game theorists, public choice economists, and Keynesians. Participants represent virtually all these schools of thought. Economists were invited to participate *because* of their diversity and were not preinstructed in how they must define *economic theory*. While all schools are not represented, particularly if the definition of schools is narrowly drawn, a diverse group certainly is.

The Role of Economic Theory: Nine Diverse Responses

The results have indeed been revealing. An appropriate place to begin is with Warren Samuels's detailed consideration of the possible roles that might be played by economic theory. Samuels exemplifies a broad approach in contrast to the more narrow focus of some of the later essays. He has chosen to be as inclusive as possible, rather than to select a particular type of theory and consider what its role might be. He begins by contemplating factors that complicate any effort at consideration of the roles of theory, such as the well-known dualisms that many of the later essays touch on as well. A major dualism involves the old problem of normative versus positive theory, already mentioned. Samuels notes that both types can be contemplated in economics but that theories often involve both and that economists typically think they are being positive when it is by no means clear that the result bears out their view. Other dualisms include the theory-fact distinction and the differing roles of induction and deduction in constructing theory.

In the first part of his chapter he considers the nature of theory, distinguishing theory from related notions—model, paradigm, and concept. Carefully differentiating validity, truth, desirability, and workability as they apply to theory, he then contemplates the part played in theory by the dichotomization of normative and positive, fact and theory, and induction and deduction. He contemplates the levels of theory, the purpose of theory, the types of theory found in economics, and the tautological character of theory.

When he focuses on the role of theory, he finds that there are many possible roles for theory to play. In addition to the generally mentioned roles of theory in explaining or helping us to understand phenomena of concern, he notes that theories may be used to describe, predict, develop hypotheses, test hypothesis, offer a conception of reality, or provide a sense of economic order. They may be used for heuristic purposes, as tools of analysis, or to play discursive or rhetorical roles. In connection with the rhetorical role for theory, Samuels suggests that theory can be used to systematize ideas, as a framework for discussion, as an organizing principle, or as mode of concentrating attention.

Another role for theory Samuels calls attention to is to facilitate manageability—such as the use of ceteris paribus assumptions. Other possible roles for theory would include as an element in a logical or epistemological structure, as prescription, as the basis of social construction of reality, or as the basis of legitimation or criticism. Theory may play a role in economics as vehicle for permitting ideology, wishful thinking, or paradigms to enter analysis. Theory may be used as a means of projection, for social control, or as psychic balm. Yet another role for theory is to tell a story that gives coherence to interrelated phenomena involving fact, theory, and values. He reminds us that theory has at least since Marshall been used to give economics the status of science.

Samuels concludes that his perspective—that theory in economics plays multiple roles—leads to the conclusion that "there is more to the world than can be encompassed within any particular theory, even the theory ... that there are multiple roles of theory."

In sum, for Samuels the possible roles are not confined to testing hypotheses developed by economists but find their origins and their justifications in political science, psychology, sociology, and aesthetics. Samuels reminds us that for many the term *economic theory* is properly applied only to neoclassical microeconomics (the crown jewel in economic theory). For others there are theories in macroeconomics, growth theory, welfare economics—in short, in every type of economic analysis. The level of generality and the structure, the relation to both reality and public policy— all these vary very much over the entire range of areas that have been subjected to economic theorizing. All these are possible if one grants Samuels's basic premise—that "there are multiple roles for theory" in economics.

One might conclude that economists' views might be similar if they could agree that the empirical record is the appropriate arbiter of otherwise abstruse debates, and that at least this would bespeak similarity in the views of the role of economic theory. Such is not the case. Consider the papers of James M. Buchanan and Lawrence R. Klein. Both agree that appeal to the empirical record is definitive. There agreement ends.

James Buchanan, cofounder (with Gordon Tullock) of the public-choice school of economic thought, presumably surveying the same history and record, concludes that experience has led citizens around the world generally to lose "the romance that collectivism-politicization might once have held" and that therefore the miracle of the market, warts and all, offers promise.

Buchanan asks why economists generally failed to predict socialism's failure and suggests that it was a mistaken view of the functioning of "an economy." Economists traditionally viewed the economy as a "maximizing paradigm," Buchanan argues. This, one presumes, led to a wrong-headed concern with objectives and the fatal effort to interfere with the operation of the economy by the use of ill-considered policy instruments; this is the hallmark of modern economists' failure as viewed by public-choice economists. Buchanan suggests that a "scientifically superior" way to view the economy and its functioning would be as a "spontaneous order." Such an economy operates automatically, thereby reducing the need for interventionist policy. By considering the modern economy from a perspective much closer to that originally taken by Adam Smith, the economy as a spontaneous order is one in which contemplation of the role of economic theory is correspondingly considerably less complex. Thus asking the objectives of the economy is not unlike asking the objectives of a perpetual motion machine. This is the essence of the noninterventionist position. The economy as an allocating mechanism, when viewed as public-choice economists view it—as a "miracle"—does not need guidance to produce the best possible allocative results. This position differs only in degree from that of most economists, who would agree that what the market accomplishes is a miracle but not so perfect a miracle as to avoid the need for all societal monitoring and any adjustment by governmental fiat. In general we may say that the debate about intervention involves two separate questions. To the first—"Left to its own devices, how acceptable is the resource allocation produced in the market?"—Buchanan, speaking for noninterventionists in general, would no doubt answer that the performance (despite warts) is acceptable. Interventionists would disagree. This could be made concrete by asking, "Is a 7 percent unemployment rate acceptable—a rate we can live with?" The answer depends on which group is replying. The second question—"Regardless of one's answer to the first question, can performance be improved by intervention?"—public-choice economists for a variety of reasons would answer in the negative. Interventionists would tend to answer in the affirmative.

At bottom, therefore, Buchanan charges most economists with regarding the economy from the perspective of the wrong paradigm. Buchanan argues that the failure of economists, especially Keynesians, to view the economy in his terms produced disastrous policy results when the depression shifted economists' attention from the microeconomy to the macroeconomy. He argues that the aggregates that "Keynes and the Keynesians provided with quasi-scientific status" have resulted in misguided interpretations and unfortunate interventionist policies. Economic theory should stick to "the domain of exchange relationships." He worries that "the management-economizing conception of economics, and especially as extended normatively to policy prescription, may not have been sufficiently exorcised." He concludes that input-output analysis is first on his list of "programs [that] offer little or no promise" for the future.

Lawrence Klein focuses on modern macroeconomic theory and, as noted earlier, comes to conclusions totally at variance with Buchanan's. He begins by tracing the development of Keynesian theory, suggesting that even Smith used macroeconomic reasoning. More immediately Frisch, Tinbergen, and Kalecki were all predecessors of Keynes who developed simultaneous equation systems of the macroeconomy. The significance of Klein's assertion lies partly in his view that Keynes's theory was very important but was only a stage in the development of macroeconomic theory. Subsequent developments do not prove that "the starting point is not right." Rather, building on solid foundations to get ever better approximations of reality in theory is the normal course to be expected.

It is clear that the relation of theory to reality is crucial to Klein because of his conviction that theory grows out of problems in the real world and is devoted to improving the derived policy with which we confront these problems. He reminds us that the difficulties faced by Germany in the 1920s, the world speculation of the 1920s, the growth of protectionism, and the massive unemployment of the Great Depression led to the development of Keynesinan theory. Thus, for Klein theory is derived from "the search for justifiable policies."

Klein notes that Keynes's theory led to an emphasis on stimulative fiscal policy but that it is an "unsophisticated interpretation" of Keynes's macroeconomics to suggest that it was simply a rationalization for public spending. It is often forgotten that in orthodox Keynesian theory the budget would be balanced or in surplus in recovery phases of the cycle.

Klein reminds us that Keynesian theory rested on three pillars—the propensity to consume, the marginal efficiency of capital, and the liquidity-preference function. After Keynes there were pedagogical improvements in the theory by Hicks and Lange. But there were important theoretical extensions as well—to make the theory open (by introducing variables dealing explicitly with international relations) and to accommodate growth in capital stock by lengthening the time horizon as is required in truly dynamic theory (which Keynes was not).

The theory was said to be demand oriented, which it was only partially. In any case, the supply side was fleshed out by including production functions and the supply and demand for labor. The latter included more explicit attention to the determination of wages and nominal prices.

In this connection, Klein goes beyond Keynes in one critical area, the notion of underemployment equilibrium. Basing his work on the dropping of Keynes's assumption of money illusion, he asserts that "a theoretical argument can be made for the existence of an unemployment equilibrium." He suggests that in a dynamic system it is possible to have a solution in a dynamic system that would involve a contradiction if equilibrium (labor supply = labor demand) were introduced in the stationary system as well.

The dynamic system would be in equilibrium but with disequilibrium in the stationary labor market. He reminds us along the way of the many institutional factors that influence labor supply. Finally, he reminds us that the Phillips curve, properly interpreted, is not a labor supply equation, but a market-adjustment equation. As commonly interpreted it abstracts from critical factors such as labor productivity.

Attention to production functions and optimization led to what Klein calls the Keynesian-neoclassical synthesis, in which Klein reminds us that in spite of the innovative aspects of Keynes's theory, he was trained as a neoclassical theorist and never developed any other approach to the microeconomy.

Klein, by reviewing the development of Keynes's theory, underscores that in his view theory is always developed and judged against the backdrop of reality and in the case of macroeconomic theory it can be tested by its forecasting ability. As such he asserts that the forty-year history of the Michigan model represents the longest record of continuous success in forecasting of any theory with which he is familiar. He specifically argues that modern Keynesian economics has been more successful than monetarism, supply-side economics, or "complete deregulation into free-market decisions."

For the future he suggests that macroeconomic theory needs to encompass more explicitly expectations, although he suggests that expectations have always been part of Keynesian macroeconomics, particularly in Keynesian econometric models. Still more can be done to include expectations (in the form of surveys) in models as endogenous variables. Second, he suggests specific attention to building futures data into macroeconomic theory. He argues that building flow-of-fund accounting or capital flows into Keynesian macroeconomic models would be useful—introducing wealth into the consumption function, cash balances into the portfolio analysis, and commercial trade flows into balance-of-payments analysis. He suggests that full integration of the national income and product accounts with the flow-of-funds accounting would be a breakthrough.

Klein has other ideas, but ultimately they are all designed to make macroeconomic theory a more accurate and complete reflection of the reality that is the macroeconomy. Along the same lines, he suggests making macroeconomic theory "green"—by including variables to cover the costs of protecting all significant aspects of the environment. Finally, disagreeing with Buchanan, he points to input-output analysis as promising for future research.

And so in the end Klein asserts that "noninterventionist policies have not worked well." Despite bedazzlement with monetarism, supply-side economics, and other approaches that are characterized by "poor theoretical underpinning," for the long run, the type of theory that has withstood the test of time is Keynesian. In the future it may be garbed in new clothes, but it will be "an outgrowth whose roots can definitely be traced."

Interventionism is embraced also by Howard Sherman, but in quite different form than one finds in Klein. Sherman has written an interesting essay in which he attempts to stake out the views of what he calls "critical Marxism." Sherman begins by contrasting the neoclassical approach with the official Marxist view. The neoclassical perspective in economics is individualist, ahistorical, and predicated on an assumption of harmony and insists on the separation of fact from theory and science from ethics. The official Marxist position, in contrast, is collectivist, has no role for individuals, is historically predetermined, is predicated on an assumption of total class conflict, and has a vision of a state run completely by the capitalist class.

Sherman notes that critical Marxism is unlike either. It is "relational" or "holistic" in that it is neither completely individual nor completely collectivist. It is historical, encompasses elements of both harmony and conflict, does include class conflict, combines both fact and theory, is predicated in scientific determinism, which includes both free will and predeterminism, and is an approach including both theory and facts and ethical values.

His analysis is Marxist, therefore, in the sense that class and class roles figure prominently in his approach to theory. He notes that in terms of numbers perhaps 80 or 90 percent of the people fall into the worker class (thus only 10 or 20 percent can be capitalists). Yet current classes cannot be distinguished easily because, Sherman is at pains to tell us, people can be blinded to their true class interests and so identify with the wrong class. Moreover, critical Marxists, unlike original Marxists, realize that in addition to class conflicts, many conflicts in society are based on race, gender, attitudes toward the environment, or whether one is an intellectual or not. Whether these categories are all independently determined and explained as sources of current conflict, or whether some are brought in as needed historically to explain what has happened, is difficult to say.

One distinctive aspect of Sherman's approach is his view that because of the Marxist distinction between the forces and the relations of production there is an "economic sphere" and a "social sphere." From this he comes to the conclusion that the interrelationship is essentially symbiotic: the economic structure is a function of the social structure, even as the social structure is a function of the economic structure.

Sherman considers a wide number of types of conflict and attempts to assess the role of democratic institutions in channeling conflict. He argues that in all conflict situations the critical Marxist is concerned with what the class relations are (if any) and how they might be related to class conflicts. In the case of critical Marxists these conflicts are invariably examined against the background of an evolving system. This view is similar to the evolutionary perspective of institutionalists, except that for Sherman some conflict leads to revolution, while some does not. Either way the resolution of conflict is carried out in an evolving system.

Sherman attempts to set Marxism in historical context and to distinguish essential Marxism from some of the distortions that, he argues, it suffered at the hands of Stalin. In the end, Sherman views Marx and Veblen as complementary and as both advancing what Sherman calls "scientific determinism."

When finally Sherman comes to consider the role of economic theory, he comes to the same conclusion that institutionalists and many Keynesians come to—that the normative and the positive are hopelessly intertwined— initially in the problems economists choose to theorize about. He argues that economists chose theory to conform to their paradigms—the initial hypothesis underlying this volume. He argues, then, that critical Marxists choose theory so as to support change. He argues that "critical Marxism is holistic or relational, class-oriented, historical or evolutionary, material-ist, determinist, and humanist." Many institutionalists would agree with all of this except for the reference to class. In the end, the role of theory for Sherman is not only to help us understand society but to change society. That is, the role of theory is to guide intervention.

Finally, one element of the radical position that is supportive of the views of both institutionalists and Keynesians—perhaps of all interven-tionists—is the notion that the mainstream noninterventionists' effort to differentiate normative and positive rigorously and to insist that economics must be positive is in the end an effort to narrow (or eliminate) a con-structive role for interventionism.

One school that is suspicious of interventionism, on grounds that all such efforts are likely to fail, is the rational-expectations approach. John F. Muth is, of course, best known for having written the article regarded as having launched what its supporters refer to as the "rational-expectations revolution." Few, if any, such efforts have received more attention from the economics profession in the past quarter century. Rational expectations has been credited with underscoring once again the critical role that be-liefs about the future play in the decisions underlying resource allocation in the modern economy. In his chapter Muth chooses to underscore the significance of expectations once again, this time along with inefficiency and innovation. By suggesting that the three concepts all "have significance in economics," he manages, implicitly, to suggest that contributions to economic theory can ultimately to be judged by what they can contribute to our understanding of how the economy functions. He adds that these three concepts lead in his analysis to conclusions about "modeling techniques" in economics.

In connection with expectations, Muth reviews a number of approaches to their inclusion in economic models, including rational expectations. Rational expectations is an approach that "assert[s] that expectations matter in a way that most econometric models mask."

He claims explicit economic models have significant advantages over the moving average and leading indicator approach to coping with economic expectations. Of the latter he asks, "Why is it important to predict an event that is difficult to determine after the fact?" Muth argues that one advantage of the rational-expectations approach is that it can be modified to cope with cognitive biases and lack of information.

While he dismisses some of the charges typically leveled against rational expectations (that they assume individuals have more information than they could possibly have) as either wrong or not very important, he suggests that the charge that actual behavior does not agree with the rational-expectations hypothesis must be taken seriously. Many researchers, including Muth himself, have found deviations in the behavior of businesspeople from what the hypothesis would predict. In the end, however, he suggests only that the hypothesis should be displaced "only . . . by something better."

Turning to inefficiency, Muth reviews the attempts by industrial engineers and economists, including Leibenstein (X-efficiency), to deal with the subject. He reminds us of the multiplicity of factors that can affect efficiency but focuses on effort. He reviews Adams's model, which introduced the inequity theory (an individual perceives a divergence between the relation of his outcomes to his inputs relative to a reference group) and considers techniques to cope with this, including the adjustment possibilities for the individuals who perceived it. He also reviews expectancy theory (Porter and Lawler). This theory is an effort to relate performance to rewards and suggests that the perceived relation depends on the actual relation. Muth notes that these theories are defective, unlike many learning and perception theories in psychology.

Lastly, he discusses technology, arguing that it "is possibly the most important single influence on productivity growth." He shares the view of Nelson and Winter that the conventional theory of the firm "is fundamentally incapable of explaining technological change. The important areas of growth and productivity change are outside the domain of theory." In a world where growth is regarded as critical and where, therefore, the emphasis must be placed on dynamic modeling, this is a considerable admission.

He considers the way economic theory typically deals with technology by considering three phenomena that economics customarily regards as empirical—learning curves, production functions, and substitution curves. In connection with learning curves, he suggests that economists concerned with theory have been remarkably uninterested in the relationship between experience and productivity improvement (cost reduction). He considers at some length a model of his own, based on four hypotheses concerning learning and how low-cost techniques get introduced into production systems. The model attempts to make explicit the major factors determining the rate at which productivity is improved through learning experiences.

He analyzes work on production functions beginning with the usual notion with which theory copes—finding efficient combinations of factors of production to produce specific rates of output. He analyzes carefully the effect of assuming (1) that the factors of production required for a given output are distributed independently of each other, (2) that the distribution of output, given the quantities, is independent of the inputs, (3) that the distribution of the output with given quantities is unbounded, and (4) that the distribution of output with given quantities is determined by the Cauchy-Pareto output distribution. He derives the Cobb-Douglas production function on the basis of these hypotheses.

In a final section he models the factors that affect the rate and manner of the adoption of innovation.

From his consideration of expectations, inefficiency, and technology he draws some conclusions concerning what its required to constitute a good theory (such as few parameters, dynamic stability, and consistency with observable phenomena), but notes that whatever the limitations any theory is replaced only by a better theory. This would presumably justify continued reliance on a number of less than adequate theories.

He concludes, finally, that theory "explains anomalies and paradoxes," "clarifies the limits of empirical laws," "simplifies the structure of knowledge," and "unifies the different parts of economics." Significantly, however, he does not regard theory as "essential for most policy determination." For the latter, Muth claims that empirical laws have historically been adequate. Because of his engineering interests, however, his views are influenced more by the history of product and process of innovation than by public-policy formulation.

A chapter that lies, in a sense, at the opposite extreme from the Samuels paper is the contribution by Andrea Boitani and Andrea Salanti. Samuels has chosen, as we have seen, to take a broad look at the possible motives for theorizing and has, therefore, attempted to classify the entire gamut of roles that theory might play. Boitani and Salanti, on the other hand, focus on Keynesian theory (that is, the work of Keynes and his legacy) as "a case study suited to throwing some light on the ambiguities surrounding the very notion of the role of economic theory." Accordingly, they analyze in some detail the causes and consequences of the differences among modern Keynesians. They begin by noting that for Keynes "the role for economic theory is to justify economic policies of interventionist kind." They suggest that all current brands of Keynesianism "share a common distrust in the virtues of laissez faire." But here the agreement ends. They suggest that different methodological perspectives in particular affect the way different groups of Keynesians view the proper role of economic theory.

In particular, they distinguish long-run Keynesians (strand 1) and short-run Keynesians, the latter in turn being divided into strands 2 and 3. Strand 1 Keynesians, typified by Garegnani and Pasinetti, focus on the long run in how economies function. They note the paradox involved in having Keynes, who was impatient of concern with the long run, inspire so much analysis of long-run effective demand. But this was the case with strand 1. For them economic theory should eschew excessive attention to ephemeral matters in order to concentrate on those underlying relations that affect long-run growth in a production economy. Initially this requires consideration of the long-run influence of consumption on investment. Ultimate these economists are concerned with the effect of technological change on economic activity. A focus on the long run inevitably means focusing on what causes fundamental movement over time in the system.

Strand 2 (Schackle, Davidson, Weintraub, Victoria Chick, and some others) regards Keynes (as does strand 3) as eschewing the general-equilibrium approach of Marshall and stresses particularly the effect of uncertainty, motives, expectations, and technological change on choice making. This makes their notion of equilibrium more transitory than the long-run equilibrium mentioned earlier. Equilibrium is always subject to revision due to changes in the factors influencing even long-term equilibrium.

This group also attempts to factor in imperfect competition in labor markets so as to bolster the Keynesian stress on wage stickiness. They do not follow through, complete the logical circle, and include imperfect competition in goods markets, an omission that, according to Salanti and Boitani, "severely weakened . . . their claim to be a coherent alternative to the new classical economics." The task of including imperfect competition in goods markets they attribute to the third strand of post-Keynesians

(Joan Robinson, Kalecki, and others), who did indeed combine Keynes and imperfect competition theory. This strand is based on the approach taken by Kalecki. It is the school that has advanced most in considering the microfoundations of macroeconomics.

Salanti and Boitani note that while Keynes's main contributions are customarily viewed as being on the "aggregate demand" side, much recent work has been on the microfoundations of aggregate supply. In particular new Keynesians today retain much of the Walrasian approach, but the new Keynesian world differs from the Walrasian world in critical respects. New Keynesians assume that economic agents do not act in a world of perfect competition and symmetric information but in "a strategic context" that involves imperfect competition and asymmetric information.

Accordingly, modern macroeconomics can explain better than Keynes how "the economy can be stuck in Pareto-inferior unemployment equilibrium, although a Pareto-efficient full-employment equilibrium exists." (On this, however, see the views of Lawrence Klein previously considered for a contrary position.) From this basis, the authors can (and do) consider a variety of models including nominal and real rigidities, policy effectiveness, unemployment equilibrium, the effect of politics on how the economy functions, and the critical operations of the capital and credit markets in an imperfectly competitive world.

In reviewing the work of economists in the Keynesian tradition, divided into these different groups, Boitani and Salanti try to reach conclusions about a proposition originally put forth by Harcourt and Hamouda: "The important perspective to take away is . . . that there is no uniform way of tackling all issues in economics and that the various strands in post-Keynesian economics differ from one another, not least because they are concerned with different issues and often different levels of abstraction and analysis." Echoing thus the views Warren Samuels, Salanti and Boitani conclude that their own research into the diverse and varied strands of modern Keynesianism appears, in their view, broadly to support the conclusion of Harcourt and Hamouda. They would add that it emerges that the nature of the links among policy recommendations, theoretical frameworks, and methodological beliefs are more complex than is usually maintained.

As Boitani and Salanti focus on varieties of Keynesian thought, so Thomas Mayer, in a carefully thought-out essay, considers varieties of monetarist thought. He begins by sketching the state of macroeconomics in the mid-1950s when monetarism first took the modern stage. He suggests that the role of money was generally downplayed if not denigrated. Today macroeconomics mostly takes the form of formal modelling: "A

priori plausibility and concordance with common sense are treated as irrelevant for scientific economics." If concern with realism marked one
a post-Keyensian or an institutionalist, Friedman, Mayer suggests, always
approached monetary theory by appeal to the empirical record. Mayer
devotes considerable attention to Friedman's quantity theory—its rhetoric, its emphasis on empirical testing, its challenge to the prevailing
Keynesian orthodoxy. Noting that Friedman was and is essentially a
Marshallian, Mayer considers the way in which Friedman dealt with his
critics. He then turns to the specifics of the quantity theory, noting that it
focuses on equilibrium in the money market. He makes a valuable distinction between true and false theories, on the one hand, and choosing
among competing research strategies, on the other. He reviews the sources
of discrepancies in the findings among researchers in the role of money in
a careful assessment of recent work. His consideration of the possible
reasons for differences in findings and conclusions is an admirable case
study in how to evaluate theory in economics.

While Mayer is concerned with whether or not monetarism is "right"
(that is, conforms to the empirical record), he belongs to those who view
an important role for theory to be "advancing our evolving understanding."
In point of fact, he notes that monetarism was claiming more and more
adherents until the 1980s when the erratic behavior of velocity, combined
with the failure of "the monetarist experiment" in Federal Reserve policy,
caused a decline in monetarist strength. Noting that Keynesians may tend
to lump monetarists together, monetarists themselves tend to consider the
school divisible into two major branches—Friedman's Chicago version and
the Brunner-Meltzer version.

The two schools do not differ in their conclusions or in their policy
implications. In some ways many schools of thought can relate to their
views as, for example, Brunner's comment that "the denial of an established fact because we lack a theory explaining it ... impoverishes our
relevant knowledge." Unlike Friedman, they place emphasis on other wealth
variables rather than focus exclusively on the money supply. They, therefore, provide an alternative intellectual route through which to consider
the effect of monetary variables on real economic activity.

In a final section dealing with monetary policy, Mayer considers the
source of divergence in contemplating the goals of monetary policy,
the relative importance to be given to unemployment versus inflation, the
inherent stability inherent in the private sector of a market economy, the
efficacy of discretionary policy, and the factors that influence central banks
in formulating monetary policy. In each of these Mayer assesses the
position of Friedman, of Brunner and Meltzer, and of those who dispute
the monetarist position.

Ultimately he concludes that "monetarism is not a doctrine that 'only money matters.'" He argues that it is much more subtle than this common description would suggest. Moreover, monetarism has not been influential, Mayer argues, not only to the extent that economists today call themselves monetarists, but beyond that to the extent that it has influenced the thinking of many economists, monetarist and otherwise. As such Mayer has employed the monetarist experience to illustrate the role of economic theory.

Eric Maskin takes the view that much theory is neither normative not positive but is, rather, concerned with providing a set of tools with which both normative and positive questions can be answered. This third type of theory he calls "conceptual theory." His main point is that conceptual theory does not focus directly on the real world (thus is what others might label "abstract theory") and that such theory, therefore, finds its justification in its usefulness in understanding economic questions and so is relevant to the analysis of both normative and positive questions.

Conceptual theory, in Maskin's view, is thus devoted to improving the tools of economic analysis. He illustrates his argument by considering two abstract concepts from modern economic theory—signaling and perfect equilibrium. In connection with the former, he considers the case of workers who self-sort themselves according to their own view of their ability, into those who can benefit from college and those who cannot. There are costs connected with college, which get weighed against the higher salaries commanded by college graduates. The result he terms an equilibrium formed by the mutually self-sustaining behavior of the talented college-graduate worker, the untalented worker who does not go to college, and the employer. The signaling involves the information passed to the employer by the decision of the workers about college. Going to college signals talent to the employer; not going signals no talent. Maskin argues that artificial as this case is, it illustrates signaling, which is a pervasive phenomenon in modern life. Maskin notes that many papers deal with the pure theory of signaling rather than with specific applications. As such he suggests it illuminates the kind of theory he calls conceptual. The examples cited illustrate the advantages of abstract conceptual theory. A similar structure can be applied in a variety of settings; it reduces the signaling structure to the essentials, while real-world economic situations must cope with a multitude of specific factors. Further, consideration in abstract theory enables the analyst to contemplate the robustness of the properties of signaling systems (that is, what are the weakest conditions under which they could occur?). Finally, because a number of equilibria are possible, examining signaling models in the abstract is useful in determining which equilibrium are most likely.

Maskin's second illustration of the value of abstraction lies in what is called "subgame-perfect equilibrium," which is a technique applied here to a two-person game. The two agents have options, each with known payoffs. Maskin considers this game under several sets of assumptions, all illustrative of subgame-perfect equilibrium. His game preserves several realistic critical assumptions from the real world (such as self-interest on the part of the players). Maskin concludes this approach can indeed increase our insight into functioning in the real world. In the end, Maskin argues that any economic concept is useful if "it helps explain the economic world or improve it."

Marc R. Tool is an institutionalist, and his critique of the current state of economic theorizing is an excellent example of how institutionalists regard the economic-theory scene in the closing years of the twentieth century. Tool's essay is an appropriate essay with which to conclude the volume because he returns us explicitly to the original focus of the book. What is the role of economic theory? In spite of the unremittingly institutionalist character of his analysis, it is appropriate at the outset to note that he nonetheless shares much with some of the earlier essays. Tool would agree that an important role for theory is to increase our understanding of how the economy actually functions. Thus, while he asserts that ultimately the justification for theory is better policy, this does not mean that he would denigrate theorizing that has the effect of increasing our understanding of the economy but does not immediately lead to policy implications. But policy implications are integrally involved in the Tool perspective: "the purpose of inquiry is to generate causal understanding of what is observed and to utilize such analytical insights to contribute to problem resolution."

Tool begins by recalling the approach taken many years ago by John Dewey in his *Logic: The Theory of Inquiry*. Economic theory as a part of all theory is above all a mode of inquiry. This approach from the outset insists that economic theory is the mode of inquiry utilized to increase our understanding about the provisioning process as it is carried out by human beings embedded as well in social, political, and cultural settings. It is a process that as a consequence cannot be abstracted from these aspects of the larger setting within which economic activity is carried out. Tool's initial concern is to spell out fully what the implications of this approach are as applied to economic inquiry, the particular province of economic theory. The result is that Tool considers the role of hypotheses, the nature of truth, the relationship of deductive to inductive inquiry, and many other aspects of the process by which economic theory is promulgated.

Tool next contemplates the approach of neoclassical theorizing, in light of his assessment of the Dewey approach. He deplores the abstraction from the institutional setting typified by the simplifying assumptions customarily included in neoclassical theory. He suggests that one result is to raise the status quo in such theory to the level of normatively sanctioned explanation.

In the second section Professor Tool considers the nature of inquiry from the perspective of institutionalism and contrasts it with that of neoclassical economic theory. He characterizes the institutionalist approach as focusing on economic problem solving, placing economic inquiry in a societal context, and broadening the scope of inquiry to ensure that it generates causal understanding. He underscores that the character of institutionalist inquiry is purposive, evolutionary, judgmental, and provisional and that the outcome of such inquiry is what Dewey called "warranted assertions"—accretions to knowledge that are deliberative, processual, cumulative, and self-corrective. In each case Tool carefully notes the neoclassical alternative.

In a final section he contemplates the consequences of dependence on the neoclassical model of inquiry. He suggests that it underscores a role for theory that stresses predictability rather than causal understanding. For the institutionalist the latter means exploring "impairments to the provisioning process." For the institutionalist the purpose of inquiry leading to theory is understanding malfunctioning of the system so that credible policy recommendations for amelioration of such malfunctioning can be devised.

Like Klein he argues that economists need to confront—in Tool's words —"horrendous problems of malperformance." This malperformance derives from "institutional malfunctions that generate inefficient production, involuntary unemployment, macroinstability, inequality of income distribution, environmental deterioration, discriminatory denial of participation, deprivation of medical care, and the like." Significantly, no mainstream economist would ever argue that it is the task of the market, however perfectly it may function, to ameliorate all of these conditions, a number of which mainstream economics would label nonmarket. But this is precisely Tool's point. Provisioning is broader and more inclusive than market allocation. The mainstream fixation on the market is what leads to defective definition of economic problems and inadequate policy recommendations. Like several of the previous interventionists in this volume, Tool insists that theory can make no rigid normative-positive distinction that will include eschewing altogether normative considerations by the theorists.

As we have noted, an insightful aspect of Tool's analysis is his critical examination of contemporary conventional economic theory. The provisioning process, unlike resource allocation in the markets of conventional theory, needs to encompass explicit concern for such things as concentrated economic power, as well as the factors influencing the givens of conventional theory—tastes, wants, technology itself, and capitalist institutions.

All of this puts Tool squarely in the camp of the interventionists who find the justification of theory ultimately to lie in the support and guidance of policymaking.

The Views of the Contributors: A Summary

In summary, contributors answered the question—"What is the role of economic theory?"—briefly as follows:

Warren Samuels argues that economic theory can play a number of roles. The significant dimension to Samuels's perspective is the recognition that, in addition to established recognized roles such as aiding in prediction or explanation, theory can play roles best thought of as sociological or psychological—as a vehicle for ideology, social control, or wishful thinking. Accordingly, there is no simple answer to the question of the role of theory.

At the other extreme, in terms of specificity, is the view of James Buchanan: "Economic theory offers an explanation of the relationships between the interactive behavior of persons and patterns of social outcomes on the presupposition that individual action is motivated by economically meaningful and conceptually measurable self-interest." In Buchanan's hands economic theory has a role driven by explaining how markets operate. Thus in considering the role of theory, Buchanan is able to conclude that "despite the effect of public-choice theory in offering a partial understanding of political failures, we do not observe an intellectual rejection of 'socialism in the small' that is anywhere remotely comparable to the near universal rejection of 'socialism in the large' in postrevolutionary settings." It seems appropriate, therefore, to conclude that the role of economic theory for Buchanan is inextricably focused on how markets allocate resources.

Lawrence Klein focuses mostly on macroeconomics. Viewing the operation of the same markets that Buchanan sees in benign terms, Klein talks not of socialism but of "noninterventionist policies" and concludes they have not worked well: "The economies of the world have been left in an unbalanced state with large deficits, persistent unemployment, growing inequality of distribution, and a great deal of public dissatisfaction with the 'magic of the market' and inaction in the face of economic deterioration."

If we conclude that both Buchanan and Klein might agree that the role of economic theory is to provide analytical insight into how resource allocation is working in the modern world Buchanan would nonetheless conclude that the role of theory is to point to the allocational successes and Klein would say that its role is to help highlight allocational failures.

Howard Sherman argues that "the methods and tools of economics are . . . partisan and not neutral." The tool kit that some economists would argue is designed to be positive (and that Maskin finds to be neither normative nor positive) is unremittingly normative for Sherman and invariably tilted toward the status quo at that. Like several contributors to this volume, Sherman argues that the role of theory is to "understand society" but unlike noninterventionists generally, Sherman argues that a critical aspect of the role of theory also is to "change society." One must conclude that the old debate concerning whether one may analyze an economy apart from having a viewpoint toward that economy is thus joined but scarcely resolved.

Consideration of John Muth's rational-expectations perspective confirms how difficult it is to define the role of theory. By implication drawn from what Muth says, theory must concern itself with issues in "the well-being of the economy"—which sounds quite normative. Echoing Maskin, he allots a role for theory in improving modeling techniques—that is, improving the tool kit. But he echoes Buchanan as well: instead of public—choice theory this time, however, it is "the rational model" that has solved several historical problems. Theories "explain anomalies and paradoxes, clarify the limits of empirical laws, simplify knowledge, and unify diverse phenomena."

Boitani and Salanti work within a smaller compass than some of the contributors, concentrating as they do on the variety of Keynesian approaches today. They, too, argue that implicitly a critical function of theory is to enhance the explanatory power of the discipline, and so they, too, can be counted among those who find explanation to be a major role for theory. While they attach considerable importance to the requirement that theory should hold to some sort of reasonable conformity with the empirical world, they would allow somewhat greater flexibility for the role of theory than some. They argue, for example, that the longer run the perspective of a theory, the smaller is the requirement that it pass short-run policy prescriptions.

As Boitani and Salanti consider varieties of Keynesian thought, so Thomas Mayer focuses on varieties of monetarism. Mayer focuses on two strands. By implication his overall view concerning the role of theory is nonetheless discernible. The effect of theory is not determined by the number of adherents to a school of thought but ultimately by how convincingly theory explains unfolding history. Thus Mayer argues for a test of relevance in judging theory. This, in turn, means that the importance of theory is bound up with the adequacy of the guide to public policy that it provides. The test of how well theory plays its role is ultimately gleaned from appeal to the empirical record produced by the application of policy (including "neutral" policy) to the problem under consideration.

Maskin, we saw, argues that the role of theory is to provide a set of tools with which both normative and positive questions can be answered. He calls such theory "conceptual theory." Theory presumably is an aid to understanding. The role of theory is to make economic tools "more effective lenses in the scrutiny of economic life."

Marc Tool would agree with those who say that the role of economic theory is to consider how the economy is functioning so as to provide a guide for public policy. Because policy is necessarily interventionist (only "no-policy" can be noninterventionist), he argues that "the pragmatic instrumentalist mode of inquiry provides philosophic bases for the creation of institutional economic theory. This model of inquiry supports and guides policy making. Its normative dimensions serve neither relativistic nor absolutist goals or interests; they serve only the furtherance of inquiry and problem solving. This perspective serves no ideological enclave."

We see how difficult it is to find common ground. Many would agree that the role of theory is to help understand "reality." Beyond that, disagreement begins. Samuels, Klein, Sherman, Boitani and Salanti, and Tool in spite of their differences would probably agree that an important role for theory is as a guide to policy making. Buchanan, Muth, and Maskin would probably agree that the most critical task for theory is to explain "reality" (either actual reality or "simulated reality"—that is, models based on "stylized facts"). The others would not agree that this is an important task. Mayer, in a somewhat intermediate position, would agree that theory has a role to play in explaining reality but would no doubt regard theory as having an additional role to play in formulating monetary policy.

There is, in sum, some agreement about the role for economic theory but also much diversity. In any case, it is time to consider the views of economic theory directly.

Reference

Phelps, E.S. 1990. *Seven Schools of Macroeconomic Thought.* Oxford: Clarendon Press.

2 THE ROLES OF THEORY IN ECONOMICS

Warren J. Samuels

Abstract

This chapter identifies some two dozen roles that theory performs in economics. It argues that the performance of a given role is not necessarily tantamount to the performance of another; for example, theory as an organizing principle, or as social control, does not necessarily constitute explanation or description.

Introduction

Theories are nets cast to catch what we call "the world": to rationalise, to explain, and to master it.

—(Popper, 1959, p. 59)

A theorist is not confronted by just one question, or even by a list of questions numbered off in serial order. He is faced by a tangle of wriggling, intertwined and slippery questions. Very often he has no clear idea what his questions are until he is well on the way toward answering them. He does not know, most of the time, even what is the general pattern of the theory

21

*that he is trying to construct, much less what are the precise forms and
interconnections of its ingredient questions.*

—(Ryle, 1954, p. 7)

*If economists forget and then stoutly deny that the production function is
a metaphor, yet continue talking about it, the result is mere verbiage. The
word "production function" will be used in ways satisfying grammatical
rules, but will not signify anything.*

—(McCloskey, 1983, p. 506)

Economics is a theoretical subject but so are all other intellectual disciplines, however much the relevant theory may be only implicit.[1] Whether
the economy exists independent of humanity or is an artifact generated
through processes of its social construction, Immanuel Kant's argument—
that we cannot conclusively know with certainty the object of study and
that the mind mediates our perception of it—signifies that we must specu-
late about the economy, we must theorize. But what is it that we do when
we theorize?

The definition of theory is not a single-headed idea. Following Webster's
New World Dictionary of American English (1988, p. 1387), theory de-
notes contemplation or speculation; systematic inquiry; statements or principles derived from inquiry, indicating apparent relationships or underlying
fundamentals that have been verified to some degree; that branch of a
science consisting in a knowledge of principles and methods rather than its
practice, that is, pure, as opposed to applied, science; but also, in pregnant
juxtaposition to the foregoing esoteric ideas, popularly, a mere conjecture,
or guess. This latter suggests Popperian epistemology, in which testing of
conjectures is undertaken with, inter alia, a rule that permits refutation.
Epistemology per se, however, is beyond the scope of this chapter, even
though epistemological considerations will continually arise.[2]

The objective of this essay is to identify the roles that theory performs
in economics and that economic theory performs in the world.[3] The inquiry is intentionally conducted in positive terms; to ascertain, whether
one likes it or not, what, in fact, are the roles of theory in economics (and
of economic theory in the world), rather than to declare what the role
properly should be. The inquiry is motivated by a belief that economists
should be alert to the different roles that theory performs and to the
nature of the differences between them. The Humean lesson should go
without saying: one cannot derive an "ought" from an "is" alone; one
needs an additional normative premise. By "economic theory" is meant
that of *all* schools of economic thought.[4]

The first part of this chapter considers certain matters relating to the *nature*, rather than the role, of theory, taking cognizance of, but putting aside, certain complications, so that the discussion in the second part of the *roles* of theory can proceed with minimal ambiguity (to minimize but not to denigrate questions such as, "But what about . . .").

To theorize, something we do all the time, is to do a considerable variety of things. The role of theory is indeed rich; economists use theory to do quite a number of things, not unlike people in other disciplines and areas of life. Not all of these roles, however, may readily comport with economists' self-perceptions of economics as a science and of what they are doing when they do economics.

The multiple roles performed by theory are not analytically equivalent. The performance by theory of roles other than explanation, for example, is often taken to constitute explanation. The performance of one role is not necessarily the performance of another. One role may misleadingly be taken for or masquerade as another. Careful attention to the multiplicity of roles and to the differences between roles, and to what the differences entail, is necessary if we are to appreciate what it is we are doing when we theorize.

The Nature of Theory

This part is intended to clear the deck, by identifying and clarifying certain considerations that might otherwise interfere with what is presented in the second part. In every case, the intention is to be inclusive rather than exclusive—which is not to say that in practice qualifications may not be called for in regard to the roles of theory presented in the second part.

Theory and Related Concepts

Theory is one generic term used in economics; three others are *model, paradigm*, and *concept*. A *model* is a set of variables structured in a particular way with regard to a specified problem, the latter often being the dependent variable. A *theory* may go beyond a model by adding a particular hypothesis (a specific formulation of the theory to be tested), specifications of the social space to which it applies, and a decision rule by which the hypothesis may be confirmed or refuted. Not all models and theories comport with these stringent specifications. The presently relevant point is that whatever is considered a model or a theory comes within the ambit of what is herein called a theory. So too with paradigm and concept, each of which can be given a variety of specifications.

Validity and Related Concepts

The differentiating essentials of four terms need to be identified: *validity, truth, desirability*, and *workability*. By *validity* is meant that a conclusion is properly derived from the premises, given the system of logic. By *truth* is meant either correct explanation or accurate description. By *desirability* is meant either that something is deemed good or bad or, given an array of goods, a prescriptive ranking. By *workability* is meant that something is deemed, by some criterion, to be effective in regard to some purpose or end. The distinction between theory and practice is, for present purposes, one way of introducing workability. The important points are that the four key terms are different and that "theory" can be used in connection with all of them, so that what is said below about theory applies to any usage involving one or more of the four.

Positive and Normative

By *positive* is meant having to do with "is;" by *normative*, having to do with "ought." Positive "is" statements generally have to do with what just above is called truth, and normative "ought" statements have to do with desirability. Theory in economics can be either or both positive and normative; it is usually both. Sometimes, perhaps typically, it is not easy to determine whether a proposition is positive or normative, or the senses or respects it is both one and the other. Indeed, it is not clear that the positivist tenet affirming a fundamental difference between the two is useful in practice, at least without a great deal of dissembling. If the economy is an artifact, a result in part of ideology and valuation, it may not be strictly possible for theory to be independent of and objective and neutral toward it. In any case, there is a difference between a positive theory of an objectively given object and a positive theory of a normatively given subject. Theory in the latter case willy-nilly contributes to a fundamental and continuing valuational process, the process through which, at least in part, the social reconstruction of reality is undertaken. Although economists have typically endeavored to achieve a positive science, it is not clear that such could be or has been accomplished. What is said below regarding the role of theory applies to both positive and normative theory.

Fact and Theory

This distinction is a common one but it is not clear that it is meaningful. Facts can be read differently, depending on perspective; differences of perspective likely involve differences of theory, or of vision; and different theories or visions in effect pose different questions. Facts, at least those of any significance, are generally theory-laden. They do not exist independent of the theory by which they are facts; and theories are what they are in part because of certain readings of the putative or ostensible facts. Among other things, descriptions embody theories. What counts as a fact depends on the background of interpretive theories; the facts by which theories are to be tested are not autonomous and self-subsistent. Theory is both derived from perception and experience, and exists prior to and helps interpret experience: the former in that theory does not occur in a vacuum; the latter in that perception and experience are derived and understood through theory. There is therefore a fundamental tautological interrelationship between a fact and its related theory, or its related interpretive perspective. Theory and evidence are subtly intertwined; facts and theory are interrelated in an hermeneutic circle.

It is particularly important to note that the concepts used to define empirical variables are themselves often implicit theories. When facts defined in terms of concepts are used to test theories, theories are being tested on the basis of other theories. Facts, or data, cannot confirm a theory if the facts are generated by the same theory or, *mutatis mutandis*, by another theory extant within the same set of theories (for example, a common paradigm). This is not to say that there are no theories or facts for which this circumstance does not significantly apply. But it is also to say that theories are sometimes, perhaps often if not typically, judged acceptable on the basis of their consonance with an accepted—perhaps the discipline's—hegemonic paradigm (accepted view of the economic universe).[5] What is said below about theories can also apply to facts that are theory-laden. The arguable dependence of a theory on the facts neither exempts nor qualifies it with regard to what is said below.

Induction and Deduction

Some theory is deductive and some is inductive. In the ambit of logical-empiricism propositions, assumptions and conclusions are subject to testing. While the theories of deduction and induction are mutually exclusive in terms of pure epistemology, in practice they are not mutually exclusive; there are deductive and inductive elements, albeit different ones, in all work. What is said below regarding the roles of theory is not vitally affected by the deduction-induction distinction.

Levels of Theory

Shackle (1967, p. 294) argues that there are three levels of thought in economic theorizing: "There is the world of what we take to be 'real' objects, persons, institutions and events; on the axis of abstract-concrete this world is at the concrete pole. There is the logical or mathematical construct or machine, a piece of pure reasoning, almost of 'pure mathematics', able to exist in its own right of internal coherence, as a system of mere relations amongst undefined thought-entities; this world lies at the abstract pole. And between these two worlds there lies the world of names, linking the real-world elements with the undefined entities of the abstract machine."[6] What is said below applies to all three levels of theory—and also to what may be considered a fourth level, the theory of economic policy, and perhaps a fifth level, whatever theory connects it with the other three levels.

The problem that Shackle identifies is truly significant in economics: the problem of applying the conclusions of abstract, highly formalized theories and models, which are largely substantively empty of institutional data, to the actual economy with all its complexities and contingencies. Theories make the real or the actual abstract and then try to make the abstract pertain to reality or actuality. The cognitive reality created by or represented in theory may or may not, typically is not, isomorphic of the real, actual economy. Often economic theorizing or analysis takes place as if there were no difference between the theories (as logical categories or thought-entities) and the real-world objects of those theories. The problem exists because the actual economy has particular institutional details, a process of working things out, and problems not within the domain of a theory, on all of which the theory is silent and to which the theory can be applied only on the basis of additional premises, implicit or explicit. This is particularly true in regard to the economic role of government in matters of legal change of institutional details, including rights governing whose interests are to count.[7] All schools of thought criticize other schools for the idealized nature of their assumptions and their uncritical applications of theoretical conclusions to the actual economy and policy.

It is the very nature of theory to be incomplete and therefore unrealistic, even reductionist. This means that all theories are necessarily limited. But such limitations do not prevent theories from performing the various roles adduced below, roles that are attributed to them by their users.

Deterministic and Other Theory

Mainstream neoclassical economic theory seeks determinate, optimal, equilibrium solutions. By no means do all economic theories have these characteristics; and of those that do many have those characteristics only because of severely limiting assumptions. A variety of other, alternative objectives are found in economics, including tendency statements and pattern models (as well as identities and tautologies). Tendency statements are probabilistic in character; pattern models identify some combination of general tendencies and regularities of structure and other properties. What is said below applies to all theory whatsoever regardless of their form and objective.

Different Types of Theory

Consider the following: general equilibrium theory, utility theory, rational expectations hypothesis, cross-elasticity of substitution, Pareto optimality, class, economic surplus, status emulation, the multiplier, accelerator, creative destruction, the Austrian theory of capital, path dependency, technological regimes and trajectories, and so on. These are all theories, but they are very different types of theory in terms of their internal structure, the level of generality at which they operate, and the domain to which they apply. What is said below applies to all these and all other economic theories regardless of these and other differences.

The Tautological Character of All Theory

Theories are tautological in two interrelated senses.[8] First, the conclusions of a theory are tautological with—that is, derived from and give effect to—its assumptions, including the specification of its central problem.[9] Theorizing by assumption constitutes implicit theory, no less significant with regard to conclusions than any other element of a theory. Second, a theory is able to answer properly only the questions that its terms allow and to answer only in those terms.[10] In other words, a theory tells a particular and more or less self-contained (theory-specific) story. The role that a theory plays may derive from any of these aspects of a theory, as well as the selective use to which a theory is put—for example, through the addition of implicit normative or other premises, including much implicit theorizing about other, subordinate subjects.

One implication of the tautological character of a theory is the possibility of excluding from it all the variables that, as complications, would otherwise prevent the desired results from being reached (see note 10). The result is the prospect of the realization (prevented by ideology or wishful thinking; see below) of a more complete theory that includes all, or all the principal, variables operative with regard to a particular problem.[11]

Aspects of Theory qua Theory

1. Theories are directly or epistemologically competitive only if they attempt to explain or describe the same phenomenon. If they attempt to explain or describe different things, they are systemically, psychologically, or sociologically competitive—in the latter case competing for social status.

2. The roles of the assumptions of a theory are multiple and complex. One role is to define the area to which a theory is relevant, including the problem dealt with by the theory. Another is to specify the variables and their relationships—that is, the basic components of the story told by the theory.

3. A distinction perhaps ought to be made between assumptions made for convenience (for example, to make the analysis manageable, which can permit a multiplicity of sins) and those that are critical to the argument. But all assumptions define the problem, social space, and the variables and their relationships, however, whatever the motivation.

4. Theories are capable of multiple specification. That is why, in the methodology of logical empiricism, inter alia, the theory to be tested must be given specific statement and the results of the theory apply only to that specific statement of the theory.

5. In an actual economy of general interdependence (or general equilibrium), coevolution, cumulative causation, and overdetermination, variables can be both cause and consequence. Variable A literally can be the cause or the consequence of variable B; so that a theory that affirms that A is a function of B can have as its correlative a theory that affirms that B is a function of A. Moreover, the relationship between A and B need not be that of simple interaction between otherwise given, independent, and self-subsistent variables; rather, each variable can itself be changed in the process.

6. Rigor has to do with the correctness and simplicity of the logic by which one moves from assumption to conclusion. Rigor thus has to do with validity and does not preclude incompleteness due to omitted variables. Rigor does not prevent the casuistic manipulation of variables so that, by omitting all variables whose operation produces results contrary to those desired by the analyst, certain conclusions can be rigorously, albeit misleadingly, reached. By failing to appreciate the limits of all analysis, theorists can engage in the nonrigorous pursuit of rigor.

The Roles of Theory

The complexity of economics as an intellectual discipline and as a corpus of "knowledge" resides in part from the multifaceted and kaleidoscopic nature of the economy and the different perspectives from which the many-sided and changing economy can approached. The complexity of economics also derives from the multiplicity of economic theories, the difficulty of refuting them, and, especially for present purposes, the multiple roles served by theory. No one theory necessarily serves all roles, and while not all the roles of theory are those of science, all are part of the human experience.

Given the multiplicity of roles that theory can serve, it is not surprising that conflicts between them arise—for example, between explanation and prediction, between tool of analysis and description, and between social control–psychic balm and heuristic. Nor is it surprising that several roles may be jointly and perhaps inseparably performed by the same theory—for example, social control, social construction of reality, vehicle of ideology, psychic balm, and so on. As Joan Robinson (1962, p. 1) wrote, economics, notably for us economic theory, "has always been partly a vehicle for the ruling ideology of each period as well as partly a method of scientific investigation."

The performance of one role does not necessarily constitute the performance of another. If description and explanation are critical roles, the performance of another role is readily taken to constitute performance of those roles; and so on. For example, one of the besetting problems of economics is that ideology functions to describe and explain as well as to legitimize reality, altogether to define reality, although it may well be serving only as a means of projection or social control in the social construction of reality.

Finally, in a very fundamental and critical way, the role of a theory is derived from the specific purpose for which it is created or used by the economist. Some of those purposes may comport with the roles herein identified, but some may be specialized and more or less particular to individual economists Theories are shaped by their builders, who are guided consciously or unconsciously by a theory's potential role in society. Theory making and theory using are decidedly social phenomena (Shackle, 1967, attempts a "theory of the origin of theories," p. 3). Politicians (including politically active economists) use, even manufacture, economic theory so as to create an aura of respectability and coherence for policies determined on ideological grounds. Among professional economists, the perceived performance of a particular function may constitute a mode of theory choice.

In the remaining pages of this part, the variety of roles that a theory may perform is identified.

Explanation

The most well recognized role of theory is that of explanation—to answer the questions "How" and "Why". A variety of meanings of "explanation" exist, some involving the notion of a governing law, and with further variety as to the meaning of *governing* and *law*. The idea of causation tends to be involved, but there is a variety of meanings of causation. Explanation has a higher status than "mere" description, although presumably explanation requires correct description (of a meaningfully generalized, hence distorted, "reality") so that what is to be explained is "known" in some sense. Indeed, different descriptions require different explanations. A principal objective, therefore, of economic theory is to explain the origin, organization, operation, and performance of the economy. Insofar as explanation takes the form of a covering, or governing law, the role of theory is either to generate such laws or to substantiate or reject conjectures as to such laws.

Description

For the origin, organization, operation, and performance of the economy to be explained, such must be described, and another principal role of theory is to describe—to answer the question "What?" Different theories generate different descriptions, thereby calling for different explanations. One subsidiary role of theory is to produce facts (theory-laden facts). Descriptions can also be at different levels of generality. A theory that correctly describes, in some sense, the object of study presumably represents it correctly (although the description may run in terms of presumptuous "stylized facts"). But each theory presents its own interpretive representation of the object. The question of the correctness of description, or of explanation, is separable from that of the functions of description and explanation.

Prediction

One function of theory is to enable prediction. Prediction, however, can also be considered not an end in itself but a means of testing an hypothesis (an as yet untested "theory") subordinate to the roles of explanation or description. For some prediction is the essence of explanation. The further distinction exists between prediction within the context and terms of a model and prediction with regard to the actual economy. The former is a matter of logic, a prediction of the logical consequences of a change, given the model; the latter, a prediction of actual events, is a matter of accuracy ("goodness of 'fit' "), given the effect of variables not included in the model. Theory serves the role of prediction in each of these respects.

Hypothesis

Whether used in connection with the roles of explanation, description, or prediction or some other role, one role of theory is to present an hypothesis, perhaps a testable hypothesis. Indeed, given the difficulty if not impossibility of the conclusive verification or refutation of a theory—theories are never conclusively "proven"—arguably all theories always remain hypotheses. The basic notion of theory as hypothesis therefore is problematicity or tentativeness. Aside from the aforementioned difficulty, the role of theory as hypothesis is to present a useful conjecture and as such nothing necessarily more.

Confirmed Hypothesis

Hypotheses that pass the accepted test (whatever it may be) are often granted the status of a theory. One role of theory, therefore, is to present a confirmed hypothesis—one that has been confirmed or verified or has passed a test permitting refutation, in accordance with some conventional procedure or criterion. If one accords the status of "theory" only to confirmed hypotheses, then hypotheses are not (yet) theories but only hypotheses, perhaps mere speculations. Given the aforementioned difficulty of conclusive verification or refutation of an hypothesis, and given too the propensity to accept the criterion of "verifiable in principle," the set of confirmed hypotheses may be small, perhaps nonexistent, but the connotation of theory as confirmed hypothesis is commonplace.

Definition of Reality

One function of a theory is to provide professional and lay people with a generalized conception or definition of what economic "reality" is all about,

with a way of seeing the world. It indicates what is and what is not important, quite aside from, although often in addition to, the substantive description thereof (treated here above as a separate function). It indicates
what problems—intellectual and practical—are worth considering, for the
purposes and as the basis of either study or policy.

Providing a Sense of Economic Order

A correlative role of theory, sufficiently distinguishable and important
perhaps to warrant the specification of a separate role, is that of providing
a sense of economic order. It is only in terms of particular theories, or
perhaps more fully only in terms of the paradigms to which they give
effect, that we have ordered conceptualizations or portrayals of the world:
the neoclassical conception of order, the Marxist, the post-Keynesian, the
Austrian, the institutionalist, the monetarist, and so on. "Order" and "orderliness' are essentially subjective; moreover, as Shackle (1967, p. 288) puts
it, "In the sciences (so-called) of men and their affairs, the investigator
may be said to impose rather than discover the orderliness which constitutes knowledge." Insofar as theories generate a sense of order, they are
essentially metaphysical,[12] but provision of order as a form of defining
reality is one of the functions performed by theory.

Understanding

There is more to "knowing" than simple or straightforward description,
explanation and prediction, and so on. One function of theory is to provide understanding in the sense of *verstehen*—that is, a comprehension of
the human or existential meaning of the object of study.

Heuristic

One function of a theory is to serve as a basis of inquiry, of search, and
thereby to guide cognition and provide suggestions for further study or
research. Theorizing is a cognitive mode, whether undertaken implicitly or
explicitly. In this regard, for example, even a false theory (one that neither
correctly describes nor correctly explains) may be useful.

Tool of Analysis

Theories are tools with which to conduct analysis.[13] The knowledge that is generated by theories considered as tools is rooted in the operations that economists perform with the tools. Conflict is possible as to whether a particular theory is an explanation, description, and so on of reality—that is, some aspect of the actual economy—or a tool with which to explore and analyze the actual economy. The instrumentalist conception of theory exists in contrast to the ontological and epistemological, but clearly the instrumental function is served by economic theories. Even if all believed in philosophical realism—namely, that theories relate to entities and relationships that are real and independent of the analyst—different individuals would likely identify those entities and relationships differently, so that the instrumentalist view would be given effect. In performing the role of tool of analysis, moreover, a theory is a means of learning (see heuristic role). Economics is readily seen as sets of tools, one group of which is economic theories, a theory being useful as a tool for some purposes and not others.

Discursive or Rhetorical Roles

Theory performs a number of closely related roles that typically are found together in various combinations but that can be separately identified:

1. *Systematizing ideas*: One role is that of systematizing ideas, in a sense to abridge and summarize data.
2. *Framework of discussion*: When economists think and analyze, they do so in terms of a theory, one theory or another (indeed, one feature of economists' self-conscious concern with making theory explicit and with rigor is their ability to tease out of a discussion the theory—perhaps as to assumptions—implicit in it). Theory serves as a mode of discourse; the terms of discourse are those of the theory used therein. Theory functions as a mode of communication, as a framework of discussion, as an organization of thoughts and therefore of thinking, as a way of identifying and looking at a problem or topic, by arranging the putative elements of the object of study in certain ways. It is, of course, of no minor significance that some or much of economic theory is a matter of metaphors (McCloskey 1953, pp. 503 and passim).
3. *Organizing principle*: Closely related to the heuristic function of a

theory is the role of theory as organizing principle. A theory as an organizing principle is the basis on which a particular story is told, the embedded plot design. It is this organizing principle that can serve as the basis of explanation, description, definition of reality, understanding, and so on. The organizing principle may reside in the identity of the independent or dependent variables or elsewhere, but it is the key to the plot of the story being told.

4. *Mode of concentrating attention*: Also close to the heuristic function as well as to the organizing-principle role, one role of a theory, but again not necessarily of all theories, is to concentrate attention on a particular facet of a topic or problem. Theory acts as a filter to focus the efforts of the discipline on certain problems; theory channels selective perception and thereby governs what can be ignored in analysis. This may be done by adopting a certain variable, factor, or force or a certain idealized abstraction of the object of study for intensive study. It is done to focus attention on a selective part of reality and to render analysis manageable; facilitating manageability is here considered a separate role. It is for this reason, if for no other, that a theory—all theories—are necessarily incomplete and therefore unrealistic, for by concentrating attention on certain variables or aspects, others are excluded from attention and the story that is produced is incomplete (and therefore unrealistic).

Facilitating Manageability

Abstraction is the very nature of theorizing, in economics and elsewhere. Not surprisingly, the Marshallian procedure of *ceteris paribus*—of impounding certain variables and dealing only with a certain few—is a trademark of economic inquiry in all schools of thought, though most highly articulated in neoclassical economics. One role of theory is to render analysis manageable, a role perhaps the counterpart of concentrating attention, with a technically different purpose but leading to the same operational result.

Element in Logical/Epistemological Structure

A theory, perhaps as an hypothesis or a tool (for example, as an assumption), though possibly also performing other functions, can perform the role of an element in a structure or process of deductive reasoning or of empirical testing. Not all theories are used in such a way.

Prescription

Theories are functional with regard to the acquisition of knowledge, in the form of explanation or description and so on; theories are also looked to for their practical implications and applications. Theories therefore can be used prescriptively for normative purposes or to serve as the basis of decision, policy, and control. The prescriptions can be developed with regard to the definition of problems of policy, ends of policy, means-end relations, techniques of decision making, and principles of policy and control. There is no doubt but that theory serves a prescriptive role.

But that role is equivocal, and the equivocality is informative as to how the role is performed. On the one hand, a positive "is" theory cannot, on Humean grounds, alone be the basis of a prescriptive "ought." On the other, theories, by virtue of the policy implications drawn from them, typically with implicit additional normative premises, are used selectively to give support to certain policies or ideologies. In various ways, for example, by the relevant choice of problem to be theorized about and by the implications for policy drawn from a theory, theories tend inevitably to have prescriptive relevance. In serving this prescriptive role, theory contributes willy-nilly to the social valuational process.

Basis of Social Construction of Reality

The concept "social construction of reality" has two different relevant connotations. In one, economic reality is an artifact, created through human action, and theory functions to provide a basis on which the action and the construction takes place. In the other, economic reality (the actual economy) exists more or less independent of human action, and the social construction is a matter of the interpretation or understanding placed by people on that reality, perhaps on the basis of religious or other ideology or material interest or disciplinary training. Both roles are akin to such other roles as definition of reality, understanding, framework of discussion, basis of legitimation and criticism (below), and perhaps other roles. Additionally, the former role is akin to the prescriptive and social control (below) roles; the latter is akin to the heuristic role. Along with explanation, description, and prediction (together constituting knowledge for its own sake), control (here the social construction of reality, in the first sense given above, as distinct from social control) has been one of the principal historically recognized objectives of knowledge—and therefore one of the principal roles of theory understood as a contribution to knowledge.

Basis of Legitimation and Criticism

Again notwithstanding the Humean injunction, theory can serve, selectively, to legitimate or to criticize.[14] Insofar as a theory represents an idealized (perhaps simplistic) version of some aspect or element of reality, and insofar as a theory stands in contradiction to its rivals, a theory can be used to applaud or to criticize existing reality and other theories. (In this manner a theory and the criticism that it enables give effect to the particular assumptions on which the theory rests.) The status quo can be, selectively, legitimized and criticized on the basis of a theory. Theories are attractive and chosen in part because of the use to which they can be put by way of legitimation and criticism. Insofar as theories perform this role, they also may contribute to the social control role (below), if not also to others. As a corollary, theory has the role of projecting perfection, or the ideal, on the world, thereby serving as the basis of legitimation and criticism; and insofar as doing so is reassuring, it is also performing the psychic balm role (below).

Vehicle of Ideology, Wishful Thinking, Paradigm

Theories are not merely a matter of the deliberate exercise of inductive and deductive reason. They also are the vehicles through which elements of ideology, wishful thinking, and paradigm enter analysis, thereby constituting a further role of theory. Theory can be constructed and chosen, deliberately or inadvertently, but no less effectively, on the basis of assumptions and conceptions utilized to permit the attainment of certain desired, congenial or habitual conclusions—for example, by ruling out all factors and all conceptualizations that would lead to different conclusions. The ideology, wishful thinking, or paradigm need not be the dominant one; heterodox or radical ones will also be served by theory. Theory can be used in conjunction with any vision or to establish, however putatively, any claim. This role is either the opposite or a constrained version of the heuristic role. Theory choice can give effect to and reenforce ideology, and so forth. (Note how far this takes us from the conventional normative-positive dichotomy.)

Means of Projection

Theory is a means whereby we project our perceptions (including those based on our fears, anxieties, and hopes) onto the actual economy. Instead of theory mirroring in some sense or way the actual economic world, theory reflects our selective perceptions of that world, the perceptions generated by us rather than by the world itself. The actual world is thereby perceived through a subject nexus of already (but not necessarily final) meanings and expectations. This role is close to but distinguishable from the psychic balm role (below). In a sense it is the opposite of the heuristic role; in other respects, it is either a constraint on or a mode of pursuing the heuristic role.

Social Control

By providing authoritative knowledge—that is to say, by providing explanation, description, definition of reality, and so on, that is proferred as or taken to be authoritative—theory serves as social control. Insofar as theory serves as the basis of the social construction of economic reality (see Samuels, 1988), insofar as it is the basis of selective legitimation and criticism of economic arrangements, and insofar as theory is the vehicle of ideology and so on, economic theory serves the social control function alongside of, and either in support of or in conflict with, religion, moral codes, and the other institutions of social control. Whether or not the vehicle of the ruling ideology, by virtue of the hold that it may have on the human mind and its understanding of what is necessary, possible, and desirable; and by virtue of its organizing, integrating, and channeling behavior, theory serves as social control.[15]

Insofar as social control is the process by which social change is governed, one of the subordinate roles of theory, perhaps worthy of its separate and independent designation as a role, is channeling the control of social change. Applied in practice, for example, to problems of legal change, theory acting as a filter to focus the efforts of the discipline on certain problems and not others, can also perform the ideological role of directing the social reconstruction of reality.

Psychic Balm

Individuals seem to have a need for a sense of order and a sense of certitude. In a disorderly and conflictual world characterized or believed to be characterized by radical indeterminacy (that the future is not presently knowable and cannot be known until we through our actions have created it), one function of theory is to serve as psychic balm. The classic statement of this function is by George Shackle, and we can do no better than quote his words (Shackle, 1967, pp. 286, 288–289):

> All we can seek is consistency, coherence, order. The question for the scientist [here, theoretician] is what thought-scheme will best provide him with a sense of that order and coherence, a sense of some permanence, repetitiveness and universality in the structure or texture of the scheme of things, a sense even of that one-ness and simplicity which, if he can assure himself of its presence, will carry consistency and order to their highest expression. Religion, science [here, theory] and art have all of them this aim in common. The difference between them lies in the different emphases in their modes of search. The chief service rendered by a theory is the setting of minds at rest. ... Theory serves deep needs of the human spirit: it subordinates nature to man, imposes a beautiful simplicity on the unbearable multiplicity of fact, gives comfort in the face of the unknown and unexperienced, stops the teasing of mystery and doubt which, though salutary and life-preserving, is uncomfortable, so that we seek by theory to sort out the justified from the unjustified fear. Theories by their nature and purpose, their role of administering to a "good state of mind," are things to be held and cherished. Theories are altered or discarded only when they fail us.

This psychic balm view of theory was essentially that of Adam Smith (1980, pp. 45–46), writing in effect about philosophy as a body of abstract theory:

> Philosophy, by representing the invisible chains which bind together all these disjointed objects, endeavours to introduce order into this chaos of jarring and discordant appearances, to allay this tumult of the imagination, and to restore it, when it surveys the great revolutions of the universe, to that tone of tranquillity and composure, which is both most agreeable in itself, and most suitable to its nature ... fitted to soothe the imagination, and to render the theatre of nature a more coherent, and therefore a more magnificent spectacle, than otherwise it would have appeared to be. According as they have failed or succeeded in this, they have constantly failed or succeeded in gaining reputation and renown to their authors.

The psychic balm role is close to that of a means of projection—projecting a systemic view of the world, a political-economic ideology, a grand value system, a class perspective, certain fears, anxieties or hopes, or whatever, including compensation for one's losses and disadvantaged position and legitimation of one's gains and hierarchically superior position, as well as salve for our senses and fears of ambiguity, indeterminacy, and disorder.

Tell a Story

Many of the foregoing roles of theory have to do, in one way or another, either directly or as a substitute, with truth in the sense of either accurate description or correct explanation. Insofar as economics can be considered a mode of discourse and system of rhetoric, or insofar as one severely discounts the epistemological (methodogical) meaningfulness of economic theory, it follows that one role of economic theory is to tell a story. Economic theory is often "an attempt to give an account of an interrelated set of phenomena in which fact, theory, and values are all mixed together in the telling" of a story (Ward, 1972, p. 180). Given in particular the fundamental nontestability of much economic theory and the difficulty if not impossibility of conclusively disproving or proving a theory, it follows that much if not all economic theory, again of all schools of thought, represents a version of social science fiction, such that the function of theory is to tell a story. Alternatively, one could follow the lead of Alfred Marshall[16] and consider economic theory a set of elegant toys, whose manipulation is the adult equivalent of play.

Give Economics the Status of a Science

From at least the time of Alfred Marshall in the late nineteenth century, economists have sought the status of science of their discipline. There have been considerable differences of opinion—in economics and in other fields, including philosophy—as to the meaning of "science." One of the functions of theory—perhaps especially, but by no means solely, highly formalized, mathematical theory and econometricized theory—has been to give to economics the status of a science, to give economics credibility as a separate professional field, and to distinguish the members of the discipline as scientists.

As a corollary, theory serves as a buffer for economists against those who would denounce the vocation and its importance. Theory serves as a means of defending and reenforcing the status of the economist as professional expert. Confidence in theory enables professional, essentially academic, economists to ignore their extradisciplinary critics, even critics from within economics, thereby maintaining the professional niche of economics.

Theory also can serve as a barrier to entry to the profession against those who would maintain neither the disciplinary nor the systemic status quo, a means of enabling professional reproduction without disciplinary change. Theory comforts minds and guards boundaries psychologically and professionally. As the basis of a science, economic theory, that of the discipline as a whole or that of a particular school, is a source of professional identity; it especially, of course, reinforces the neoclassicist identity of economists (see below) because neoclassicism is the hegemonic school.

Theory also provides a sense of confidence in the face of existential ambiguity, radical indeterminacy, Godelian undecidability, and the like.

In each of these ways, economic theory serves the psychic balm role. Many of these considerations constitute part of the sociology of economics— ironic in view of the generally denigratory attitude that many economists have toward sociology, in part because it does not have (in the view of those economists) anything resembling "theory."

Refer to Neoclassical Economics

The term *theory* is also used to refer to neoclassical microeconomics, sometimes to refer to both microeconomics and macroeconomics. Given the honorific status of the concept "theory" in economics, this has the effect of giving those bodies of theory, especially microeconomic theory, a privileged hermeneutic and disciplinary position and to treat invidiously all other forms or schools of economic thought.

The foregoing can be partly illustrated by example. Consider the quantity theory of money (as a generic category with several different specific versions). The quantity theory is an attempt at explanation of the determination of the price level in terms of monetary variables. It constitutes description in terms of monetary variables and a definition of reality in terms of the price level. It offers certain hypotheses and predictions. It represents a sense of economic order in terms of price stability. It is a mode of concentrating attention, framing discussion, and systematizing ideas by emphasizing price stability rather than, for example, unemployment, telling one story rather than another. By doing so it also is the basis of prescription, of legitimization and criticism, and the social construction of reality. It thereby serves a social control function. In organizing thought and providing a sense of what monetary phenomena are all about it provides a sense of economic order, serves as a vehicle of ideology and projection of fears and hopes, serves as psychic balm, and gives economics something of the status of a science. Much more is involved than the "simple" relationship between the supply of money and the price level.

Conclusion

Theory in economics is a very powerful artifact and instrument. In addition to being more comprehensive than the usual (neoclassical microeconomics) connotation recognizes, theory is more powerful and certainly richer, in terms of its diverse roles, than is often acknowledged.

The conventionally understood goal of theory, under the aegis of the philosophy or theory of science, is truth (explanation and description). But theory involves more than the quest for truth per se, in economics and in other disciplines. There also is more to the role of theory in economics than a preoccupation with deterministic theory seems to permit.

Apropos of the epigraph taken from Gilbert Ryle, economists are engaged in a process of working out, consciously or otherwise, what questions they are answering in their research. The determination of what roles they are performing is typically not a totally self-consciously cognitive matter for economists or other scholars. Among the "ingredient questions" of a theory, however, must be included the roles that the theory performs willy nilly. The intellectual meaningfulness of a theory resides not solely in what it says but also in the roles that it plays.

Economists are known to disagree. Disagreements can be paradigmatic, conceptual, and technical. They include the nature and substance of fundamental economic processes, the definition of "problem," the nature and origin of actual economic problems, and the solutions to problems. These differences arise from many sources, some that involve the multiplicity of roles that theory in economics performs.

The roles that theory performs in economics can be performed by other means. The definition of reality, understanding, framework of discussion, social control, psychic balm, and other roles can be and have been performed, for example, by societal myths. It may also be the case that theory in economics sometimes subtly gives effect to these myths, as theory serves the role of being a vehicle for the entry of ideology and wishful thinking.

With theory in economics having multiple roles, the case for theoretical pluralism and a deep sense of the limits of a theory is further strengthened (see Samuels, 1993, for the Hicksian case). But before that can be appreciated, economists need to overcome their myopia about theory and what theory is all about. There is more to theory than epistemology or philosophy of science seems to recognize. There is more to the world than can be encompassed within any particular theory, even the theory on which this article rests—that there are multiple roles of theory.

Acknowledgments

With the assistance of Diane Bruce, Ibrahim Halil Canakci, Larry A. Carver, Jiun-Young Chiang, Aliou Diagne, John Duncan, Laura M. Geis, Steven Hughes, Michael D. Kloha, Dongin Lee, Wing-Fai Leung, Leo Paul Loetscher, Tariq Mahmood, Kahlil Rowter, Dan Schoen, Chen Shyuee, and Im Kyung So; and with the help of comments by Jeff Biddle, Michael Spagnuolo, and Philip A. Klein.

Notes

1. It is tempting to think that economics is a more theoretical subject than, say, sociology, or that economists are more self-consciously theoretical than sociologists. Although economists tend to make more of a show of their formalist determinate solutions, both (all) disciplines are at bottom theoretical in terms of the roles adduced below to theory in economics.

2. Among the numerous relevant topics (and associated controversies) not considered are theory evaluation and choice; the relations between correspondence with reality, logical coherence, and clarity of expression as tests of a theory; the limits of empiricism, positivism, and logical empiricism, including verification; causality; universality and eternality of truth as a requisite characteristic (among other criteria of adequacy, etc.); the self-referentiability of a theory; metaphysics; common sense; the relative meaningfulness of analytic and synthetic statements; the relation of speculation to science; conflicts among putative roles, for example, theory as definition of reality and as tool, and related issues, such as objectivity versus advocacy; formalism; internalism versus externalism, or absolutism versus relativism, with regard to the origins of theories; the importance of acknowledging the limits of any theory; and, inter alia, progress in theory.

The question also arises whether economics, and therefore economic theory, is different from theory in the natural, biological and physical sciences. Surely two differences are, first, that the material of economics—human beings and their actions—are sentient and can reflect and act upon the findings of economics; and second, that the economy presumably is made and remade through human action. As Shackle (1967, p. 130) puts it, "Surmise and assumption about what is happening or about to happen are themselves the *source* of these happenings, men make history in seeking to apprehend it."

The present topic is also relevant to the question and the cases for and against theoretical pluralism, which deal with the question of multiple theories, not multiple roles performed by either a particular theory or theory in general. In my view the multiplicity of the roles of theory strengthens the case for theoretical pluralism, but that is another matter. This matter is touched on in the concluding section but is not treated in detail. Regarding John R. Hicks's case for theoretical pluralism, see Samuels (1993).

Two other points: First, many of the technical terms used herein have variegated meanings in different philosophical systems. It would be very burdensome to explore them and it is unnecessary to do so. Technical terms are used in their common or general meanings. Second, there is considerable controversy whether a particular economic theory is to be identified with one role or another; for example, whether a theory is an explanation in some sense or a set of comments, or indeed whether a body of thought is a theory at all or just a set of comments. For that and comparable reasons I generally avoid giving examples.

3. I have been thinking about this subject for many years. Although I have accumulated

numerous debts, I have tried to keep the number of references to a minimum, recording only those that have significantly entered my thinking as I have prepared this chapter. I am indebted to the graduate students in my history of economic thought course, Economics 841C, Fall 1991, whom I coerced into thinking and writting about the nature and role of theory in economics. Their papers were very helpful and suggestive, though the principal outline of this paper was prepared before I received their papers.

4. I specifically include historicism and institutionalism. The argument, advanced on both sides of the issue, that these schools are not economic theory, or not theoretical, derives from the identification of theory with microeconomic (and macroeconomic) theory and with neoclassical economics. These identifications are simply wrong. All schools of thought are theoretical. They differ in regard to their respective central problems, scope of variables, and paradigm. Nonetheless, one role of "theory" in common practice in economics is to refer to neoclassical microeconomic theory (and sometimes macroeconomic theory) and sometimes to neoclassicism per se.

5. It is also the case that economists doing econometrics generally experiment with a number of functional forms until they find the one that best fits the available data, and then adjust the theory to justify the functional form that was chosen.

6. Shackle (1967, p. 287) also writes that theorizing discerns "essential likeness amongst essentially diverse patterns, so as to embrace many formerly distinct stereotypes into one more general form. Its means will be the invention of axioms concerning entities or elements which in the first place will remain undefined except by the interrelations imposed upon them by the axioms. Upon these axioms it will construct systems of further propositions obtained from the axioms by logical inference. Finally a likeness will be sought between the structure of some such system and some observed stereotype, whose composing elements may then be identified with the elements or concepts of the logical system, and the inferential properties of the latter ascribed to the background of real events within which the stereotype was discerned." The problem posed by the juxtaposition of otherwise empty formal logical categories or concepts to real-world entities with particular institutional details is discussed in the text in the next paragraph.

7. For example, conclusions derived from theories or models of pure markets that lead to noninterventionist policy implications are non sequiturs. In the real world there are no pure markets, only markets that are a function of and give effect to institutions. These institutions are in large part a function of law and subject to legal change; and the only way a noninterventionist policy recommendation can be issued is to assume the propriety of the already existing set of legally based arrangements, which involves an assumption added to the theory or model. Economic theories and models are frequently applied to issues and problems for which they are unable to provide unequivocally dispositive answers and solutions. But the fact that they are so applied does mean that theory performs certain roles. See the second part of this chapter.

8. In addition to theories that are essentially metaphysical and incapable of being tested, even in principle, because they deal with absolutes, invariables, nonobservables, and especially nonconfirmables.

9. The conclusions of a theory or model, when considered in regard to the real (actual) world, are driven by two different engines, such that the conclusions are tautological with both: on the one hand, the endogenous independent variables; and on the other, the exogenous variables. Formally, assume that a model is structured by A as the dependent variable and by B, C, and D as the independent variables, with E, F, and G as the exogenous variables. In the actual world economy, the combination of A, B, C, and D is driven by the combination of E, F, and G simultaneously with A being a function of B, C, and D.

10. Rigor, highly valued by economists, has to do with the conduct of deduction/induction

and validity. The circumstance, for example, that a conclusion is rigorously derived from its premises says something only about its validity; the conclusion, the entire apparatus of the theory, may be and very likely is incomplete. This incompleteness makes the theory and the conclusion amenable to scientific and ideological (that is, policy-oriented) casuistry. For example, let A be a function, in the actual economy, of B, C, D, E . . . N variables. A theory that rigorously explores A as a function of C necessarily suspends the operation of the other variables (or places them in Alfred Marshall's pound of *ceteris paribus*). As a matter of deductive logic, pursuit of A as a function of C is quite permissible. As a matter of ideology, concentration on A elevates the problem represented by A above all other problems (for example, those represented by B or C, or X). Also as a matter of ideology, A as a function of C may be pursued in the service of an antecedently given political agenda, using ad hoc assumptions that render all the other variables nugatory, so that the policy implication drawn follows only from A considered as a function of C. Economics is replete with this practice. See note 11.

11. I should perhaps be specific here. I have in mind, for example, Say's law and the Coase theorem. Each reaches its special result by virtue of assuming away all the situations that would prevent the law and the theorem, respectively, from being reached, whereas in reality the assumptions likely do not hold, so that the actual result likely bears no relation or resemblence to that stipulated in the law or the theory. In the case of Say's law, for example, it is assumed that money is only a medium of exchange; that the interest rate equates saving and investment; that all prices are sufficiently flexible to be market-clearing; and that all wants are insatiable. The point is the same that Schumpeter (1954, pp. 472–473) made with regard to Ricardo, of whom he wrote that "he then piled one simplifying assumption upon another until, having really settled everything by these assumptions, he was left with only a few aggregative variables between which, given these assumptions, he set up simple one-way relations so that, in the end, the desired results emerged almost as tautologies." One is tempted to say that economists preach, and to some extent practice, rigor but are not rigorous about the use, and therefore the limits, of rigor.

12. "The hallmark of a metaphysical proposition is that it is not capable of being tested. . . . It can never be proved wrong, for it will roll out of every argument on its own circularity; it claims to be true by definition of its own terms. It purports to say something about real life, but we can learn nothing from it" (Robinson, 1962, p. 3). The last phrase is not quite true, or true only by definition. See above with regard to the tautological character of theory.

13. Economic theory as a set of tools was the view of Joseph Schumpeter and John R. Hicks. Schumpeter (1954, pp. 6–20) understood economic theory as the technology of economics. For the views of Hicks, on theories, models, assumptions, concepts, and so on as tools, see Samuels (1993).

14. "Legitimation 'explains' the institutional order by ascribing cognitive validity to its objectivated meanings. Legitimation justifies by institutional order by giving a normative dignity to its practical imperatives. . . . Legitimation not only tells the individual why he *should* perform one action and not another; it also tells him why things *are* what they are" (Berger and Luckmann, 1966, pp. 93–94). The objectified institutional order need not be the existing order; it can be a reified or absolutistically formulated idealization thereof or of some alternative. Criticism is implicit in this usage of legitimation. Hicks believed that economic theory is critical theory (see Samuels, 1993). The concepts of reification and absolutist formulation pertain here; insofar as theory performs them as corollary roles, they also perform other roles, such as definition of reality, basis of social construction of reality, and so on.

15. The classic statement of this admittedly controversial, but to me conclusive, position is in Robinson (1962, pp. 1–25).

16. "Much of 'pure theory' seems to me to be elegant toying: I habitually describe my own pure theory of international trade as a 'toy'" (quoted in Coats, 1967, p. 413).

References

Berger, Peter L., and Thomas Luckmann. 1966. *The Social Construction of Reality*. New York: Doubleday.

Coats, A.W. 1967. "Alfred Marshall and the Early Development of the London School of Economics: Some Unpublished Letters." *Economica*, N.S., 34 (November), 408–417,

McCloskey, Donald. 1953. "The Rhetoric of Economics." *Journal of Economic Literature*, 21 (June), 481–517.

Popper, Karl R. 1959. *The Logic of Scientific Discovery*. New York: Basic Books.

Robinson, Joan. 1962. *Economic Philosophy*. Chicago: Aldine.

Ryle, Gilbert. 1954. *Dilemmas*. New York: Cambridge University Press.

Samuels, Warren J. 1988. "An Essay on the Nature and Significance of the Normative Nature of Economics." *Journal of Post Keynesian Economics*, 10 (Spring), 347–354.

———. 1993. "John R. Hicks as Historian of Economic Thought." *History of Political Economy*, 25 (Summer), 351–374; extended version in Warren J. Samuels, Jeff Biddle, and Thomas Patchak-Schuster, *Economic Thought and Discourse in the Twentieth Century*. Brookfield, VT: Edward Elgar, 1993, 1–86.

Schumpeter, Joseph A. 1954. *A History of Economic Analysis*. New York: Oxford University Press.

Shackle, G.L.S. 1967. *The Years of High Theory*. New York: Cambridge University Press.

Smith, Adam. 1980. *Essays on Philosophical Subjects*. Edited by W.P.D. Wightman and J.C. Bryce. New York: Oxford University Press.

Ward, Benjamin. 1972. *What's Wrong with Economics?* New York: Basic Books.

Webster's New World Dictionary of American English. 1988. Third College Edition. New York: Simon & Schuster.

3 ECONOMIC THEORY IN THE POSTREVOLUTIONARY MOMENT OF THE 1990s

James M. Buchanan

Abstract

Why did economists, generally, fail to predict socialism's failure? This chapter suggests that such failure is due to economists' acceptance of a maximizing paradigm as applicable to "the economy" as a whole, when the alternative conceptualization of "the economy" as a spontaneous order would have been scientifically superior. The approach derived from the theory of games should have been helpful but was dominated for three decades by the maximizing paradigm.

Introduction

Economic theory offers an explanation of the relationships between the interactive behavior of persons and patterns of social outcomes on the presupposition that individual action is motivated by economically meaningful and conceptually measurable self-interest. Economic theory, as such, does not embody the behavioral hypothesis that persons do, in empirical reality, act so as to further measurable self-interest. To the extent that they

47

do so, economics offers the source of hypotheses that often withstand the falsifiability test. But such falsification, if it occurs, should not be inter-preted as refutation of the underlying theoretical construction, although it would suggest limits of practical usefulness.

In this elementary sense, economic theory has been vindicated by the events of this century, culminating in the revolution that has signaled the failure of the great socialist experiments. Socialism, as an inclusive system of organizing economic activity, did not achieve the objectives that its advocates defined at its inception. Socialism did not produce the goods, defined as the economic values that can emerge ultimately only from the preferences of individual participants. Economic theory explains the fail-ure of socialism through its focus of attention on incentive structures, on informational requirements, and on the necessary uncertainties in the linkage between choices and consequences. The ex post explanation does not, however, excuse economists, generally, from their apparent failure to predict the consequences that did, in fact, occur. Why did the revolutions that marked socialism's death take place before more than a tiny minority of practicing, professional economic theorists made predictions of systemic failure?

I suggest that this woeful record of economists' performance stems from a set of scientific errors that must be put right before economic theory can begin to exert a productive influence on the hard problems of transition from socialism to alternative structures. We know, of course, that these scientific errors were, in part, driven by the ideological bias that economists shared with intellectuals generally. But the errors in scientific understanding can be divorced from the ideological setting. It is possible to discuss the role of economic theory, as such: first, in its failure to predict socialism's demise; second, in its widely accepted explanation for the antisocialist revolution, ex post; and third, in its potential contribution to problems of transition in the postrevolutionary moment of the 1990s.

It first is necessary to lay out the general domain for discussion. I define my own understanding of economic theory in the sense used in this chapter and sketch out familiar territory in the history of ideas, with emphasis on the eighteenth-century discovery of the spontaneous order of market interaction, the discovery that sparked the genuine intellectual excitement of the classical political economists. Then I discuss, briefly, the classical economists' presuppositions for the constitutional framework necessary for an effective functioning of economic order and trace out the collapse of the classical-neoclassical understanding of the working of an economy, a collapse that was influenced by the challenge of Marxian socialism, by the implicit acceptance of political idealism and by the loss of systemic evaluation and analysis. I note the emergence of the maximization or allocationist paradigm, as aided and abetted by the particular mathematics of the calculus, and at the expense of emphasis on the catallactic subject matter of market organization, and the effect of game theory as a complement to a catallactic approach. Finally, I examine the elementary, but essential, contribution that economic theory can bring to participants, academic and lay alike, who have not experienced the history of market institutions. The genuine "miracle of the market" that did, indeed, excite the classical economists can offer a basis for an enthusiastic public philosophy in postrevolutionary societies, a philosophy that the cynical, jaded, and intellectually soft citizens in Western nations may have lost forever. As economists in the West, we, too, must recover our *raison d'être* as political economists-cum-political philosophers and not as social engineers. Our science has much to answer for but also much to contribute.

The Relevant Domain

As the definition in the first sentence of the introduction implies, the subject matter of economic theory is a set of relationships among choosing and acting persons and the patterns of results or outcomes that these relationships generate. An alternative way of placing the emphasis here is to say that economics offers a theory of organizational-institutional *order*. The theory tells in a generalized and pattern predictive sense "what will tend to emerge" under this and that set of circumstances, conditions, and constraints. We use economic theory in precisely the same way that we use much other knowledge. We explain why there is tropical fruit—say, bananas—on the supermarket shelves a thousand miles from the location where the fruit is grown. We use economic theory here just as we use physics to tell us why water runs down hill. We do not, of course, claim that theory enables us, in advance, to predict that bananas, as identified, will be on the market's shelves. Nor would we use physics to predict that the liquid substance to run down that ravine will be water. Economics allows us to predict that whatever people want to purchase will be available for purchase. Economic value will tend to be created in the form that people prefer, as driven by the same persons in their dual role as producers. The grower, the shipper, the distributor, the market manager, the shelf stocker, the cashier—all these put bananas on the shelves because they expect that, in so doing, they can exchange bananas for money, which will, in turn, allow for their own purchases of the goods that they desire, goods that will, in further turn, be put on the store shelves by those of us who purchase the bananas.

My purpose here is not to bore you with a summary of first-week elementary economics. But I should insist that those of us who are professionals in the discipline often neglect these elementary principles at our peril, and especially when we recognize that only a very small minority of nonprofessionals possesses even a generalized understanding of how the economic order works.

If my summary seems perhaps too elementary as well as too conventional, let me contrast my definition of the subject matter with more familiar claims. Economics or economic theory is *not* about "the allocation of scarce means among alternative ends" (Robbins, 1932). This familiar means-end formulation draws attention, first, away from the creation of value as opposed to some allocation or utilization of value that is presumed to be in existence, and, second, from the interactive relationships among persons that define the order of an economy. Biblical mythology is helpful with reference to the first point. After the expulsion from the Garden, the lot of humans requires that they create economic value if they are to survive at all. Absent such creation, or production, there are no resources, no means, to allocate among ends or purposes. And if humans move beyond self-subsistent existence, production as a means of securing ultimate consumption must involve the establishment of exchange relationships with others. Economics allows us to construct a generalized understanding of the complex set of exchange relationships.

As noted earlier, economic theory in its essential respects is no different from other scientific knowledge, within the appropriate limits of its enterprise. These limits are transgressed, however, when attempts are made to move outside the constraints imposed by the human subject matter and to objectify economic reality on some presupposition that values can be divorced from the subjective consciousness of participants in the order. To recall Gertrude Stein's comment about Oakland, "there is no there there" in the sense of an objectifiable economic universe that lends itself to scientific observation and evaluation, a universe that exists separately and apart from the interlinked set of human choices and actions that bring "the economy" into being. At best, therefore, the economist as scientist is restricted to potential explanation of patterns of results, and especially when noneconomic motivations for human actors are necessarily incorporated in what may be observed.

The enterprise of economics is, however, sufficiently open-ended to allow the potential for genuinely exciting scientific advances, which will be influenced, in part, by the events of history. The unexpected and dramatic collapse of communist totalitarian regimes has renewed and reinforced the attention of economists in incentive compatibility in varying institutional

structures, in the informational characteristics of choices made under uncertainty.

Order without Direction

Economic theory, as such, was born with the scientific discovery of the
spontaneous coordination that emerges from the separated, locally directed,
and self-interested actions of participants in a nexus of exchanges. Prior to
this breakthrough in the eighteenth century, there could scarcely have
existed an "economic science," properly understood, since there was no
reasoned understanding of the observed patterns of the order that resulted
from human behavior directed toward economic purpose. Production,
exchange, and consumption could, of course, be observed, but there was
no integrating vision that allowed the separated actions to be related.

At this point, we confront etymological confusion that has plagued the
discipline from its beginnings, a confusion that is not, to my knowledge,
matched in any other science. *Economics*, as a term, finds its origins in
Greek and refers to management or to economizing, yes, to the utilization
of scarce means *by a decision-making unit*. In this accurately derived
etymological use of the term, economics was, of course, always with us,
and there were preclassical theories of economic management in which the
direction of the national household by the king, the prince, the bishop, or
some other sovereign became the subject matter for learned discourse.
German cameralism provided a set of precepts for the prince to follow in
arranging the economic affairs of the principality, and the economizing on
the use of scarce resources was central to any such exercise. Although
mercantilism, as a descriptive term applicable to systems, was coined by
Adam Smith, we find this term useful to refer to those sets of policy
directed principles that offered guidance to those who "managed" the
national economy, who established specific objectives such as national
accumulation of treasure, national rates of growth, and national levels of
employment.

It is not surprising that Keynes found the mercantilist writers to be
kindred souls, since in his attempt to shift the emphasis of economics back
to macroaggregative management, Keynes necessarily moved away from
the central thrust of the whole explanatory enterprise. The macroeconomic
theory of midcentury was strictly within the management tradition and
consistent with the etymological origins of "economics" as a term.

Adam Smith (1937) himself perhaps added to the ultimate confusion
by the selection of the title for his treatise. *The Wealth of Nations*, read

descriptively from the title's words alone, suggests that nations are the units that are wealthy or poor, and, by inference, that increases in nations' wealth are desirable. Smith did not, of course, have such a reading of his title in mind, since the whole thrust of his argument is that individuals, not nations, are the relevant units and that wealth consists in whatever it is that individuals desire. And Adam Smith's work was the channel through which economic theory in the sense used in this chapter was established, a theory of the spontaneous coordination achievable through an interlinked network of market exchanges and a theory that demonstrates the inefficacy of attempted economic management for a whole society.

Throughout the two and a quarter centuries of its history, economics, as a theoretical science, has been burdened with its two-track and mutually contradictory analytical cores. More than mere bifurcation is involved here. The approaches required for analysis in the two research programs are categorically different. A theory that offers an explanation or understanding of the coordinating properties of an exchange network cannot be harnessed into "economizing" service in any strict managerial sense, although, of course, such a theory becomes an essential component in any design and construction of the framework of rules like constitutions within which economic interaction is allowed to operate.

My own resolution of the confusion in economics is clear from my discussion. Economic theory, properly defined, is limited to the domain of exchange relationships, and the behavior within those relationships, along with the institutional structures that emerge or are constructed to constrain those who are participants. If progress is to be made, economics must, once and for all, throw off its etymologically influenced interpretation. Ideally, we should replace the very name; *catallaxy* or *catallactics* is etymologically descriptive (see Buchanan, 1979).

The Constitutional Framework

As people in the Soviet republics are finding out in 1992, the free market does not accomplish the coordination promised by some of its naive advocates in the absence of a set of constraints that may be considered to be the rules or the constitution for the market game. The classical discoverers of the coordinating properties of markets did not sufficiently emphasize the necessary presence of such rules or institutions. If no such rules exist, the chaos that the nonsophisticate in economics more or less naturally imagines may, indeed, become descriptive of reality.

The elements of the constitutional framework are familiar, and these need not be discussed in any detail here, but a summary statement is required in order to ensure that there are some common bounds for subsequent analysis. The political-legal order must embody security of person and property, and the basic rights that define such security cannot, in themselves, emerge from an exchange-like process, despite the pronouncements of the libertarian anarchists. Without some prior agreement on or acknowledgement of what is mine and thine, how could you and I even commence a trading or exchange relationship (see Buchanan, 1975)? Once we are secure in rights of ownership, we are free to make exchanges in rights, in the expectation that those received in trade will themselves be genuinely owned, once possessed. A regime in which rights are severally assigned, mutually acknowledged, and legally protected defines the broad boundaries of the playing field for the inclusive economic interaction process.

A corollary of the ownership and control of person and possession is the enforcement of voluntary contracts of exchange, once made. The political-legal order must operate so as to ensure that individual contractors abide by the terms of agreed on, but not fully implemented, exchanges of rights. And, as with the initial assignments, we could scarcely expect effective contract enforcement to emerge, itself, from contractual foundations, although the libertarian argument here is somewhat more persuasive than in the former case.

There are additional, and supplementary, elements in a constitutional framework that allow a market order of an economy to function effectively. These elements, some of which remain subject to ongoing scientific debate (for example, monetary arrangements), need not be treated in this summary. My point here is to emphasize only that it is the constitutional framework (the laws and institutions, the constraint set) that becomes the appropriate focus for those who seek to reform or to improve the operation of the social process in its economic aspects.

The eighteenth-century discovery of the ordering properties of market exchange was a discovery of such properties *within* rather than independently from the political-legal structure. And classical political economy, the emerging science that elaborated this discovery, at least in early form, was interpreted as a challenge to the whole enterprise of economic management. Laissez-faire—to leave alone—applied negatively to politicized effort to interfere with, and to improve on, the workings of markets. It should never have been extended to the criticism of the necessary political effort aimed at establishing and maintaining the constitutional framework. The categorical distinction between these two levels or stages of politicization was never clearly articulated, and this ambiguity compounded that discussed earlier that involved the meaning of terms.

The Loss of Wisdom

What happened to economics after the fourth decade of the nineteenth century? We know that the excitement of scientific discovery that characterized classical political economy did not survive. Somehow the basic theoretical understanding of market order seemed to slip away, at least partially, and we observed a peculiar melange of scientific progress and scientific retrogression.

Several sources of difficulty can be identified. The classical economists' understanding of market coordination was seriously incomplete. There was no plausibly acceptable theory for the pricing of productive inputs. The cost-of-production theory for the pricing of outputs offered the basis for the Ricardian-Marxian backward extension to input pricing and notably to labor. The theory of surplus value, allegedly produced by but not fully received by labor, was used effectively by Marx to undermine the efficacy of markets, even within the attitudes that embodied the earlier discoveries. The distributional implications of market coordination were moved to center stage, providing grounds for revolutionary political proposals that were well beyond any mercantilist schemes for political management of national economies. The Marxist argument tended to weaken economists' normative evaluation of their whole scientific enterprise.

In this respect, it is singularly unfortunate that the theory of input pricing that emerged as a consequence of the 1870s marginalist revolution in economic theory could not have been developed a mere half century earlier. Such a time shift might have forestalled the Marxist critique, which was clearly based on straightforward scientific error, and the consequences that we all know might not have occurred at all.

Quite apart from the Marxist extension of classical principles that indirectly caused economists to lose confidence in their own *raison d'être*, developments in moral philosophy were also of major importance. Influenced by the ideas of Hegel, philosophers lost the eighteenth-century skepticism about the operations of political-collective institutions, a skepticism that we can interpret to have been squarely based on both analytical and empirical hypotheses. As a substitute, there emerged a romantic model of the state, a model that came to be increasingly dominant, an idealist vision of an omniscient and benevolent collective entity. Both common-sense observation and theoretical understanding were lost. Alongside idealism in political philosophy, and especially in Great Britain, classical utilitarianism provided the framework for normative evaluation of alternative policy propositions, with the effect of drawing attention away from problems of implementation through the realities of politics.

Political idealism and utilitarianism are important because, even in those societies that were not so directly influenced by the Marxian challenges, the romantic model of the state became the source for totally unwarranted comparisons between the market order, as observed in operation, and the state, as idealized. Developments in economic theory did identify and classify institutional and operational failures in the workings of markets, as against the laissez-faire idealizations, but no comparable failures of politicized corrections were brought within the canon of political science until the public-choice revolution of the last half of this century.

Maximization, Mathematization, and the Theory of Games

Genuine scientific progress has been made in economic theory since the moment of its eighteenth-century origins in discovery. The marginalist revolution, and particularly the theory of input pricing that emerged in consequence, tended to complete, in broad basic outline, the theory of market coordination. Even in this respect, however, the contributions of axiomatic general equilibrium theory midway through this century were necessary to round off the whole enterprise. But, as I also noted, the management or economizing conception of subject matter, and applied at the level of the national economy, has never been absent from economists' professional tool kit.

The potential for intellectual confusion was enhanced by some of the methodological implications of the marginalist revolution itself. In voluntary market choices made by participating individuals, values are determined at the relevant margins of adjustment, and the very idea of marginal comparison of values stems from mathematics, the central logic of the calculus. It is not then at all surprising that economic theory, as developed throughout this century, should have use of more and more sophisticated mathematical tools. And, as applied to the decision making of individuals, the calculus of utility maximization is helpfully explanatory. But the availability of the applied mathematics surely generated a bias toward artificially forced and unwarranted extension beyond individual choice to collectivities, to macrounits, to society, to the economy. Social engineering became one of the several postmarginalist versions of mercantilist economic management. As also noted, the Depression inspired shift of attention to movement among economywide macroaggregates, a shift that Keynes and the Keynesians provided with quasi-scientific status, added powerful complementary force to economic management as the ultimate motive impulse for the formulation of economic theory itself.

Even without macroeconomics, however, the increasingly rigorous efforts to define the hard core of economic theory would have ensured an emerging economizing framework, as readily mathematized through the maximization paradigm. Post-Marshall economics became the theory of allocation of scarce resources or means among competing ends, a formulation that lends itself more or less directly to a marginalizing calculus. Emphasis was shifted away from the coordinating properties of interlinked markets, in which the separate participants may, indeed, be modeled as utility maximizers, and toward properties of markets conceptualized as if they were alternatives to or substitutes for economic management schemes for inclusively defined aggregations.

A major change of direction in economic theory may have occurred in midcentury when the theory of games provided an alternative mathematics to the marginalist calculus, a mathematics that carries important implications for the very way that economists conceive what their enterprise is all about (von Neumann and Morgenstern, 1944). In the theory of games, attention is immediately focused on the interaction process, as such, with participants modeled as taking separate actions within specified rules (the constitution), and out of which some solution emerges that is chosen by no one, either individually or collectively. During the second third of the century, the ongoing dominance of the maximization paradigm tended to obscure the potential contribution that game theory's elegance can make toward restoring, indirectly as it were, the catallactic focus of economic theory, a focus that was never totally absent. Only within the last three decades of the century did game theory's economic emphasis shift from the choices of strategies of separate players to the search for solutions and to properties of alternative solutions and then, by inference, to the effects of alternative sets of rules on solutions, the domain of constitutional economics.

The Miracle of the Market

I have found it useful to organize this chapter as a history-of-ideas narrative of the development of economic theory, as personalized through my own definition of the science as stated at the outset. In one sense, therefore, the whole discussion to this point becomes prefatory to the main purpose of the assignment, as suggested in the title of the chapter itself. What role can economic theory play in those societies that have experienced genuine revolutions, in which socialist organizational structures have been explicitly rejected, both in practice and in idea, but in which market-like institutions have not emerged, at least in forms similar to those observed in Western mixed economies? What role should economic theory play in the necessary transition from socialism? The 1990s are properly classified as a postrevolutionary moment in history. Will economic theory be of value in this moment?

I suggest that we can look for an answer in the historical epoch that describes economic theory's finest hours, the few decades that span the turn between the eighteenth and the nineteenth centuries, the period of classical political economy. The ideas of Adam Smith may or may not have themselves influenced events directly as initiating causes of political changes. (I do not engage George Stigler on this point here.) But we cannot deny the role that these ideas played in the undermining of the intellectual foundations, the putative legitimacy, of the eroding mercantilist structure of national economic management. The economists were effective in convincing political leaders, and a sufficiently large number of citizens, that an economic order without politicized direction could not only be imagined but could also be expected to increase the well-being of the economy's participants generally. The central role played by economic theory during this whole epoch seems clear enough. Persons had to be, and were, convinced that a market economy would work, and work with tolerable efficiency, before they would begin to feel comfortable in unstrapping the complex harness of politically controlled economic management.

The eighteenth-century skepticism about the motivation as well as the predicted efficacy of political-collective action in furthering the interests of citizens provided fertile ground for the acceptance of the economists' ideas. The potential constitutional function of market arrangements was for the first time understood, separate and apart from any concern with any prospect for efficiency in generating valued product. In retrospect, we can understand why the classical economists, along with their media and lay supporters, were so enthusiastic about the potential value of the newly emergent science of political economy.

The setting in the postrevolutionary societies in the 1990s is in many respects similar to that of the emerging industrial economies in the late eighteenth and early nineteenth centuries, at least similar enough to warrant speculation about the positive role that might be played by the more sophisticated, and more complete, modern theory or science of economic order. To the citizenry generally, to the intelligentsia, to newly enfranchised political leaders, all of whose history has dispelled any and all of the romance that collectivism-politicization might once have held, the miracle of the market, warts and all, offers promise. The observable consequences of socialism leave little space for the motivation of strictly distributional criticisms of market capitalism.

The timing seems ripe for an emergent and newfound enthusiasm for a Central and Eastern European *Wirtschaftwunder*, an enthusiasm that can be jointly grounded in a loss of faith in politicized economic management and a generalized understanding of economic theory in its most basic, and elementary, sense. The highly sophisticated analyses of potential market failures, as evaluated against nonattainable perfection, can be put on the shelf for those who understand the current relevance of the hard-core principles. To citizens in this postrevolutionary moment, simple analyses of market successes offer the essential components of attainable dreams. Vaclav Klaus, minister of finance in Czechoslovakia, is reported to have called for a "market without adjectives," and it is perhaps only in a postsocialist setting that we might have expected such comment from a highly successful political leader. Can we even imagine his United States counterpart, Secretary of Treasury Bentsen, making such a statement?

As noted, economic theory can provide postrevolutionary intellectuals with a much more sophisticated understanding and explanation of a market order than that which effectively energized the followers of classical political economy two centuries ago. And the body of doctrine incorporated in modern economic theory is sufficiently inclusive to offer continuing challenge to those scientists attracted by the aesthetics of new ideas. The hard core can excite the intelligentsia while the several research programs around the periphery offer promise to the practicing scientists.

For those who seek to use economic theory for more specific reform purposes, the critical distinction between adjustments in the constitutional framework, the constraints within which economic activity takes place, and attempted politicized interferences with market results remain of critical importance. The postrevolutionary institutional settings are in flux; rights have not been fully assigned and acknowledged; legal rules and norms of behavior have not been fully established; contracts among traders have not evolved through a commercial history. And, significantly, a culture of reciprocal exchange is not descriptive of social reality, a culture that is embedded in our subconscious in Western economies (see Buchanan, 1991). The most elementary of all economic principles—there exist mutual gains from trade—remains to be absorbed by people in postsocialist societies. The teaching of economics becomes socially productive in these societies in ways that we can scarcely appreciate in Western cultures.

In my definitional introduction to this chapter, I stated that economic theory, as such, is not itself an empirical science but that it does provide the source for hypotheses that may be subjected to falsifiability tests. The dramatic events that have taken place, and others that will follow, in postrevolutionary economics must surely offer empirically minded economists wonderful opportunities for examining the implications of simple hypotheses. Never in history have economists been offered such near laboratory conditions and on so enormous a scale. Almost regardless of methodological preferences, the economist who concentrates on postrevolutionary societies must be excited about his or her scientific enterprise.

I should acknowledge that my interpretation and prediction of the role that economics and economic theory will play in the postrevolutionary moment are tinged with hope. My response is really to the question "What role can economic theory play?" rather than to the more neutral question "What role will economic theory play?"

The management-economizing conception of economics, and especially as extended normatively to policy prescription, may not have been sufficiently exorcised, and I am concerned that economists in postrevolutionary societies will import many of the wrong or misguided research thrusts of Western economics rather than select carefully for potentially helpful research directions. Without attempts to be exhaustive here, I can list (alphabetically) several research programs that would seem to offer productive insights to professionals in the new postrevolutionary economies: Austrian economics, catallaxy, constitutional economics, game theory, general equilibrium theory, experimental economics, law and economics, new institutional economics, property rights economics, public choice. By comparison and by contrast, the following programs would seem to offer little or no promise and, indeed, may be distracting elements: input-output analysis, industrial policy, linear and quadratic programming, optimal control theory, optimal growth theory, optimal taxation, social choice theory, social welfare functions, theories of planning.

Economic Theory in the West

As an end note to the chapter, it is appropriate to ask the question "What is the role for economic theory in the mixed economics of Western countries that have not experienced revolutionary changes in institutional structures?" I am much less sanguine here than in response to the same question posed earlier for postrevolutionary societies. Western economists, as practicing scientists, tend to take the elementary principles of their discipline too much for granted, and they devote far too much effort, interesting though it may be, to esoteric intellectual puzzles that often have little relevant content, even in some remote sense. (The exception, as noted, may be in modern game theory, where the intricacies of the analytics may be required to force belated recognition of the foundational shift in approach to economic process.)

Economists forget that, quite unlike the other sciences where professionally agreed on principles command authority beyond the scientific community boundaries, economics must be made convincing to the public and its political leaders, a task that requires continued teaching of the elementary verities. "Every man his own economist is a plague that has been with economics since its inception as an independent body of thought. As a result, the failure of the theory's professionals to renew the principles allows interest-driven politicization to intrude continuously into the operations of the market order.

We observe little enthusiasm for the principles of markets based on a widening understanding of the market's efficacy in producing and delivering valued product. And, despite the effect of modern public-choice theory in offering a partial explanation or understanding of political failures, we do not observe an intellectual rejection of "socialism in the small" that is anywhere remotely comparable to the near universal rejection of "socialism in the large" in the postrevolutionary settings.

The relatively pessimistic conclusion is that the future role of economics and economic theory lies with the postrevolutionary societies rather than in the sometimes tired science that is academically established in the West, and, merely by way of such establishment itself, will devote resources to the maintenance of whatever role serves its own interests.

Acknowledgment

I am indebted to my colleague, Viktor Vanberg, for helpful comments.

References

Buchanan, James M. 1975. *The Limits of Liberty: Between Anarchy and Leviathan.* Chicago: University of Chicago Press.

———. 1979. *What Should Economists Do?* Indianapolis: Liberty Press.

———. 1991. "Tacit Presuppositions of Political Economy: Implications for Societies in Transition," Center for Study of Public Choice, George Mason University, Fairfax, Va. Mimeo.

Neumann, J. v., and O. Morgenstern. 1944. *Theory of Games and Economic Behavior.* Princeton: Princeton University Press.

Robbins, Lionel. 1932. *The Nature and Significance of Economic Science*, London: Macmillan.

Smith, Adam. 1937. *The Wealth of Nations.* New York: Random House.

4 THE ROLE OF ECONOMIC THEORY: KEYNESIAN MACROECONOMICS

Lawrence R. Klein

Abstract

The core of Keynesian macroeconomic analysis supports the policy pre-scriptions of high employment and economic stabilization. Balanced policy mixtures for different situations are explained in terms of Keynesian theory, relating back to its inception more than half a century ago and brought forward by subsequent enhancements to the original analysis of *The General Theory*.

The Evolution of Formal Macroeconomics

Macroeconomic analysis has always been a part of economic reasoning, but it was not treated as a separate branch of economics in a formal sense of classification until the period after World War II. By then, the teaching curriculum recognized macroeconomics as a separate subject, but some people still insist that it is simply an extension of microeconomics, obtained by adding up people, establishments, and goods and services.

Adam Smith certainly used a great deal of macroeconomic reasoning, although he is most remembered by devotees for his concept of the "invisible hand" for analysis of goods and services and markets at the microeconomic level.

Macroeconomics as a separate subject was not discovered or invented by Keynes, but his analysis certainly provided the groundwork for guiding economics into the macroeconomics channel.[1] It was fascination with the Keynesian system that generated postwar macroeconomics as a distinct subject, both for teaching and research.

The development may have occurred outside the environment of social accounts and mathematical and statistical models, but these were the vehicles that carried the message of macroeconomics. Keynes was a proponent of social accounting within the British government during World War II (Stone, 1984).

Predecessors of Keynesian macroeconomics were Frisch (1933), Tinbergen (1959), and Kalecki (1935), who independently built self-contained simultaneous equation systems of macroeconomics. Another predecessor who was perhaps less widely known among economists was the mathematician Griffith C. Evans (1934), who built an interesting two-sector (producer and consumer goods) theoretical model of the macroeconomy.

Following the publication of Keynes's *General Theory* (1936), there were interpretive models of Keynesian economics by Lange (1938), Hicks (1937), and others, but they mainly made the nonmathematical exposition of Keynes more logical and understandable; they did not independently propose theoretical macroeconomic models. Wicksell (1907), Irving Fisher (1911), and others dealt with important macroeconomic relationships, especially for price-level and interest rates, but they did not build self-contained models of the economy as a whole.

The study of the macroeconomy was generally classified as business-cycle analysis. Ultimately, nearly all business-cycle scholars reached a point in their theories or statistical investigations at which they looked at the phase and amplitude positions of the economy as a whole, clearly a macroeconomic consideration, although some may have reached this point by adding up various parts. Keynes, on the other hand, opened the way to go directly to the macroeconomics of the matter, both theoretically and statistically. Keynes was not particularly strong on the systematic investigation of business cycles; he was more interested in explaining why the overall economy was at any particular position, without going deeply into the dynamic sequencing of states of the economy. It was left to others to make the Keynesian theory truly dynamic, from a self-contained point of view.

The Correspondence between Theory and Policy

In this chapter I look at the relationship between Keynesian theory and Keynesian policy, without implying that other theories lack such correspondence; they simply are theories that I believe to be inferior to my chosen variety.

The theory of Keynesian economics grew out of an attempt to deal with the problems of the day—the breakdown of the economic restrictions imposed on Germany by the Treaty of Versailles, the speculative waves of the 1920s, the growth of protectionism, the appearance of mass unemployment, and the persistence of the Great Depression. It is not unusual for theory to grow out of practical problems. The search for justifiable policies to deal with these massive problems gave rise to the Keynesian theory.

Briefly put, the Keynesian policies involved a strong fiscal stimulus to pull countries out of the Depression. The emphasis was on public spending but could have been focused to some extent on forms of tax relief, where taxes were sufficiently punitive. Monetary policy could have been part of the overall package, but the emphasis was on public works spending. It is unfortunate that unsophisticated interpretations of Keynesian economics assume that it is simply a rationalization of public spending; that is certainly not imbedded in the theory.

Keynes was not the only person who recommended public spending as a policy to lead major industrial countries out of the Great Depression. Also the thinking was not devoted solely to depression economics, although that provided the impetus. It was recognized that public budgets should go into surplus, or at least balance, during strong recovery phases—after the initial expansion became well established.

The principal theoretical development for support of public spending policies was the discovery of the *multiplier* principle by Richard Kahn (1931) and possibly other associates in the Keynesian circle. It is true that we know much more about the multiplier now—its dynamics, its need for monetary accommodation, its balanced-budget version, its supply-side aspect, and its uncertainty—but it was a breakthrough discovery.

The main theoretical contribution of Keynesian economic policy was that it needed explanation in terms of a total system, for the economy as a whole, in other words a complete national model. It was recognized that policy should not be based on intuitive and subjective reasoning, that indirect as well as direct effects should be included. In order to provide this, Keynes had to develop an entire system. This system, as explained so well by Oskar Lange (1938) and John Hicks (1937), rested on three pillars

—the propensity to consume, the marginal efficiency of capital, and the theory of liquidity preference.

If to these three pillars, we add public budgets and a monetary authority controlling the supply of money to the system, we have the necessary ingredients for the formulation of fiscal (spending *and* taxing) and monetary policy.

The early theoretical renditions explained this system in terms of three equations (Lange) or two equations (Hicks) with some exogenous policy variables (or parameters) added. These theoretical formulations greatly improved the pedagogical treatment of the theory. It was suggestive or indicative for policy formation, but it needed much more work for careful implementation.

No economic theory should be frozen in its tracks. This is particularly true in macroeconomics, where approximation occurs on such a large scale. The next version of a theory generally leads to improvement, and I interpret the evolution of Keynesian economics in this light.

How Did Keynesian Theory Evolve?

Some critics view every amendment to a theory as a sign that the starting point is not right. In this subject it is normal to build on the latest renditions of a theory in order to get the next (better) approximation to reality.

The first extensions of Keynesian theory were to make it open by introducing international trade in the form of propensity to import relationships and export relationships. Also, Keynes assumed that the stock of capital could be taken as given, in the short run. This is surely unduly restrictive in a system that is driven by positive capital formation (investment). The time horizon was lengthened to encompass growth prospects, capital expansion, and long-term evolution of the economy—both in terms of trends and cycles. Not only were cycles introduced, but they were generated by *nonlinear* processes (Hicks, 1950; Kaldor, 1940; Goodwin, 1955) as well as by linear dynamics (Samuelson, 1939; Tinbergen, 1939). Frisch (1933) and Kalecki (1935) had already opened the vista for stochastic effects.

The Keynesian theory was said, as noted above, to be a theory of Depression economics; that was obviously incorrect, but it was a popular conception. It was also said to be entirely demand oriented. That was partially correct. The theory was extended by introduction of a supply side, in terms of production functions, labor supply and demand, and dynamic features that could encompass all phases of the business cycle in addition to long-term growth.

Another extension was to deal more directly with the problem of determination of nominal prices and wage rates. In this connection, a clearer picture of unemployment determination and either unemployment equilibrium or medium-term persistence of unemployment became a possibility. What became known as the Phillips (1958) curve, introduced by me in 1947 (Klein, 1947) and again in 1950 (Klein, 1950) enabled one to close the system and to have a theoretical model that could effectively challenge classical monetarism.

Keynesian Theory and the Existence of Underemployment Equilibrium

Some economists think that Keynes will be remembered mainly for his analysis of *effective demand*; others will emphasize the theory of money and interest (*liquidity preference*). I, as an econometrician, think that the lasting contribution is the specification of a macro model that shows how the main aggregates are determined. The general citizenry will remember Keynes more for his contribution to public policy in terms of fiscal policy (public spending and taxation) and monetary policy. Keynes left his analysis at a point at which others, often associates or disciples, were able to add international and growth modules to his edifice, thereby rendering it more useful and realistic.

There is, however, one piece of Keynesian analysis that remains and, in my opinion, that did not receive definitive treatment at the hand of Keynes—namely, the existence of an *underemployment equilibrium*. This has both theoretical and empirical aspects, the latter being associated with public policy. Keynes asserted that an equilibrium in the economy could exist with persistent involuntary unemployment (Keynes, 1936, p. 249). In theory, classical economics *assumes* the existence of full-employment equilibrium. In practice, a person supporting the classical view might argue that observable unemployment is all voluntary or frictional; whereas its observable persistence may indicate to others that Keynes was correct in pointing out the existence of an underemployment equilibrium.

To state the classical view, let us describe the economy, in Walrasian terms, as a system of supply (S) and demand (D) functions that depend jointly on a complete vector of relative prices $(p_1, p_2, \ldots, p_n)$. A classical model can be written as

$$S_i(p_1, p_2, \ldots, p_n) = D_i(p_1, p_2, \ldots, p_n)$$
$$i = 1, 2, \ldots, n.$$

The solution to this system is one that clears all markets $(1, 2, \ldots, n)$. The introduction of money and the determination of absolute prices completes this system but is not relevant to the present discussion.

A subset of the n equations, above, describes supply, demand, and market-clearing in the labor market. *Equilibrium*, in this sense, means the existence of a vector of prices that makes supply equal to demand in the labor market; hence there is no unemployment because all labor services offered at prevailing prices are demanded.

There is no explicit dynamic process for finding equilibrium in this system, and one would have to appeal to Wald, Arrow-Debreu, McKenzie, and other general equilibrium theorists to show that a solution exists. Apart from this theoretical literature, it was generally assumed that a situation of full employment prevailed in equilibrium. Many of the time-honored propositions of economics—the optimality of free markets, the gains from free international trade—assume implicitly that full employment prevails.

I believe that a theoretical argument can be made for the existence of an unemployment equilibrium, but to establish this proposition it is necessary to go beyond the analysis of the *General Theory*. Also, I believe that it is an empirically validated argument that is very important for providing guidance to economic policy.

In the classical theory, there is no money illusion; so all supply and demand functions depend on relative prices. The original Keynesian analysis suggested that labor supply was nonhomogeneous—that is, that money wage rates, rather than real wage rates, determined labor supply. It is possible to show the existence of unemployment as a solution to an equation system with Keynesian specifications if labor supply depends on nominal wage rates instead of real wage rates, and if it is assumed that nominal wage rates are "sticky" as a result of trade union power and attitude. There is, however, a question whether such a solution can be called *equilibrium*. If wage rates were to be made flexible and if there were no money illusion, the underemployment solution would not exist, in theory.

Contrary to Keynesian thinking (from the *General Theory*), let us assume that labor supply is not based on money illusions:

$$L_t^s = f(w_t/p_t).$$

This exposition is explicitly dynamic and, of course, compact. There are a number of other plausible arguments that could be included in the labor-supply function. Such variables as vacancies, prevailing unemployment (discouraged-worker effects), age-sex-race demographics, and training are significant, but they do not introduce money illusion, and they do not affect the core of the present argument. In addition to these other variables dealing with labor market conditions and demographics, there could also be other real prices, such as capital rental prices, in the labor supply function.

Correspondingly, there is a labor demand function that can be written as

$$L_t^D = g(w_t/p_t).$$

This equation is derived from optimizing behavior of the firm. It is a homogeneous function and could have other arguments such as real output level and different real factor prices. Also, quality and types of labor vary across the population, so that various real wage rates may simultaneously affect labor demand functions.

In serious empirical investigation of such equations as the two above, significant lags or expectations may be relevant for the explanatory variables.

Finally, we have an equation for wage determination. Instead of using static equilibrium analysis, we have an explicit dynamic equation for wage determination:

$$\frac{dw_t}{dt} = h(L_t^s - L_t^D, \frac{dp_t}{dt}).$$

Like the labor supply and demand functions, this equation should also have other arguments. Labor force demographics, social insurance systems, wage drift, and other variables should be introduced. All three equations being considered here are not necessarily linear; in fact, they are likely to be highly nonlinear, and in the analysis of inflation, the nonlinearities play important roles, especially in the wage-determination equation. This equation is stated in terms of the nominal wage, but that does not mean that money illusion is assumed to be present. If

$$\frac{\partial \frac{dw_t}{dt}}{\partial \frac{dp_t}{dt}} = 1,$$

there is no money illusion. It is an empirical matter whether econometric estimates of this equation indicate no money illusion. The crucial issue is whether this equation satisfies

$$0 = h(0, 0).$$

It is entirely possible to have a dynamic system that generally provides a solution as long as the system is in motion but fails to have a *stationary* solution. If unemployment is allowed as a separate variable, empirical models can find a stationary solution, but if $L_t^s = L_t^D$ is also imposed, we may have a contradiction, and a solution may not exist. This is what I find in empirical models.

One may not want to call such a solution an equilibrium solution, since $L_t^s \neq L_t^D$ at a stationary point, when all rates of change in the system are zero, but that is purely semantic. There is no reason to assume that all economic variables are stationary in the time series sense or in the sense of satisfying static versions of dynamic systems.

Following ideas of Tinbergen that wage rate and unemployment variables are related in a macro model equation, I introduced a theoretical equation associating wage change with unemployment as early as 1947 but was actually working with such an equation in model building much earlier. It was finally published in a book describing early efforts at reviving U.S. macro model building, following on Tinbergen's earlier effort. What is now called the Phillips curve is important for demonstrating the possibility of the existence of equilibrium. Apart from the issue of homogeneity (money illusion), it became a vital component of Keynesian analysis but was, unfortunately, not properly interpreted.

It is not a labor-supply equation, as many scholars have assumed or tried to show. It is a market-adjustment equation similar to those used by Oskar Lange (1944) to dynamize and supplement general equilibrium systems, of the form

$$\frac{dP_{it}}{dt} = F\left(S_i\left(\frac{P_{it}}{P_t}, \ldots, \frac{P_{nt}}{P_t} \right) - D_i\left(\frac{P_{it}}{P_t}, \ldots, \frac{P_{nt}}{P_t} \right) \right)$$

$$P_t = \sum_{i=1}^{n} w_i P_{it} \; ; \sum_{i=1}^{n} w_i = 1$$

General equilibrium theorists have extended their analyses to such systems but did not investigate the problem of unemployment in that connection.

In a later study, Ronald Bodkin and I used an estimate of the wage-change/unemployment relationship to see if

$$\Delta w_{it} = h(u_{it}, \Delta p_{it})$$

satisfied

$$0 = h(0, 0).$$

We concluded that unemployment would have to be as high as 10 percent in the United States in order for inflation and wage change to be zero.

Although this estimate of unemployment was scoffed at, as being ridiculously high, it has, in fact, been found to be in the appropriate neighborhood.

One of the misconceptions about the Phillips curve is that it ought to show the (inverse) relationship between inflation and unemployment, but Phillips and I both treated it as a relation between wage change and unemployment. Strict conditions on labor productivity would have to be imposed in order to make a wage-change equation equivalent to an inflation equation. I consider a Phillips curve, properly augmented with demographic and other variables, to be a basic structural equation of market adjustment, while an inflation-unemployment equation is more properly viewed as a *derived* tradeoff equation embedded in a more general system of simultaneous equations. Tradeoff equations can be derived from macro models by fixing all but one (or a combination) of exogenous variables and then varying that one exogenous variable so as to generate a series of unemployment values and a series of inflation variables. Their plotted covariation defines a tradeoff curve, given the fixed values of other exogenous variables. It may or may not produce an inverse relationship—that is, a tradeoff—if some kinds of exogenous variables are isolated as the key factor. If they generate supply-side shocks, we may get positive instead of negative relationships, but that has no effect, by itself, on the structural Phillips curve. Some economists have tried to interpret the existence of "stagflation" in the presence of supply-side shocks as a contradiction of the structural Phillips curve, but this is quite incorrect. The relation between inflation and unemployment may well be positive, while the structural equation associating wage change with unemployment in a bargaining relation is inverse.

The introduction of optimizing equations based on production functions, expanded the strict Keynesian system to what I prefer to call the Keynesian-neoclassical synthesis. This is a long-winded expression but is quite appropriate in view of Keynes's neoclassical training in Cambridge, at the turn of the century.

The theory is, thus, in place, but to show that the various approximations at the macro level are closely related to neoclassical behavior at the micro level, it is necessary to build bridges between the two levels through distribution theory—the size distributions of income, wealth, demographic characteristics, and others. These are partly handled by specifying sector behavior, parameters, or other statistics of distributions and by testing the theory against actual observations of the economy. It is no surprise that Hicks and Lange modeled Keynes with just two or three equations, while modern econometric models use numbers in the hundreds or thousands in order to get the flavor of specificity and, in some cases, aggregative results.

The longest known record of forecasting power is the forty-year history of the Michigan model, which under various operators has been generating macroeconometric forecasts, steeped in the theory of Keynesian economics—extended as noted above—since 1952. It has weathered trying times with the Korean War, Vietnam War, breakdown of Bretton Woods, oil shocks, the Cold War (with its ending), the Persian Gulf War, and many other major events. A remarkable picture was presented by Stephen McNees (1988) a few years ago, but it seems to improve with age and experience. This model representation of Keynesian-neoclassical macroeconomics has earned the present operator, Saul Hymans, the top national forecasting award twice. I know of no other theory that has held up so well, for so long, in the midst of an ever-changing economic environment. Of course, McNees's article refers to GNP prediction, but scores of other magnitudes are carefully generated, in a replicated manner, at the same time.

A great deal of economic theory concerns what ought to be—sometimes in generality and sometimes in the minds of economists who fail to test their theories. A theory should be judged on its ability to predict, and theorists ought to be making frequent, careful validation tests. Keynesian macroeconomics, unlike many of the alternative expositions of economics or schools of thought, is operational and can be checked against data. This does not mean that it is proven to be the sole theory with explanatory power, but it does mean that it has a clear advantage against other approaches.

Some Lines of Future Development

When macroeconomics became a separate subject for the teaching of economics, both at the elementary and advanced levels, the predominant mode of expression was the Keynesian model and extensions of it. During the last two decades there have been challenges. It is my opinion that none of the challenging positions has been validated and put to the same battery of tests to which Keynesian economics has been subjected. Nevertheless, other theories about macroeconomics have become popular in higher education and scholarly meetings. When it comes to the application of these theories for management of the macroeconomy, none has withstood the test of time. They have all made fallible predictions and misled decision makers. Such concepts as supply-side economics or monetarism or complete deregulation into free-market decisions (without macroeconomic policy guidance) have seemingly had short spurts of success but eventually have broken down with legacies of heavily indebted public bodies, persistent unemployment, uneven balances among countries in external payments, long-term currency misalignments, and prolonged recessionary phases of the business cycle. Governments have fallen as a result of being too closely wedded to some failed concepts of theoretical macroeconomics.

By and large, Keynesian medicine served the world well for more than twenty-five years after World War II. This, together with careful validation tests, provided a fruitful link between economic theory and application in the form of policy guidance at the macro level. There were some favorable episodes of policy formation along Keynesian lines after 1973, and there will be more to come, but there are still challenges in the form of theory building in constructive ways to make the Keynesian-neoclassical synthesis work even better.

First, let us consider the subject of *expectations*. This subject was treated in an interesting way by Keynes and was taken further theoretically by Shackle (1949) and empirically by Tinbergen (1939). Expectations have always played a prominent role in Keynesian macroeconomics and also found explicit expression in econometric model building along Keynesian lines.

A popular concept among the younger generation of economists is that of *consistent* expectations—that is, expectations that are generated by the model itself even though the estimation of the model must use the same expectations. This model has defined solutions, although there can be a multiplicity of accepted solutions. This approach has the advantage of making expectations endogenous and capable of being explained without adding to the model except in computational complexity. Subject to the above-mentioned cases of multiplicity of solutions, computational difficulty is not particularly a serious obstacle. A more serious difficulty is the plausibility of this approach to expectations formation, and the lack of a "track record." I know of no instance in which consistent expectations have been found to lead to superior predictions or validated insight about the functioning of the economy. There is nothing to match the forty-year forecasting behavior of the Michigan model.

There are, nevertheless, important avenues of research in the field of expectations formation that can lead to future improvement in the Keynesian-neoclassical synthesis. In the first place, there are numerous sample surveys of expectations—prices, investment plans, housing starts, orders for goods, and similar anticipatory variables that need to be incorporated explicitly in the systems of Keynesian macroeconomics.

It is easy enough to collect these objective, but sometimes indirect, measures of expectations and use them as exogenous information—with a validity horizon of less than one year. That is all too short. These anti-cipatory magnitudes must be related in estimated equations to other vari-ables of the system and thereby generated endogenously within the model. There are many instances of such treatment of anticipatory variables, but they need more research and work experience.

A second, and related, avenue of future investigation involves the use of *futures* data, especially forward prices. The spot-forward spread for primary commodity prices can be related to the inventory position and other important variables of the system.

There may be other methods of getting at subjective expectations, but the two methods mentioned here look very promising and are capable of being treated operationally.

A second line of new theory building is to integrate flow-of-funds, or capital flows, or balance-sheet items into the macroeconomics of Keynes and the neoclassicists. Pieces of such theory integration have been widely investigated. I have in mind the introduction of wealth or liquid assets in the consumption function, the treatment of holding of cash balances as an element of total financial portfolio analysis, the extension of commercial trade flow analysis to complete balance-of-payments analysis. These are all parts of the total exercise, but what is needed is a full integration of the national income and product accounts (NIPA) with a complete flow-of-funds accounting (F/F). Each sector's balance sheet (household, nonfinancial business, banks, other financial institutions, public authorities, rest-of-the-world) should be generated endogenously by the extended theory, in some detail, together with the elements of NIPA. That would represent true frontier work—far more important than the excessive preoccupation of young theoreticians with such things as consistent expectations. It is the direction for the next constructive step in the tradition of Keynesian eco-nomics. Some elementary systems have been built along these lines, but a finished and comprehensive product is not yet in hand.

Along the same lines as the above discussion about integrating F/F with NIPA is careful attention to specific issues in international finance, not only to explain a country's international balance of payments but to delve into analysis of everyday operations on international financial markets. Vast sums of money to finance exchange of assets (existing as well as new), speculation on foreign-exchange markets, and speculation on commodity markets are important for explaining movements in the international spectrum of interest rates, bilateral exchange rates, and prices of basic commodities.

People and businesses may hold money and other assets in many differ-ent countries simultaneously. They are influenced by foreign interest rates, prices, and business conditions, as well as by those at home. This means that the liquidity preference and savings functions of Keynesian theory depend on many different international variables and not simply one interest rate, one inflation rate, one index of exchange rate, and one aggregate activity level. Many such variables across countries matter for making economic decisions, on a twenty-four-hour global basis; therefore a great deal of theory building is required. It will surely involve putting together larger, more complicated systems along innovative lines.

I have spoken of international trade and international capital flows; these are very important, but even more important are international people flows—immigration. Large-scale movements of people have been very important in the economic lives of entire countries or continents. In some cases, an influx has been important for understanding economic performance, as in the United States, Canada, Australia, and, more recently, Western Europe. Immigrants have made enormous contributions to the economic life of the United States. At the same time, outward migration has been of extreme importance for Japan, Western Europe at an earlier stage, India, China, Africa, and other countries or continents. Labor shortages have been relieved; scarce skills have been transported; and diverse tastes for economic output have been introduced into societies to bring them cultural diversity. People cannot generally move freely, but they do sometimes move on a large scale and have a great deal of economic impact.

Total analysis of demography, covering births, deaths, aging, working, studying, and many other people activities need to be treated carefully in the extended Keynesian system. For the most part these are trend-like variables and not strongly cyclical. They are needed for long-run analysis, but immigration is subject to short-run swings and contributes both to cyclical and secular analysis. As was noted earlier, the distribution bridge between micro- and macroeconomics must have large demographic content, but demography is important, too, for theory building at the purely macroeconomic level.

The third social accounting system, in addition to NIPA and F/F, is the input-output (I-O) system that portrays the use of intermediate inputs in the technical production process. The most effective way to treat disaggregation by sector (not *within* sector) is to combine a detailed input-output (I-O) system (Leontief, 1952) with the NIPA and F/F system. Then the Keynesian-neoclassical synthesis becomes a Keynes-Leontief-neoclassical model. The I-O system brings short-run operating characteristics of the production process into the overall theoretical framework.

Finally, at least for now, a next concern for economic model building is a combination of standard economic classifications and issues with environmental affairs. By this, I refer to the natural environment, spanning air, water, waste, and congestion. The theory will have to be "green." There will have to be variables to cover the costs of protecting the natural environment, and macroeconomic indicators will have to reveal a qualitative as well as a quantitative dimension. The taxation-subsidy system will provide policy handles for taking public action in the interests of protecting the environment. This area of economic reasoning will come under pressure for a great deal of policy action in the future, and the policy makers will have to be able to refer to a solid theoretical base for implementing their decisions.

A Return to Keynesian Policy

Noninterventionist policies have not worked well. The economies of the world have been left in an unbalanced state with large deficits, persistent unemployment, growing inequality of distribution, and a great deal of public dissatisfaction with "magic of the market" and inaction in the face of economic deterioration. To a large extent, this situation came about because of poor theoretical underpinning for such things as monetarism and supply-side economics.

For a successful return to Keynesian-type macroeconomic policy to restore good growth with full employment and adequate price stability, an extended Keynesian system will have to be called on. The simple system of three pillars is fine for pedagogical purposes, but a much more comprehensive and complex system will have to be built and used for policy guidance. If the extensions that were mentioned in the previous section are put into place, it is inevitable that the system will have to be large. Computer-based systems of hundreds or thousands of interdependent equations can be handled with modern facilities. Gone are the days of back-of-the-envelope calculations. The largest systems for which databases can be built and that can be managed by humans will be required. These will become ever larger as computer and related technology advances, but the next generation of Keynesian economics will not look like its antecedents, although it is an outgrowth whose roots can be definitely traced.

Note

1. For early usage of macroeconomics, see de Wolff (1941) and Klein (1946).

References

de Wolff, P. 1941. "Income Elasticity of Demand: A Micro-economic and a Macro-economic Interpretation." *Economic Journal*, 51, 140–145.

Evans, G.C. 1934. "Maximum Production Studied in a Simplified Economic System." *Econometrica*, 2, 37.

Fisher, I. 1911. "The Equation of Exchange, 1896–1910." *American Economic Review*, 1, 296–305.

Frisch, R. 1933. "Propagation Problems and Impulse Problems in Dynamic Economics." In *Economic Essays in Honour of Gustav Cassel*. London: Allen and Unwin.

Goodwin, R.M. 1955. "A Model of Cyclical Growth." In E. Lundberg, ed., *The Business Cycle in the Postwar World*. London: Macmillan.

Hicks, J.R. 1937. "Mr. Keynes and the 'Classics': A Suggested Interpretation." *Econometrica*, 5, 147–159.

———. 1950. *A Contribution to the Theory of the Trade Cycle*. Oxford: Clarendon Press.

Kahn, R.F. 1931. "The Relation of Home Investment to Unemployment." *Economic Journal*, 41, 173.

Kaldor, N. 1940. "A Model of the Trade Cycle." *Economic Journal*, 50, 78–92.

Kalecki, M. 1935. "A Macro-dynamic Theory of Business Cycles." *Econometrica*, 3, 327–344.

Keynes, J.M. 1940. *How to Pay for the War*. New York: Harcourt Brace.

———. 1986. *The General Theory of Employment, Interest, and Money*. New York: Harcourt Brace.

Klein, L.R. 1946. "Macroeconomics and the Theory of Rational Behavior." *Econometrica*, 14, 93–108.

———. 1947. "Theories of Effective Demand and Employment." *Journal of Political Economy*, 55, 108–131.

———. 1950. *Economic Fluctuations in the United States, 1921–1941*. New York: Wiley.

Lange, O. 1938. "The Rate of Interest and the Optimum Propensity to Consume." *Economica*, 12.

———. 1944. *Price Flexibility and Employment*. Evanston: Principia Press.

Leontief, W. 1952. *The Structure of the American Economy, 1919–1939*. New York: Oxford University Press.

McNees, S.K. 1988. "The Accuracy Keeps Improving." *New York Times*, January 10, Business, p. 2.

Phillips, A.W. 1958. "The Relation between Unemployment and the Rate of Change of Money Wage Rates in the United Kingdom, 1861–1957." *Economica*, N.S. 25, 283–299.

Samuelson, P.A. 1939. "Interactions between the Multiplier Analysis and the Principle of Acceleration." *Review of Economic Statistics*, 21, 75–78.

Shackle, G.L.S. 1952. *Expectation in Economics* 1949. (2nd ed.). Cambridge: University Press, 1952. 1st ed. 1949.

Stone, Richard. 1984. "Autobiographical Statement." In *Les Prix Nobel*. Stockholm: Almqvist & Wiksell.

Tinbergen, J. 1939. *Business Cycles in the United States of America, 1919–1932*. Geneva: League of Nations.

———. 1959. "An Economic Policy for 1936." In L.H. Klaasen et al., eds., *Jan Tinbergen Selected Papers*. Amsterdam: North-Holland.

Wicksell, K. 1907. "The Influence of the Rate of Interest on Prices." *Economic Journal*, 17, 213–220.

5 METHODOLOGY OF CRITICAL MARXIAN ECONOMIC THEORY

Howard J. Sherman

Abstract

Three paradigms are distinguished: neoclassical economics, official Marxian economics, and independent or critical Marxian economics. The critical Marxian paradigm is holistic or relational and does not reduce everything to psychology or economics. It investigates both conflict and harmony, not assuming either one. It finds three levels of class conflict—economic, political, and ideological. It is evolutionary and historical, rather than static and ahistorical. It is opposed to positivism and sees a unity of facts and theories as well as a unity of theories and ethical judgments. It rejects free will as well as predeterminism, believing that human beings make their own history within certain historically given conditions. It believes that the role of theory is to understand the political-economic system in order to change it.

Introduction

Following the approach of Thomas Kuhn (1962), a *paradigm* may be defined as a set of basic assumptions, methodological stances, and theories that are taken for granted by most of the practitioners of a discipline. The economic theories and empirical assumptions of different paradigms in

77

economics have been thoroughly discussed elsewhere (see Sherman, 1988). Here, the focus will be on methodology—that is, the approach to society and the philosophy of science of economics.

The dominant paradigm in U.S. economics may perhaps be called "neoclassical economics," interpreted broadly to include many neo-Keynesians as well as monetarists. Those opposed to the neoclassical position include the institutionalist, post-Keynesian, and Marxian traditions. In the Marxian tradition, there is a split between the official Marxism of the old USSR or of China versus the *critical Marxists*, that is, all those Marxists who are independent of and critical of the old, traditional, official Marxism. This chapter concentrates on the critical Marxian approach—but it should be stressed that this approach is very close to the radical institutionalist view (see Dugger, 1989) and to the radical post-Keynesian view (see Sawyer, 1989).

To make the contrast among current paradigms in economics clear, the tendencies in the different paradigms in methodological approaches may be summed up very briefly. Neoclassical economics tends toward (1) an individualist approach that always begins with individual psychology; (2) universal, ahistorical laws; (3) an assumption of harmony, excluding conflict; (4) the complete separation of empirical fact from theory; (5) the free will of consumers; (6) the complete separation of "science" from ethics. Official Marxism tended to the opposite extreme: (1) a collectivist approach that began with class and economic structures, giving individuals (such as consumers) no role to play; (2) a completely predetermined historical set of stages of society; and (3) an assumption of total class conflict with no elements of harmony or cooperation in capitalism, so (4) the state was run completely by the capitalist class.

Critical Marxian economics is quite different than either of those paradigms and tends toward (1) a relational approach (similar to the holistic approach of many institutionalists) that prohibits reduction to either psychology or economics standing alone; (2) an historical approach (similar to the evolutionary approach of institutionalism); (3) conflict as well as harmony; (4) class analysis of conflict (on this point, liberal institutionalists will tend to disagree, while radical institutionalists may agree); (5) an approach combining empirical fact with theoretical framework, which excludes both empiricism and rationalism; (6) a scientific determinism, which excludes both free will and predeterminism; and (7) an approach combining theory-and-facts with ethical values. The rest of the chapter explains these abstract terms and provides concrete examples. These thumbnail sketches have left aside all of the differences within each paradigm, so one could say that any such listing is a strawman. The object here, however, is not a comprehensive history of thought but merely an ideal model of what the extreme positions and options are in the current methodology of economic theory.

The Holistic or Relational Approach

Official Marxism, under Stalinist domination, tended to interpret Marx's historical materialism as saying that everything can be reduced to economics, and that economics determines in the last analysis all of the politics and ideas of a society. Most of the recent commentators who have written in depth on historical materialism, however, have agreed that there is a two-way interaction of ideas and economics (see the outstanding books by Larrain, 1986; Wolff and Resnick, 1989: Rigby, 1987; Sayer, 1987; and Callinicos, 1988; also see the pioneering contribution by Sartre, 1968).

In a relational (or holistic) view, critical Marxian economists examine the relations between ideas and economics as a multiple-causation relationship in a society that is an integrated whole. By contrast, the psychological reductionism of neoclassical economics and the economic reductionism of official Marxism both start from a premise that there are various isolated spheres in society, with a one-way causation running from one to another. In the relational view of critical Marxian economics, society is to be seen as a unified organism, not a set of isolated spheres, so social scientists should always begin with relationships in the whole society, including integrated political, sociological, psychological, and economic analyses. Thus, critical Marxian economists do not isolate economics but always examine the whole social framework, including issues such as class conflicts as well as all aspects of racial and gender discrimination.

Critical Marxian economists distinguish two spheres of society—the social structure and the economic structure. The *social structure* includes by definition all ideas and all noneconomic institutions. The *economic structure* includes by definition both the forces of production (land, labor, capital, technology) and the class relations of production (who owns, who works, who gets the product). For example, the class relations would include relationships between slaves and slave owners or between farmers and collective farm bosses.

In this framework, there are two basic aspects to the social-economic process. First, the ideas of human beings clearly affect, shape, and influence the relations and forces of production. For example, ideas affect politics and politicians make laws, which determine property ownership. Moreover, human ideas result in technological innovation. In this sense, *the economic structure is a function of the social structure.*

Second, it is also the case, however, that the economic structure (including human relations of production a as well as forces of production) affects, shapes, and influences the social structure. For example, the birth control pill (a technological innovation) has profoundly changed human sexual views and behavior. Some technological advances, such as the use of fire or of writing, affected practically every aspect of human social structure. In addition, one's position in the relations of production, such as whether one is a slave or a slave owner, shape a person's way of thinking as well as one's style of life. In the United States today, there is an enormous difference between the viewpoint of a frequently unemployed worker and that of a millionaire corporate executive. Thus, *the social structure is a function of the economic structure.*

One qualification is necessary. Our social structure is partly a function of the economic structure, but it is also a function of its own previous evolution. For example, our literature is influenced by its social-economic environment, but it is also influenced by the whole past history of literary technique.

Similarly, the economic structure is a function of both the social structure *and* its own previous evolution. For example, the inventing and building of the atomic bomb resulted partly from previous technological advances but partly from the political-military pressures of World War II. To sum up, the social and economic structures are functions of each other, but each is also influenced by its own history.

These functional relations, however, are quite vague and general. If we try to think of these functions as "laws" like the usual kind of scientific law, then they would have to specify given parameters in a given time and place. That is exactly what radical economists explore in their detailed studies. But if—in an attempt to be scientific and verifiable—these vague, general laws are transformed into very specific statements about a given time and place, they lose a large part of their usefulness. Is the only alternative to leave them as vague "laws" (or statements) about social reality?

Rather than being vague laws with questionable scientific credentials, it is better to think of the relational approach as a set of guidelines or methods of approaching difficult problems. As a nondogmatic approach to social problems, the relational view teaches some important lessons. It is not a set of answers, but a set of questions. These questions suggest the best way to approach any social issue; the questions are based on the previous experience of social science.

For example, if an economic event is to be explained, then one should ask questions not only about the previous economic structure, but also about the social structure that interacts with it. Similarly, to explain an event in the social structure, one should consider not only the previous social structure but should ask questions about the economic structure with which it interacts.

To understand the evolution of ideas, the relational approach suggests that one should ask, "What social process produced these ideas or selected these ideas to be dominant, and how did the previous ideological evolution produce this form in the ideas?" To investigate political institutions, ask, "How are the politics of the era shaped by the relative power of different classes in the relations of production?" To investigate the forces of production, ask, "How do the relations of production hold back or stimulate advances in the forces of production?" To investigate the class relations of production, one question is, "How much does the level of the forces limit the possible class relations of production? How do ideology and political institutions affect class relations?" Questions about class relations are at the heart of Marx's relational method.

Types of Conflicts

The relational method of critical Marxism does not assume conflict in all societies at all times. It is possible for relations to be harmonious or conflictual or any combination thereof. Critical Marxian economists do insist that these questions should always be asked: "Are the class relations of this society conflictual ones? Are there other conflicts as well?" Critical Marxian economists have explored not only class conflicts but conflicts between big business and small business, racial conflicts, gender conflicts, nationality conflicts, and environmental conflicts—as well as the relationships of all of these in a given society.

There is nothing in critical Marxism that says that class conflict is the only conflict or even that it is always the most important. Class relations and class conflict are considered the best beginning point to understand the structure of any society—though the answer may be very simple if the society is not divided by classes. Without understanding the social and economic structure of a society, one cannot understand race, gender, or nationality within it. Having found and examined class conflicts, however, critical Marxian economics insists that one must then study separately racial, gender, and nationality conflicts. Of course, one must examine how each of these conflicts are affected by class conflict—but one must also examine how class conflict is affected by race, gender, and nationality conflicts.

Here, discussion begins with the three main levels of class conflict: the economic, the social and political, and the ideological. Official Marxists may sometimes speak as if one only had to pay attention to the economic level of class conflict, but critical Marxists insist on a careful investigation of all three levels.

Class Conflict in the Economy

The U.S. class structure reveals a small class of capitalists in conflict in different ways and different degrees with professionals and managers as well as with the large class of workers (plus the unemployed, small farmers, and so forth, see Wright, 1985). Where critical Marxian economists see class conflict, neoclassical economists tend to deny it. Liberal institutionalists find many conflicts and many fights for power in capitalism, but not along class lines.

Official Marxists have usually used a model of only two classes. No critical Marxist claims there are only two classes in modern capitalism; there are many classes and strata. It is true there has been polarization, however, in two significant ways. In 1840, the small farmers, small businessmen, and independent professionals constituted perhaps 90 percent of the populace. Today, those groups are only 7 or 8 percent, while 80 to 90 percent of Americans are in the working class, including both poor and well paid, both low-status and prestigious, both manual and mental workers. Because of this objective polarization, the main political issues—such as unemployment benefits or capital gains taxes—are also polarized around a capitalist position versus a workers' position. Issues involving farmers or small business exist but are more peripheral and may be seen as one of many secondary conflicts in society. Of course, there are also issues on which average workers may be opposed by professionals, technicians, or supervisors according to their own interests.

Within the productive process, there are several modes of class conflict. The conclusion of radical economic theory is that capitalists exploit workers by extracting profits from the values created by the workers' toil. Workers resist this exploitation by individual slowdowns, by tossing monkey wrenches in the productive process in many ways, and by organized activity such as collective bargaining and strikes. In many industries the collective arm of the workers—their unions—meets head on against the collective arm of capital, whether a single monopolistic giant or a trade association. The strength on either side—modified by supply and demand conditions—determines the split between wages and profits. Obviously, these class conflicts are neither random nor accidental; they are internal to the normal working of the productive process.

These class conflicts are partly reflected in and partly intensified by workers' alienation. Workers are alienated from their product by capitalists who own it and sell it at a profit, thus exploiting the workers. Workers are alienated from their work because each worker does only a tiny, routinized part of the whole job. Subjectively, workers are alienated, not only from capitalists but from each other as the result of competition against each other in the labor market.

Social-Political Class Conflicts

The class conflict at the productive level is modified by the class conflict within all social and political institutions. For example, when Californians debated a proposition to reduce the progressive state income tax, the change was attacked by the AFL-CIO and other working-class and middle-class organizations but was supported by the California Manufacturers Association, Builders Association, Farm Bureau Association, Real Estate Association and Chamber of Commerce. Obviously the defense and attack is not random but represents class interests.

This second level of class conflict includes political struggle for control of the government (see Sherman, 1988, ch. 7; and Sawyer, 1989, ch. 10). Neoclassical economics says little on the state but usually assumes that issues are decided on a rational basis by voters. At the other extreme, official Marxism contends that in capitalism there are only two classes locked in combat (thus precluding any real democracy), while in socialism there is only one class and it governs (providing democracy by assumption).

Critical Marxian economics considers that, under capitalism, capitalist, working-class, and other class interests and views clash within the media of propaganda, the churches, the education system, the legal system and the courts, and the legislative and executive branches of government. In all of these institutions, capitalist interests tend to be dominant, though there is more or less pressure from and expression of working-class interests and the interests of other classes—with differing degrees of success by the non-dominant classes.

There are innumerable ways in which the economic power of big business is translated into political power, such as control of the media, churches, universities, candidates, and political parties through the direct use of wealth. In addition, the structure of capitalism forces all politicians to follow the interests of capital, regardless of ideology. For example, when Chrysler corporation was on the verge of bankruptcy in the late 1970s, labor supported a government bailout for Chrysler Corporation to protect jobs.

Under either capitalism or socialism, one cannot say that democracy "exists" or "does not exist"; it exists *to some degree*. Where there is formal democracy but capitalist ownership, the degree of democracy for most people is very low; there are "democratic" struggles amongst factions of the capitalist class, with only a small amount of "outside" pressure exerted by farmers and industrial and professional workers. Certainly, the converse is also true: where there was government ownership but no formal democracy and the universal vote was allowed only for the purpose of endorsing a single party, the degree of democracy for most people was close to zero. This was the case in the Soviet Union before Gorbachev, though some pressure was always exerted by the nonruling groups in various ways. A high degree of democracy requires both a formal democratic process *and* democratic control of the economy—that is, public or workers' cooperative control of much industry to ensure a high degree of equality of economic power.

The conflict between the economic power of the capitalist class and the formal right to vote of the other classes is analyzed by Samuel Bowles and Herbert Gintis: "Liberal democratic capitalism is a system of contradictory rules, empowering the many through . . . citizen rights—and empowering the few through property rights" (Bowles and Gintis, 1990, p. 39). They define "citizen rights" to be the formal freedoms fought for by the working class, women, and minorities; while they define "property rights" to be the legal representation of the actual economic power used by the capitalist class. They show that the history of capitalist democracies is the history of conflict between citizen rights and property rights. The result has been formal equality, as in the civil rights acts, but actual continuing inequality for workers, women, and minorities.

Bowles and Gintis stress the clash between "two fundamental historical tendencies. The first is the expansionary logic of personal rights, progressively bringing ever wider spheres of society . . . under at least the formal . . . rubric of liberal democracy. The second tendency concerns the expansionary logic of capitalist production, according to which the capitalist firm's ongoing search for profits progressively encroaches upon all spheres of social activity" (Bowles and Gintis, 1986, p. 29). On the one hand, working-class parties extended the suffrage to all U.S. white males regardless of property in the early nineteenth century, the women's movement extended suffrage to women in the early twentieth century, and the African American civil rights movement extended effective suffrage to minorities in the late twentieth century. On the other hand, corporations grow larger and larger, with more power over government, as shown in the counterrevolution of the Reagan years, which rolled back many previous reforms.

Critical Marxian economists also stress the crucial importance of racial and gender conflicts in our society. The civil rights movement, including all minority organizations and minority theorists, has shown with great clarity that racial conflicts shape and are shaped by politics and class conflict (see the extensive discussion of the literature in Sherman, 1988). The women's movement, including organizations and theorists, has shown with equal clarity that gender conflicts shape and are shaped by politics and class conflict (see, e.g., Nancy Hartsock, 1985, as well as Sherman, 1988).

Ideological Class Conflict

The third level of class conflict is the reflection of class conflicts in clashing ideologies. There are very real conflicts between ideologies. Examples include the arguments between those for and against taxation of capital gains, between feminists and sexists, and between the defenders of the ecology and the growth-at-any-cost school. Moreover, each of these ideologies develops with more and more sophistication and elegance. The path of development of each opposing idea is partly determined by the battle with its opposite. Yet these internal developments of ideologies are not independent of class relations but are both highly influenced by changing class relations and highly influential on the course of class relations. Thus the fact that prevention of pollution could cause loss of profits for powerful capitalists has a great deal to do with the promotion of conflicting ideologies on pollution. On the other side, the surge of interest in ecological protection was related to the involvement of intellectuals in the civil rights and antiwar movements of the 1960s.

It should be noted that no class in history has ever had a simple, narrow, materialistic ideology that values things simply for its own class interest. On the contrary, the majority of each class usually believes that its desires represent the good of the whole of society. Thus, the bourgeoisie did not lead the French Revolution on the basis of what was good narrowly defined for its own interests but as a crusade for liberty, equality, and fraternity (or the brotherhood of all men)—while the bourgeoisie in the American Revolution fought for life, liberty, and the pursuit of happiness.

Therefore, in each social-economic investigation, critical Marxian economists ask, "What are the class relations, if any? What are the types of class conflicts, if any? Are there economic, political, ideological class conflicts? Are there conflicts within classes? Are there racial, gender, or nationality conflicts? Are there conflicts between developers and the ecology movement? How are the nonclass conflicts related to class conflicts in the society? Are the relationships all of conflict, or all of harmony, or do the relationships involve both harmony and conflict in varying degrees." Note that the questions about conflict are a subset of the questions about relations, not a new and different approach.

Main Features of the Historical (or Evolutionary) Approach

Institutionalists have always approached the evolutionary process in terms of the conflict between institutions and technology (see, e.g., Samuels, 1977). A similar view of the evolutionary and revolutionary historical process may be found among critical Marxists (such as Callinicos, 1988, p. 94). First, if productive forces develop, they will eventually be inappropriate to the existing class relations. Second, the result is a crisis of some sort, which is often reflected in stagnant or declining productive forces. Third, this tension may then result in class conflict; which will be reflected only in part in direct economic form but also in political and social conflict and in ideological conflicts. These social and political conflicts may be expressed as religious, racial, gender, or national conflicts—and the racial or gender conflicts may themselves have an independent life, exacerbating the class conflicts.

Fourth, the outcome of the class conflict will depend on the exact nature of the class interests and class power of a multitude of classes. Yet radical economists (including critical Marxists, but *not* official Marxists) also emphasize that class interests must be reflected in the actual subjective outlook of the majority of a class, or else they are of no actual consequence. Critical Marxists (in a large number of studies, see, e.g., Callinicos, 1988, p. 184). have studied the conditions under which the individuals of a class will have the desire to make a change. Most critical Marxists do find that under the right circumstances, revolution is a rational choice for most workers. The first Soviet revolution in 1917 showed that workers (with the help of intellectuals) could make a successful revolution against capitalist and feudal rulers. The second Soviet revolution in 1991 proved that workers (with the help of intellect workers and some managerial workers) could make a successful revolution against a ruling class consisting of the top Communist Party leaders, the generals, the leaders of the Soviet government, and the leading economic planners.

As is the case with the relational view, the historical approach is better seen as a methodological suggestion for approaching problems than as a set of laws—since the "laws" would be rather vague generalities. As Engels put it, "Our conception of history is above all a guide to study, not a lever for construction after the Hegelian manner" (Frederick Engels, quoted in Rigby, 1987, p. 104). The historical approach suggests asking certain questions; it does not give specific answers. The historical or evolutionary method asks the question, "How is this political-economic system, and each part of it, evolving?"

Thus, faced with a particular situation or problem in political economy, it is usually useful to ask, "How has this problem evolved? Toward where is it evolving?" Of course, Marxian economics suggests as the entry point to an understanding of a specific political-economic evolution the nature of the class conflict at that time. Therefore, it is necessary to investigate as closely and concretely as possible exactly the class structure, how it relates to the problem at hand, and the strength of the opposing classes. The direction of change in social-economic process can usually be understood only by investigating both its internal tensions and its relation to the rest of the social world.

In summary, the historical approach asks

1. From where did this system evolve, how is it now developing, and in what direction may it evolve? Who is helped and who is hurt by the present tendencies?
2. What are the present conflicts, what relationships are involved in those conflicts, and how are those relations changing?
3. More specifically, are there tensions between the productive forces and the productive relations (as defined by Marx)?
4. Are these structural tensions causing class conflicts, ethnic or racial conflicts, or gender conflicts?
5. Are these conflicts leading toward a revolutionary situation?
6. If there is a revolution, what new relations and conflicts may replace the present ones?

Materialism, Empiricism, and Rationalism

The medieval period in Europe was a period of religious superstition and idealist mystification. The term *idealism* in this context means the notion that reality is not material but is a set of absolute ideas or an idea of God. To avoid confusion, note that this concept of idealism has no relation to the statement that someone is idealistic in moral terms. There was a long period of struggle against superstition and idealism, led by British and French philosophers, such as Locke and Diderot.

Marx's materialism represents an evolution from these early materialists. Engels said that materialism means only this: "to comprehend the real world as it presents itself to everyone who approaches it free from preconceived idealist fantasies" (Engels, 1966, 1878, pt. 4). In the materialist view, science can probe deeper and deeper into the complexities of nature and society—and there is no limit to human knowledge, no mysterious line beyond which we may not go.

As a method, materialism means the directive to the social scientist that he or she can derive scientific knowledge only from observation and experiment—more generally, participation—in the real world. The scientist cannot prove anything from religious authorities or revelations—but also cannot accept any authority, such as Aristotle or Marx, as being beyond contention or disproof in the ordinary way. Moreover, mere assertion of an idea proves nothing but may be used as an hypothesis, to be proven or disproven. Critical Marxian economists agree with the concept of John Dewey (1957) that science is a process involving researcher and world, practice and theory, at every moment.

Marx's "materialism" is not a theory of what the universe is "really" like "beyond" science—though some official Marxism in Stalin's era sounded that way. It is merely an affirmation of a method of approach, treating every theory in a nondogmatic and tentative way, testing every generalization against the facts, and assuming only that there is no supernatural, mysterious area beyond our understanding.

The need for testing and attempting to verify all theories against the facts, gained through experience and practice, is an area of agreement of critical Marxian economics with the empiricist tradition. But materialism opposes the empiricist or positivist notion that there are "facts" out there completely separate from our general theories. The "facts" must be chosen from an infinite number of facts according to some theory, they must be collected and tested in particular ways determined by theory, and they must be interpreted by a theory. Materialism is equally opposed, of course, to any rationalist attempt to conjure up a theory without ever consulting the facts.

The Dilemma and the Road to a Solution

It appears that critical Marxian economists must know the facts before they can formulate any theories or definitions. Yet it also appears that critical Marxian economists cannot investigate the facts until they have some theory and definitions. How can one get out of this dilemma?

The way to remove the dilemma is to approach scientific research as an historical process, not a static either-or situation (which comes first, the chicken or the egg?). Thomas Kuhn's work (1962) on the history of science, and the enormous literature discussing Kuhn's work, points to a concrete process of how change occurs in fact and theory.

The history of science is not one of simple accumulation of facts and linear improvement of theories. On the contrary, natural scientists accept a paradigm for some time and normally do research taking it for granted; but there are occasionally revolutions in which one paradigm replaces another, with more or less resistance. Resistance cannot be overcome by any single experiment because single hypotheses are embedded in a web of related theories and assumed (often unobserved) empirical "facts." In economics, there is even less chance to prove—or disprove—some hypothesis conclusively because we cannot hold other things constant but can only abstract certain past statistical behavior. In addition, economic paradigms reflect vested interests, as shown brilliantly by both Veblen and Marx. Any change in economic theory affects policy. For this reason, such arguments as that over the empirical validity of Milton Friedman's monetary hypotheses seem likely to go on forever.

Yet paradigms do change and are replaced. How does this occur? How does any one of us choose a paradigm? Economists may choose which paradigm to follow based on (1) which is most helpful in providing fruitful paths for research, (2) which explains the most facts that we find relevant, and (3) which best suits our own biases and interests, as conditioned by the society about us. Thus, old economic paradigms usually do not die, but—very slowly—fade away. Only when a whole society changes very drastically, as in Eastern Europe in 1989–1991, will economists be so shaken as to give up an old paradigm. Thus, the very same economists in Eastern Europe and the former Soviet Union, who professed to believe in central planning in 1982, were singing the free-market tune in 1992 (and were even higher in their praise of market systems than those who had long lived under them).

Scientific Determinism

Institutionalists and critical Marxists have written extensively on how human ideas ("human nature") arise from given structures and conflicts within socioeconomic institutions. At the same time, institutionalists and critical Marxists avoid economic or technological determinism by emphasizing that human beings, guided by their own ideas, are the makers of institutions and events at a given time. There is a reciprocal interaction. As Marx wrote: "Men make their own history, but they do not make it as they please; they do not make it under circumstances chosen by themselves, but under circumstances directly encountered, given and transmitted from the past" (Marx, 1963, p. 16).

Neither the dogmatic view called predeterminism (or fatalism) nor the equally dogmatic view called free will (or voluntarism) are defensible. A scientific determinism must oppose both, while using the grain of truth in each. Predeterminism claims that humans are a puppet of fate, God, economic forces, or whatever, which leads to the position of fatalism. Fatalism cannot be defended because people do make choices and do affect events. The free will position claims that history is accidental, there are no laws, humans can do anything, which leads to voluntarism in politics, religious mysticism, or opium dreams, and it also cannot be defended (because people must always act within given conditions).

A scientific determinist position simply asserts that everything—not only natural but also social events—is explainable on the basis of observed relationships, *including the existing psychology and behavior of humans*. In this view, humans make their own history; that is, humans can make their own decisions on the basis of their own ideas and psychologies, but under given natural and social constraints. "Scientific determinism is the view that every event occurs in some system of laws . . . *if* we knew [all] these laws and the state of the universe at any time, then we could explain the past and predict the future. This frame of reference includes, as it consistently must, human actions which, therefore, can be the object of scientific study" (Brodbeck, 1968, p. 669). The fact that human actions and human choice can be studied and explained does not reduce our freedom of action. On the contrary, such knowledge allows us to act more rationally.

The term *laws*, as used here by Brodbeck, merely means the observed regularities of behavior in nature or in society. One must distinguish the actual laws or regularities of nature and society from those observations or "laws" stated by scientists. Laws stated by scientists—or scientific laws—reflect the actual behavior of nature and society, but only to the extent of our present limited knowledge, so the laws we state are always limited, imperfect, and subject to revision.

Of course, we can never know all of the laws of the universe, nor the complete state of the universe at a particular time, so our explanations and predictions must always be partial, although we may hope that they will improve as we learn more laws. Furthermore, "laws" are not absolutes given forever (as religions claim for revealed truths), but merely our best description of certain regularities as presently known. The future will take place in some particular way, but our knowledge of social "laws" and our predictions based on them are always limited. We are constrained at any given time by (1) the extent of known facts, (2) the analytic theories available (including restricted mathematical knowledge), (3) our imperfect reasoning power, (4) the time available to research a problem, and (5) the fact that we are part of the social process and therefore, have limited or biased views of it (see Kemeny, 1959, p. 78). Social scientists know *something* about social laws at any given time, but not everything.

Some skeptics have argued that economics cannot be determinist because social situations are not exactly repeated or recurrent. They conclude that economists can draw no precise unconditional predictions. This is simply another limitation of our predictive ability; it is not a telling argument against a reasonable or scientific determinism. In fact, even in the natural sciences, none but the very simplest situations can be exactly repeated in the laboratory. Outside the laboratory, natural situations also do not exactly repeat themselves. Scientists base "laws" on what is common to many situations or individuals. The fact that each situation or individual is unique does not mean they have nothing in common. Thus, each consumer is affected by his or her income, even though other variables may affect that reaction in each case. We can formulate laws, but they are limited by the degree to which each new individual or situation includes the common aspect on which the law is based. This variability limits predictive power for both the natural and social sciences, and the difference is only one of degree.

Critical Marxists (unlike official Marxists) have always emphasized that human beliefs and actions must be included as a dynamic determining factor of social analysis. Certainly, humans are "free" in the sense that they may make any decision they care to make and may act on it: "The individualist truth that people are the only moving forces in history—in the sense that nothing happens behind their backs, that is, everything that happens, happens in and through their actions—must be retained" (Bhaskar, 1989, p. 81). On the other hand, humans are "determined" in the sense that their decisions are predictable as a statistical probability for an entire group within the limits of social science knowledge. In the same way, the weather is predictable as a statistical probability within the limits of current human knowledge of natural science, as well as our fact-gathering technology. The fact that weather is unconscious while human beings are conscious does not change the common characteristic that both show certain regularities of behavior—and these regularities may be stated as conditional statements or laws. It is worth repeating in this context that one's freedom of choice is not limited by the fact that we may follow certain regularities of behavior and may be predictable.

Decisions by groups of human beings are predictable (within the limits stated above) because they result from human ideas and psychological states. These ideas and states are determined for each individual by his or her experiences from birth to the present (and his or her inherited physiology). Knowing a group's history and environment, social scientists can predict its behavior (within the limits stated above), but that does not make the group or the individual member any less free or their actions any more predetermined by some outside plan. Of course, humans can carry out their decisions only within biological, physical, and political-economic conditions inherited from the past. Humans make their own history, but under given ("determining") conditions, and in predictable ways, although our predictive powers are limited in the ways stated above. The fact that we behave in somewhat predictable ways only means that we behave somewhat rationally with respect to conditions, not that we are coerced.

It is thus perfectly consistent to be determinist in the sense that economists may investigate and discover the laws of social-economic history, while acknowledging free will in the sense of urging individuals to participate in political struggles to affect history. We cannot change history in the sense that there is no predetermined history to change, but we can make history in the sense that history is always made by human beings acting under certain social and natural conditions. There include our present (1) technology and capital, (2) resources and natural environment, (3) social, economic, and political institutions, and (4) ideas, including each individual's psychology.

Human beings are free to make (or not make) a revolution, but our actions are predictable by a knowledge of present and previous conditions, *including our psychologies*, and the laws or regularities of human behavior under these conditions: "To say that the revolution is inevitable is simply (in Marx's scheme) to say that it will occur. And it will occur . . . not in spite of any choices we might make, but because of choices we will make" (Addis, 1968, p. 335). The prediction of socialist revolution, however, must be expressed as a probability rather than a certainty because of our limited knowledge of the conditions and the laws.

Critical Marxian Economic Theory and Ethics

Critical Marxian economists maintain that every statement in political economy must contain both a positive statement and a normative or ethical statement; the two can never be disentangled, nor should one try to state them separately. This Marxian humanist view is discussed in Marc Tool (1982, 1983), Philip Kain (1988), John Elliott (1987), and John B. Davis (1983).

An economist cannot do positive science alone because, in the process of choosing a research project, carrying it out, and interpreting the results, every social scientist must apply some ethical framework. That framework may be humanist or antihumanist, in sympathy with the oppressed and exploited groups or in sympathy with the elite, pro or anti the status quo, but some ethical viewpoint must guide the researcher. The economist *must* choose in every investigation what problem to tackle, what facts to select, and how to interpret the facts, in order to decide what policies to support. The choice may be make consciously or unconsciously, implicitly or explicitly, but a choice must be made in every case.

It is also true, however, that if a radical economist tries to follow a humanist ethics with no scientific basis, then it is merely a vague aspiration. The goals may be commendable, but they are no help in understanding the real world or in changing that world.

Conclusion: The Role of Economic Theory

What is the role of economic theory? Why is it important? What does it matter if the theory is good or bad? The role of economic theory is quite different in different paradigms. The role of good neoclassical theory is to explain and justify the status quo in capitalism. For this purpose, its theory is excellent. A theory that is individualist, psychologically reductionist, a-historical, and assumes no conflict but rather a tendency to an equilibrium point optimal for all is perfect for the purpose for which it is used. It is sometimes said that neoclassical theory is so unrealistic that it is useless for understanding current problems. But that is incorrect. It does set all of those problems within its framework in such a way that the answer is always that market capitalism is the best system. Do we need national health care? No, a market capitalist solution is better. Do we need some kind of democratic planning for full employment? No, market capitalism will automatically reach full employment.

Similarly, the former Soviet ruling class distorted Marxism so that it became an apologia for whatever the Soviet Union did. Was there anything wrong with executing thousands of people? No, it was a necessary class policy! Thus, although it had no recognizable relation to Marx's Marxism, it was perfect for the use to which it was put.

Finally, critical Marxism is holistic or relational, class-oriented, historical or evolutionary, materialist, determinist, and humanist because those are the necessary tools for its purpose. The purpose of critical Marxian economics is to examine the status quo critically, to explain the situation from the viewpoint of the oppressed (workers, women, minorities) and the long-run interests of humanity, and to advocate ways of changing the present system towards a better one from that viewpoint.

The methods and tools of economics are thus seen to be partisan and not neutral. The tools and methods of critical Marxian economics could not be used to improve neoclassical economics because such "improve-ments" would be contrary to its purpose. Similarly, the tools and methods of neoclassical economics cannot be used to improve the critical Marxian economic approach because they are contrary to its purpose (though one may use bits and pieces of any theory if it is sufficiently transformed to fit a different paradigm). Obviously, in the critical Marxian approach, the role of economic theory is not only to understand society but to change society.

References

Addis, Laird. 1968. "The Individual and the Marxist Philosophy of History." In May Brodbeck, ed., *Readings in the Philosophy of the Social Sciences.* New York: MacMillan.

Bhaskar, Roy. 1989. *Reclaiming Reality.* New York: Verso.

Bowles, Samuel, and Herbert Gintis. 1986. *Democracy and Capitalism.* New York: Basic Books.

———. 1990. "Rethinking Marxism and Liberalism from a Radical Democratic Perspective." *Rethinking Marxism,* 3 (3–4) (Fall–Winter), 37–45.

Brodbeck, May, ed. 1968. *Readings in the Philosophy of the Social Sciences.* New York: MacMillan.

Callinicos, Alex. 1988. *Making History.* Ithaca, N.Y.: Cornell University Press.

Davis, John B. 1983. *Marx's Conception of the Status of Ethics in Capitalist Society.* Ph.D. dissertation, University of Illinois, Urbana-Champaign.

Dewey, John. 1951. *Reconstruction in Philosophy.* Boston Press.

Dugger, William, ed. 1989. *Radical Institutionalism.* New York: Greenwood Press.

Elliott, John. 1987. "Marx's Moral Critique of Capitalism." In Warren Samuels, ed., *Annual Research in History of Economic Thought and Methodology.* Greenwich, Conn.: JAI Press.

Engels, Frederick. 1966. *Herr Eugen Duehring's Revolution in Science (Anti-Duehring).* New York: International Publishers.

Hartsock, Nancy. 1985. *Money, Sex, and Power: Toward a Feminist Historical Materialism.* Boston: Northeastern University Press.

Kain, Phillip. 1988. *Marx and Ethics.* New York: Oxford University Press.

Kemeny, John. 1959. *A Philosopher Looks at Science.* Princeton, N.J.: D. Van Vostrand.

Kuhn, Thomas. 1962. *The Structure of Scientific Revolutions.* Chicago: University of Chicago Press.

Larrain, Jorge. 1986. A Reconstruction of Historical Materialism. London: Allen and Unwin.

Marx, Karl. 1963. *The Eighteenth Brumaire of Louis Bonaparte.* New York: International Publishers.

Rigby, S.H. 1987. *Marxism and History*. New York: St. Martin's Press.

Samuels, Warren. 1977. "Technology vis-a-vis Institutions: A Suggested Interpretation." *Journal of Economic Issues*, 11 (December), 867–895.

Sartre, Jean Paul. 1968. *Search for a Method*. New York: Vintage.

Sawyer, Malcolm. 1989. *The Challenge of Radical Political Economy*. Savage, Md.: Barnes & Noble.

Sayer, Derek. 1987. *The Violence of Abstraction*. New York: Basil Blackwell.

Sherman, Howard. 1988. *Foundations of Radical Political Economy*. New York: M.E. Sharpe.

Tool, Marc. 1982. "Social Value Theory of Marxists, Part, I." *Journal of Economic Issues*, 16 (December), 1079–1107.

———. 1983. "Social Value Theory of Marxists, Part II." *Journal of Economic Issues*, 17 (March), 155–173.

Wolff, Richard, and Stephen Resnick. 1989. *Economics: Marxian and Neoclassical*. Baltimore: Johns Hopkins University Press.

Wright, Eric Olin. 1985. *Classes*. New York: Verso.

6 DOES ECONOMICS NEED THEORIES?

John F. Muth

Abstract

Theories seldom play as important a role in engineering design or public policy formulation as empirical laws. Even inaccurate empirical information can be tolerated as long as experimentation is possible. Theories do, however, perform important functions. They explain anomalies and paradoxes, clarify the limits of empirical laws, simplify knowledge, and unify diverse phenomena.

Introduction

This chapter discusses theories in three areas that have some significance in economics: expectations, inefficiency, and technological change. Expectations are, of course, involved in almost all realistic choices, particularly those that affect business fluctuations, growth, or development. Expectations and their formation have a role in modeling for all these areas that is just as important as tastes and opportunities.

Inefficiency is inconsistent with the rational model, which is the explicit

97

optimization of a utility or a profit function, usually under conditions of certainty, perfect markets, and equilibrium. Technological change is a phenomenon that has never been satisfactorily addressed by the rational model or by economics in general. Yet this and its consequences, such as productivity improvement, are among the most important and pervasive economic phenomena.

Expectations

The forecasting of economic conditions possesses some similarities with that of weather. Both affect the everyday life of almost everyone, both are widely reported in the press, and both may be wildly incorrect. Weather forecasting was originally limited to the use of climatological data and visually recognizing approaching weather systems, although the Bible reports some instances of divine insight.

Over a century ago, new telegraphy systems allowed better predictions because the easterly movement of weather systems at about 20 miles per hour means that weather in Indianapolis resembles that of Kansas City a day earlier. Careful study of weather maps made with information from hundreds of locations allows better projections about both the movement and formation of weather systems.

In 1911, Lewis Richardson (1881–1953) envisioned an orchestra of human computers numerically solving systems of partial differential equations representing the behavior of the atmosphere as it was understood at that time. Weather fronts were discovered in Norway during World War I, and jet streams were discovered in northwestern Europe and Japan during World War II. Radar, electronic computers, and models reflecting a better understanding of atmospheric phenomena now allow improved predictions of the formation of weather systems, such as the 1993 winter storm on the east coast of the United States.

Economic Expectations

A wide variety of techniques have been used to make economic predictions. Important approaches include surveys of attitudes and intentions. My comments, however, are limited to certain mathematical models.

Roughly analogous to the use of climatological data are moving averages and their generalizations in time-series analysis. Simple moving averages have been used a long time to smooth economic data, but exponentially weighted moving averages are of more recent origin. Cagan (1956) and Friedman (1957) apparently introduced the model in economics, and it was used at about the same time in management science. Many statisticians study time-series forecasting as well. Box and Jenkins (1970) developed particularly important generalizations.

The simplest model is based on

$$\frac{dy}{dt} = \alpha(x - y), \tag{6.1}$$

where x is the variable being predicted and y is the forecast. If

$$x = \sin\omega t, \tag{6.2}$$

then the forecast is given by

$$y = \frac{\alpha}{\sqrt{\alpha^2 + \omega^2}} \sin(\omega t - \phi), \quad \phi = \tan^{-1}\frac{\omega}{\alpha}. \tag{6.3}$$

High-frequency fluctuations are filtered out with a phase lag of up to $\pi/2$ radians. Moving averages thus forecast the future by looking backward and function by reducing the level of random variability over that in the series being predicted. They are theoretically appropriate for time series consisting of permanent and transitory components (Muth, 1960). On the other hand, they run the risk of introducing spurious time lags and cycles in the models utilizing them.

Leading economic indicators (Burns and Mitchell, 1946) are roughly analogous to the easterly movement of weather systems. This system appeals to the intuition of many but has some limitations. The criterion of a turning point is very sensitive to random variation and, indeed, is not determined for several months after the event. Why is it important to predict an event that is difficult to determine after the fact?

Some of the leading indicators possess the transport lag of weather systems (e.g., building permits for construction activity). For others, such as the change in sensitive materials prices, the variable possesses a phase lead arising from differentiation:

$$y = \frac{dx}{dt}. \tag{6.4}$$

The value of one variable is equal to the time derivative of another. If x is a defined by equation 6.2, then

$$y = \omega \sin(\omega t + \frac{\pi}{2}). \tag{6.5}$$

Hence y is a leading indicator of x. The factor ω indicates that the amplitude increases with the frequency, so the predictor tends to be sensitive to random variability. Hence it predicts by doing almost the opposite of moving averages.

Atmospheric models now seem to offer the most accurate weather prediction. Despite their limitations, explicit models of the economy seem to offer the best hope for genuine prediction of economic conditions. This is not to say that the present state of the art is very good. Particularly difficult to capture is the influence of events in the political arena. The influence of new products and new manufacturing processes and other factors driving productivity change are also significant. It is reasonable to expect phenomena as yet undiscovered to be important as well.

Economic models ordinarily need to include some variables for expectations. They could be moving averages, survey data, and so on. The rational expectations hypothesis (Muth, 1961),

$$y = \mathscr{E}x, \tag{6.6}$$

is another. There are several plausibility arguments for it, including announcing the prediction of the model will not change anyone's mind and hence invalidate the original prediction. It asserts that businesspeople and consumers tend to learn something about the world in which they live. It is a public forecast in the sense of Simon (1954) and Grunberg and Modigliani (1954), but rational expectations differs from these models by dealing with a multiperiod problem under risk.

Theoretical Contributions

Government policy is influenced by predicted consequences of its effects. Mankiw (1990) states that the accepted model of the economy was the IS-LM model with a Phillips curve of some sort appended to explain the adjustment of prices. A typical ingredient of the IS-LM model is Keynes's "fundamental psychological law." Such systems are largely based on empirical laws—that is, empirical regularities.

Through much of this century most engineering design was based only on empirical laws (Newton's, Hooke's, Boyle's, Ohm's). They are usually true under limited conditions. Newton's laws are valid only for speeds well below the speed of light; Hooke's is valid only until the elastic limit is reached; Boyle's only if gas molecules are small.

The same is true of empirical regularities in economics. A well-known example, not related to rational expectations, is the marginal propensity to consume. By using a rational optimizing model, Modigliani and Brumberg (1954) were able to explain why the marginal propensity to consume estimated from time series differed from that estimated from cross-section data. A related model of Friedman (1957) also explained differences in the propensity to consume among occupations.

Friedman (1968) and Phelps (1968) are credited with observing that the Phillips curve breaks down if exploited. They reason that the equilibrium, or natural, rate of unemployment depends on labor supply, labor demand, optimal search times, and other microeconomic considerations and not the average rate of money growth (Mankiw, 1990). Lucas (1972) then showed that adaptive expectations do not lead to the natural rate of output but that rational expectations do. He then concludes that the natural rate has nothing to do with the Phillips curve.

Sargent and Wallace (1975) analyzed alternative monetary policies in a macroeconomic model with rational expectations about prices. They compare the effect of pegging the interest rate and pegging the money supply on a quadratic loss function. The probability distribution of outcomes is independent of the money-supply rule used. Under the interest-rate rule the price level is indeterminate. These results have been interpreted as predicting the ineffectiveness of monetary policy. Instead, they may point out that the standard model used is defective. They also emphasize the sensitivity of policy conclusions to expectations of the future.

Kydland and Prescott (1977) show that even if there is a social objective function and policy makers know the effects of their actions, then a discretionary policy does not maximize the social objective function. The reason for this apparent paradox is that economic planning is not a game against nature, but a game against rational economic agents.

Empirical regularities built into econometric models have implicit assumptions about expectations built into them. If a significant policy change is made, expectations will change, and so will the empirical relations. Moreover, the effects of public policy are very sensitive to the expectations model that is used. The theories then clarify the limits of empirical laws.

Criticisms of Rational Expectations

The conclusions above do not depend on the validity or truth of the rational-expectations hypothesis. They only assert that expectations matter in a way that most econometric models mask. But the truth of rational expectations has been questioned on a number of grounds.

The rational-expectations hypothesis assumes all individuals in the economy have unlimited computational ability and know how to make use of the information that they possess. As a former student and colleague of Herbert Simon, I believe he would find the cognitive requirements most difficult to swallow (see, however, Simon, 1986, and the references contained there). The first assumption is possibly truer today than it was thirty years ago. The second is probably not. Humans are not very good intuitive statisticians, so we should expect cognitive biases of the sort identified by Tversky and Kahneman (1974) and others. These effects appear to be rather durable and may not dissipate with improved business and economic education.

Shiller (1978) and Taylor (1985) raise two additional points: multiple equilibria and convergence. They contend that except for degenerate cases, these models allow an infinite number of rational-expectations equilibria. The problem is that convergence conditions for infinite series must be considered, along with attention to boundary and transversality conditions. Techniques appropriate for the initial-value problem with linear differential or difference equations are not always appropriate. For a further discussion and references, see Evans (1989).

They also feel that it is unrealistic for an economy to converge to a rational-expectations equilibrium in a reasonable time, if at all. Taylor makes the related observation that the hypothesis implicitly assumes that agents expect other agents to have the same view of the economic environment as they do. Several studies have been concerned with this problem, but I do not think it is very important. As models of the economy gradually improve, however, one might be concerned with adaptation of expectation.

Shiller also believes that the models assume individuals have more knowledge about the economy than they could possibly have. An instance of imperfect information was examined in my 1961 paper.

The question that must be taken more seriously is whether actual behavior agrees with the rational-expectations hypothesis or models using the hypothesis. Studies by Lovell (1986) and Levine (1993) indicate that although the expectations of motivated individuals in the aggregate may not deviate too markedly from rationality, closer examination of individual or firm behavior indicates substantial deviations. Muth (1985) found similar deviations on the part of business professionals. Their forecasts did not agree with the exponential, extrapolative, or naive models, either. Only the expectations revision model used by Meiselman (1962) agreed with the data. Some agreement was found with an errors in variables model, which is a combination of the rational and the implicit expectations model (Mills, 1962).

The accuracy of expectations is generally easy to determine and feedback is relatively fast. Expectations should therefore be subject to rapid improvement compared with most other economic decisions. If expectations are not rational, what behavior is?

Despite its limitations, the rational-expectations hypothesis should be displaced only by something better. The error in variables model is a possibility, but it does not go far enough. Incorporating cognitive biases and limited information are directions that have some potential, however.

Inefficiency

Efficiency has been a concern of the industrial engineering and management professions since the turn of the century. Frederick W. Taylor (1856–1915), Frank B. (1868–1924), and Lillian M. Gilbreth (1878–1972) were early researchers in methods and time study. They and later industrial engineers found that substantial improvements were not unusual or difficult to achieve. By the late 1950s interest in the subject among industrial engineers waned in favor of mathematical modeling.

At that time, Michael Farrell (1957) introduced the subject of measuring productive efficiency into the economics literature. He recognized the distinction between allocative inefficiency, which is choosing factor combinations improperly reflecting their relative prices, and technical inefficiency, which is everything else. Almost a decade later, Harvey Leibenstein (1966) introduced the concept of X-efficiency, which focused on mismanagement. His writings emphasized relaxing maximizing behavior, inertia, incomplete contracts, and discretion.

Aigner and Chu (1968) and others started to estimate cost and production functions with statistical models recognizing unilateral errors (inefficiency). A decade later, Charnes, Cooper, and Rhodes (1978) developed a model, called data envelopment analysis, to measure relative efficiency. Other linear programming models have been developed by Byrnes, Färe, and Grosskopf (1984) and others. The measurement literature is now quite extensive.

Numerous empirical studies indicate that inefficiency is too pervasive a phenomenon to be ignored. They also suggest that technical inefficiency is more significant than allocative inefficiency.

Productive efficiency is governed by a number of factors, including work methods, workplace layout, tools, materials, product design, skill, and effort. Effort, in turn, depends on motivation (and, undoubtedly, human physiological limits). Satisfaction as an explanation of effort has apparently been disproved. Motivation may in turn depend on such factors as wage incentives, job variety, responsibility, autonomy, and opportunities for personal growth. The influence of wage incentives (external rewards) is examined further below.

Just how motivation affects performance is subject to considerable controversy, and several models have been proposed. Models that have been proposed include two factor (Herzberg, Mausner, and Snyderman, 1959), aspiration level (March and Simon, 1958), positive reinforcement (Skinner, 1953), inequity theory (Adams, 1963), and expectancy theory (Porter and Lawler, 1968). Most of these are summarized by Filer (1986). I discuss the two most recent models in the context of the influence of wage incentives on performance and compare it with a standard economic model.

Economic Model

Assume that an individual's satisfaction S in a job setting depends on his rewards R and his productivity P.

$$S = f(R, P), \tag{6.7}$$

where f_R is presumably positive. Rewards, in turn, depend on productivity:

$$R = a + bP, \tag{6.8}$$

where a is the hourly rate and b is the incentive rate.

Setting the total derivative of S with respect to P equal to zero gives:

$$\frac{dS}{dP} = f_R b + f_P = 0, \tag{6.9}$$

with the additional condition that

$$\frac{d^2 S}{dP^2} = f_{RR} b^2 + 2 f_{RP} b + f_{PP} < 0. \tag{6.10}$$

Taking differentials with respect to a, b, and P, we obtain:

$$(f_{RR} b^2 + 2 f_{RP} b + f_{pp}) dP + (f_{RR} b + f_{RP})\, (da + Pdb) + f_R db = 0 \tag{6.11}$$

If a change in the wage system is such that the total payment is unchanged at prior performance levels,

$$da + Pdb = 0, \tag{6.12}$$

then the incentive rate and performance necessarily change in the same direction.

Inequity Theory

The inequity-reduction model of Adams (1963) has had an important role in modeling human productivity. Numerous empirical studies give moderate support to his predictions, but because they are experimental, these studies have questionable external validity.

The basic hypothesis is that inequity exists for a person whenever he or she perceives that the relationship of his or her outcomes to inputs differs from that of some reference group. The presence of inequity creates tension or dissatisfaction in the person, which motivates him or her to eliminate or reduce it. One way to reduce inequity is to alter his or her inputs.

A person may vary inputs, either increasing them or decreasing them, depending on whether the inequity is advantageous or disadvantageous. Increasing inputs will reduce felt inequity if

$$\frac{O_p}{I_p} > \frac{O_a}{I_a}, \tag{6.13}$$

where O refers to outputs (rewards), I to inputs (effort directed toward productivity and quality), the subscript p the person, and a to the reference person or group. Conversely, decreasing inputs will be effective if

$$\frac{O_p}{I_p} < \frac{O_a}{I_a}. \tag{6.14}$$

Tension is proportional to the magnitude of the inequity present. By equating dissatisfaction with tension, we then have the relation:

$$S = g\left(\frac{O_p}{I_p} - \frac{O_a}{I_a}\right), \tag{6.15}$$

where g has a maximum at the origin. Without loss of generality, we can take $O_a/I_a = 1$.

In studying the effect of wage incentives, we let the outcome be the wage rate O_p, which is a nondecreasing function of productivity, P:

$$O_p = a + bP, \tag{6.16}$$

and the effort input is some function of productivity and quality Q:

$$I_p = f(P, Q), \tag{6.17}$$

where the partial derivatives f_p and f_Q are positive. Then equation 6.15 can be rewritten as

$$S = g\left(\frac{a + bP}{f(P, Q)} - 1\right).$$
(6.18)

Tension would tend to be removed if

$$f(P, Q) = a + bP,$$
(6.19)

at which point we would also have

$$S = g(0).$$
(6.20)

Equations 6.19 and 6.20 constitute the equilibrium conditions for Adams' system. Since the number of variables exceeds the number of equilibrium conditions, the system is indeterminate. Equation 6.19 merely specifies the productivity-quality tradeoffs associated with any given reward level.

Adams' predictions, on the other hand, are the following: (1) if people perceive that they are overpaid (underpaid) on an hourly basis, they will increase (decrease) performance; (2) if they are overpaid (underpaid) on a piece basis, they will decrease (increase) performance and improve (reduce) quality. Adams' predictions do not follow from the model. The reasons for the discrepancy are unknown because he never gave his "derivation," only his conclusion.

Expectancy Theory

The expectancy theory of Porter and Lawler (1968) has also had a great influence on empirical research in organizational behavior. Numerous empirical investigations, mostly field studies, tend to support at least part of the model. The lack of experimental controls limits the informative value of the studies.

The theory asserts that performance is an increasing function of the effort expended by the individual, which in turn is an increasing function of the perceived effect of performance on rewards and the value of the reward. The perceived effect of performance on rewards (instrumentality) depends on the actual association of performance and rewards—say, $h(P, R)$. The value of the reward (valence) depends on actual satisfactions. Hence, performance depends on S and $h(P, R)$, or

$$P = f(P, R, S) = f(P, a + bP, S).$$
(6.21)

Satisfaction depends on extrinsic rewards $R = a + bP$ and intrinsic rewards, which depends on P. Thus we have

$$S = g(P, R) = g(P, a + bP) \qquad (6.22)$$

Productivity thus depends on the total magnitude of rewards and not on its composition. Porter and Lawler appear to predict, however, that an increase in the hourly wage rate would have no effect.

How can it be that the expectancy model predicts the same effect for hourly and piece-rate systems when the motivational mechanism explicitly considers the instrumentality of a given behavior resulting in a reward outcome? It may seem obvious that an increase in the hourly rate has no motivational effect on performance, while an increase in the piece rate does have such an effect. The problem is that the model is expressed as a block diagram in which the inputs to the motivational mechanism are merely the total value of the rewards, not its composition by hourly and piece rates. There is a fundamental difference between stating that a variable depends on another and that it depends on the entire shape of a function.

Hence we have a rather curious situation in which rational modeling techniques can help explain inefficiency phenomena, which are inconsistent with the (rational) theory of the firm. In this instance, behavioral modeling techniques are ineffective because their predictions appear to differ from what their authors claim. The expectancy model also appears to use a variable to describe the properties of a function. In certain areas of psychology, notably learning and perception, theory development is quite sophisticated, but it is not in organizational behavior. Problems in theory development are not, however, limited to economics and psychology. Birkhoff's theory of gravitation, for example, requires the speed of light to equal the speed of sound (Will, 1974).

Technology

Technological change is possibly the most important single influence on productivity growth, which in turn is a determinant of increased economic standard of living. Abramowitz (1956) and Solow (1957) attempted to explain productivity growth in terms of improved inputs, capital-labor substitution (allocative efficiency), economies of scale, with the unexplained residual being attributed to technological change. Economic models have relied on economies of scale and externalities to explain economic growth.

The theory of the firm has been criticized by Blaug (1980) and Simon (1986) for not being consistent with certain phenomena. Despite its limitations, microeconomic theory explains several anomalies and paradoxes of value. The theory of the firm alone explains certain puzzles in wages and interest. In so doing, however, it leaves some puzzles unanswered and creates some of its own.

I share the view of Nelson and Winters (1982) that the theory of the firm is fundamentally incapable of explaining technological change. The important areas of growth and productivity change are outside the domain of the theory.

To illustrate the gaps, consider three phenomena that have generally been regarded as being purely empirical—namely, learning curves, production functions, and substitution curves. The first and last of these topics have no role in the mainstream theory of production, as represented by Samuelson (1947) or Shephard (1970). The second has generally been regarded only as a datum for "real" economics.

Learning Curves

The manufacturing progress function asserts that the relation of unit labor hours or production costs to the total number of items produced is linear in the logarithms of these variables. Letting x represent the labor hours for the n'th item produced, the function is:

$$x = Kn^{-a}, \tag{6.23}$$

where K and a are positive constants. The phenomenon was first reported by Wright (1936) and was widely reported in the production of aircraft and merchant ships during World War II.

The phenomenon of cost reduction or productivity improvement with experience is generally regarded as a purely empirical one, possibly having some applications in the management of a business firm. Despite the fact that the experience phenomenon is a very large effect, there has been a remarkable lack of interest in theoretical explanations. Of scores of articles on the subject (Yelle's 1979 survey lists ninety-three references), only seven have attempted such modeling.

Arrow's famous 1963 article on "learning by doing" is concerned not with explaining learning but with drawing some of its implications. The model is deterministic, with improvements in capital goods taking place exogenously. A model of Oi (1967) purports to explain learning curves but really deals with economies of planned volume of production, a distinction recognized by Alchian (1959).

Deterministic models explicitly attempting to predict the manufacturing progress function were developed by Levy (1965), Sahal (1979), and Kantor and Zangwill (1991). Stochastic theories have been developed by Crossman (1959), Roberts (1983), Sahal (1979), Venezia (1985), and Muth (1986).

The last of these will be described here. It is related to the theory of job search (see Lippman and McCall, 1976) and to certain economic models of research and innovation (Evenson and Kislev, 1975; Telser, 1982). While job search is concerned primarily with conditions under which a person stops searching and starts working, the learning model is mostly concerned with the rate of improvement as experience accumulates. Unlike most models of research and innovation, it is based on the statistics of extremes.

The basic model relating productivity improvement to experience is based on four hypotheses:

1. Cost reductions are realized through independent random sampling (search) from a space of (technological, managerial, or behavioral) alternatives. The cumulative distribution function of hours or costs is denoted by $F(x)$.
2. Lower-cost techniques for each manufacturing operation are adopted when discovered. A manufacturing process consists of one or more independent operations.
3. The distribution of unit costs approaches a power function at a lower bound (denoted by x_0). That is,

$$\lim_{x \to x_0} \frac{F(x)}{(x - x_0)^k} = c, \text{ a constant.} \tag{6.24}$$

Furthermore, the lower bound is zero ($x_0 = 0$).
4. Search is prompted by production activity. It may also be carried out before actual production and may terminate completely when the rate of improvement becomes sufficiently small.

The first two hypotheses imply that costs for a single operation are associated with the minimum of a sample of n observations. Let X_n be the minimum of n independent random variables, each with the distribution function $F(x)$. Then the distribution function of X_n, $G_n(x)$, is

$$G_n(x) = 1 - [1 - F(x)]^n. \tag{6.25}$$

The probability that the minimum is no less than x equals the probability that no observations are less than x.

Regardless of the distribution for the initial learning rate, a common one is approached for all underlying distributions satisfying hypothesis 3. The limiting, extreme-value distribution was discovered by Fisher and

Tippett (1928). It was used by Weibull (1939) to explain the size effect in the strength of materials. It is also used in the statistical theory of reliability.

It can be shown that $G_n(x)$ converges in the mean (and hence in probability) to the exponential form,

$$G(x) = 1 - \exp[-nF(x)]. \qquad (6.26)$$

(see Gnedenko, 1943, or Galambos, 1978).

The sample minima are eventually small. For such values of x, $F(x)$ is approximated by its limiting form according to equation 6.24:

$$G(x) = 1 - \exp\{-[(cn)^{1/k}(x - x_0)]^k\}. \qquad (6.27)$$

Thus the variable $t = (cn)^{1/k}(x - x_0)$ has the Weibull distribution. The mean value of x is

$$\mu = x_0 + \Gamma(1 + 1/k)\ (cn)^{-1/k} \qquad (6.28)$$

It is often approximated by the expected fractile of the minimum, which is

$$\mu = x_0 + (cn)^{-1/k} \qquad (6.29)$$

By hypothesis 4, cumulative output is identified with cumulative search activity. Hence the derivation of the power function relation, equation 6.23, is complete.

Production Functions

In the theory of the firm, cost phenomena are explained jointly by market and technological transformations. Although various structures leading to the market transformations have been examined, production functions characterizing the technical transformations have generally been studied only from the standpoint of empirical estimation. They have seldom been explained in terms of more fundamental concepts.

Engineering production functions (Chenery, 1949; Ferguson, 1951; Kurz and Manne, 1963; Smith, 1957) might be regarded as exceptions. However, these are not very satisfactory as explanations because they are based on empirical laws, such as Boyle's law, rather than theories, such as the kinetic theory of gases.

The problem of finding efficient combinations of the factors of production for a specified rate of output is discussed first. This is a vector minimization problem whose solution gives the isoquants of the production function. Random sampling from a space having a very simple structure leads to isoquants of the production function proposed by Cobb and Douglas (1928).

5. The factors of production required for a given rate of output are distributed independently of one another.

This would seem to rule out substitution among the factors, but it does not because the boundary of the set of efficient combinations is the object of interest, not a regression line through the possible combinations.

Let u_n be the minimum observation in a sample of size n from an infinite population uniformly distributed in the unit interval. Its expected value is

$$\mathscr{E}u_n = n\int_0^1 u(1-u)^{n-1}\,du = \frac{1}{n+1} \qquad (6.30)$$

This is the expected extreme fractile. Let $F(x)$ be the cumulative probability distribution of factor combinations x to achieve a given output rate. Then u_n can be regarded as the probability $F(x)$ after sampling n times. Letting

$$F(\xi) = \mathscr{E}(x), \qquad (6.31)$$

we then have

$$F(\xi) = \frac{1}{n+1}. \qquad (6.32)$$

The independence specified by hypothesis 5 implies

$$F(\xi) = \prod_{i=1}^{r} H_i(\xi_i). \qquad (6.33)$$

The power function approach to the lower bound $x_0 = 0$ according to hypothesis 3 gives

$$H_i(\xi_i) = K\xi_i^{k_i}. \qquad (6.34)$$

Substituting equations 6.33 and 6.34 into equation 6.30 leads to the main conclusion of this section:

The factor combinations required to produce a given (mix of) output after sampling n possibilities is characterized by

$$\prod_{i=1}^{r} \xi_i^{k_i} = \frac{K}{n+1}, \qquad (6.35)$$

where n is an integer and K is a constant. This evidently gives, after a specified amount of search, the tradeoffs allowed by the Cobb-Douglas production function.

Output possibilities can now be integrated with those of the factors of production. The joint distribution of inputs, x, and output, y, is $F(x, y)$, which refers to the left tail for x and the right tail for y. There is no maximum output rate.

The tradeoffs after a given amount of search is the solution to

$$F(\xi, \eta) = \frac{1}{n + 1} \tag{6.36}$$

for ξ. The joint distribution of inputs and output is the product of the conditional and marginal distributions:

$$F(\xi, \eta) = G(\xi|\eta) \, [1 - H(\eta)]. \tag{6.37}$$

Its expected value, according to equation 6.30, is $1/(n + 1)$, so that

$$G(\xi|\eta) = \frac{1}{(n + 1) \, [1 - H(\eta)]}. \tag{6.38}$$

It is now assumed that

6. The distribution of output given the quantities of input factors is independent of the inputs.

The assumption of independence contained in hypothesis 6 is, as is the distribution of factor inputs, very strong. Nevertheless it leads to commonly observed production relations and might serve as a basis for further generalizations of production functions. Under this assumption, the conditional distribution $G(\xi|\eta)$ is equal to the marginal, $G(\xi)$. Consequently, the production function has the form

$$\eta = H^{-1}\left(1 - \frac{1}{(n + 1) \, G(\xi)}\right)$$

$$= H^{-1}\left(1 - \frac{K}{(n + 1) \displaystyle\prod_{i=1}^{r} \xi_i^{k_i}}\right) \tag{6.39}$$

provided the inverse function exists. Note that H^{-1} is monotonically increasing wherever it exists.

It is not reasonable to assume that the outputs are necessarily bounded, so somewhat different limiting distributions may be involved. This hypothesis is suggested:

7. The distribution of output given the quantities of the input factors is unbounded.

Distributions without a finite bound on the values of the variates have either the Cauchy limit or the exponential limit. Consider the case of the Cauchy limit:

8. The distribution of output given the quantities of the input factors has the limiting form:

$$1 - H(\eta) = K\eta^{-k}, \qquad \eta > 0. \tag{6.40}$$

With the Cauchy-Pareto distribution of outputs, the production function is

$$\eta = K[(n + 1)\, G(\xi)]^{1/k} = K(n + 1)^{1/k} \prod_{i=1}^{r} \xi_i^{k_i/k}, \tag{6.41}$$

where n is an integer. This, of course, is the Cobb-Douglas production function, except for the factor involving the number of observations.

Adoption of Innovations

Diffusion of information is the predominant theory of the adoption of innovation. It is often represented by a logistic function, which is modeled after a theory of autocatalytic chemical reactions (see Lotka, 1925) and the spread of epidemics in a population (see Bailey, 1957). It is used in the literature of economics (Griliches, 1957; Mansfield, 1961), sociology (Coleman, Katz, and Menzel, 1957), and marketing (Bass, 1969). Other models of innovation are based on interfirm profitability differences, competitive structure, and uncertainty resolution.

The logistic model always possesses an initial period of slow growth, sometimes called the introductory phase. Models with contagion from the source need not exhibit this phase, however. The models all predict eventual market saturation with no subsequent decline.

Studies of the product life cycle indicate that many innovations peak out at something less than the entire market, that several technologies exist at the same time, that adoptions eventually decline, or that other shapes, such as a bimodal one, exist. All these phenomena are inconsistent with the diffusion theory and are consistent with search theory.

The main theory for explaining adoption of innovations or forecasting new-product demand and technological change is based on the diffusion of information from the source or other adopting organization. This theory leads to a combination of the exponential and logistic functions, although several similar curves have been empirically fitted.

A model based not on information but search follows. Let x be a value that indexes the state of technology (that is, cost or some other figure of merit) and let $p = F(x)$ be the probability of achieving the value x in one trial. Then with independent random sampling, the number of trials until the first event occurs has the geometric distribution

$$P_n = (1 - p)^{n-1}p. \tag{6.42}$$

(Other distributions, such as the negative binomial, may be used if a more complex search process is used.) The probability of success in n trials or less is the cumulative distribution, which is identical with equation 6.25:

$$G_n = 1 - (1 - p)^n. \tag{6.43}$$

To determine the probability density for an innovation with a criterion value in the interval $(x, x + dx)$, we take the derivative of G_n with respect to x, obtaining

$$\frac{dG_n}{dx} = n(1 - p)^{n-1}\frac{dp}{dx}$$
$$= n[1 - F(x)]^{n-1}f(x). \tag{6.44}$$

Equation 6.44 is the basic relation for the distribution function of the number of adopters of a narrowly defined innovation. It is expressed in terms of "quanta" of search activity, however, and not in calendar time.

Conclusions

The requirements of a good theory are demanding and seldom realized. A theory needs to be complete and consistent, with well-defined and preferably unique predictions. It should have few free parameters, be continuous in its parameters, and be dynamically stable. A theory should, of course, be consistent with observable phenomena, at least over a limited range. Typically, a theory is displaced only by a better one.

What does theory contribute to policy and design? It explains anomalies and paradoxes. This has been one of the great achievements of micro-economics. Similarly, it clarifies the limits of empirical laws. In macro-economics, work of Modigliani, Friedman, Phelps, Lucas, Sargent, Wallace, Kydland, Prescott, and many others achieves this end.

Theories simplify the structure of knowledge. Rather than cluttering up microeconomics with all sorts of marginal conditions, we only have to deal with a simple optimization problem from which all these relations flow. Moreover, the same general problem can be applied in other areas, such as explaining the effect of wage incentives on individual performance.

Theories also unify different parts of economics. The theory of the household is, for example, essentially the same as the theory of the firm (Samuelson, 1947). Learning curves, production functions, and the adoption of technological change are interrelated phenomena, some of whose features can be explained by essentially identical models.

Theories are not essential for most policy determination or engineering design. Empirical laws have historically been sufficient for most design problems. Inaccurate empirical information can be tolerated and, indeed, prevailed through much of the nineteenth century. Generally required, however, are experimentation and practical testing, which are not standard features of government policy formulation.

Acknowledgments

I am indebted to James H. Patterson for his comments and suggestions.

References

Abramowitz, M. 1956. *Resource and Output Trends in the U.S. since 1870.* National Bureau of Economic Research, Occasional Paper 52.

Adams, J. Stacey. 1963. "Towards an Understanding of Inequity." *Journal of Abnormal and Social Psychology*, 67, 422–436.

Aigner, D.J., and S.F. Chu. 1968. "On Estimating the Industry Production Function." *American Economic Review*, 17, 826–839.

Alchian, Armen. 1959. "Costs and Outputs." In M. Abramowitz et al., eds., *The Allocation of Economic Resources.* Standford: Stanford University Press.

Arrow, K.J. 1963. "The Economic Implications of Learning by Doing." *Review of Economic Studies*, 29, 679–693.

Bailey, N.T.J. 1957. *The Mathematical Theory of Epidemics.* Griffin, 1957.

Bass, Frank M. 1969. "A New Product Growth Model for Consumer Durables." *Management Science*, 15, 215–227.

Blaug, Mark. 1980. *The Methodology of Economics: or, How Economists Explain.* Cambridge: Cambridge University Press.

Box, George E.P., and Gwilym M. Jenkins. 1970. *Time Series Analysis: Forecasting and Control.* San Francisco: Holden-Day.

Burns, Arthur F., and Wesley C. Mitchell. 1946. *Measuring Business Cycles.* New York: National Bureau of Economic Research.

Byrnes, P., R. Färe, and S. Grosskopf. 1984. "Measuring Productive Efficiency: An Application to Illinois Strip Mines." *Management Science*, 30, 671–681.

Cagan, Phillip. 1956. "The Monetary Dynamics of Hyperinflation." In M. Friedman, ed., *Studies in the Quantity Theory of Money.* Chicago: University of Chicago Press.

Charnes, A., W.W. Cooper, and E. Rhodes. 1978. "Measuring Efficiency of Decision Making Units." *European Journal of Operational Research*, 1, 429–444.

Chenery, H.B. 1949. "Engineering Production Functions." *Quarterly Journal of Economics*, 63, 507–531.

Cobb, C.W., and P.H. Douglas. 1928. "A Theory of Production." *American Economic Review*, 18, 139–165.

Coleman, J.S., E. Katz, and H. Menzel. 1957. "The Diffusion of an Innovation Among Physicians." *Sociometry*, 20, 253–270.

Crossman, E.R.F.W. 1959. "A Theory of the Acquisition of Speed Skill." *Ergonomics*, 2, 153–166.

Evans, George W. 1989. "The Fragility of Sunspots and Bubbles." *Journal of Monetary Economics*, 23, 297–317.

Evenson, R.E., and Y. Kislev. 1975. "A Stochastic Model of Applied Research." *Journal of Political Economy*, 84, 265–281.

Farrell, M.J. 1957. "The Measurement of Productive Efficiency," *Journal of the Royal Statistical Society, Series A (General) 120, Part III*, 253–281.

Ferguson, A.R. 1951. "An Airline Production Function" (Abstract). *Econometrica*, 19, 57–58.

Filer, Randall K. 1986. "People and Productivity: Effort Supply as Viewed by Economists and Psychologists." In Benjamin Gilad and Stanley Kaish, eds., *Handbook of Behavioral Economics.* JAI Press.

Fisher, R.A., and L.H.C. Tippett. 1928. "Limiting Forms of the Frequency-Distribution of the Largest of Smallest Member of a Sample." *Proceedings of the Cambridge Philosophical Society*, 24, 180–190.

Friedman, Milton. 1957. *A Theory of the Consumption Function.* Princeton: Princeton University Press.

———. 1968. "The Role of Monetary Policy." *American Economic Review*, 58, 1–17.

Galambos, J. 1978. *The Asymptotic Theory of Extreme Order Statistics.* New York: Wiley, 1978.

Gnedenko, B. 1943. "Sur la Distribution Limite du Terme Maximum d'une Série Aléatoire." *Annals of Mathematics*, 44, 423–453.

Griliches, Z. 1957. "Hybrid Corn: An Exploration in the Economics of Technological Change." *Econometrica*, 25, 501–522.

Grunberg, Emile, and Franco Modigliani. 1954. "The Predictability of Social Events." *Journal of Political Economy*, 62, 465–478.

Herzberg, F., B. Mausner, and B.S. Snyderman. 1959. *The Motivation to Work*. New York: Wiley.

Kahneman, Daniel, Paul Slovic, and Amos Tversky, eds. 1982. *Judgement under Uncertainty: Heuristics and Biases*. Cambridge: Cambridge University Press.

Kantor, Paul B., and Willard I. Zangwill. 1991. "Theoretical Foundation for a Learning Rate Budget." *Management Science*, 37, 315–330.

Kurz, M., and A.S. Manne. 1963. "Engineering Estimates of Capital-Labor Substitution in Metal Machinery." *American Economic Review*, 53, 662–681.

Kydland, Finn E., and Edward C. Prescott. 1977. "Rules Rather than Discretion: The Inconsistency of Optimal Plans." *Journal of Political Economy*, 85, 473–491.

Leibenstein, H. 1966. "Allocative Efficiency vs. 'X-Efficiency.'" *American Economic Review*, 56, 392–415.

Levine, David I. 1993. "Do Corporate Executives Have Rational Expectations?" *Journal of Business*, 66, 271–293.

Levy, F.K. 1965. "Adaptation in the Production Process." *Management Science (B)*, 11, 136–154.

Lippman, Steven A., and John J. McCall. 1976. "The Economics of Job Search: A Survey." *Economic Inquiry*, 14, 155–189, 347–368.

Lotka, Alfred J. 1925. *Elements of Physical Biology*. Williams & Wilkins, reprinted by Dover Publications, 1956.

Lovell, Michael C. 1986. "Tests of the Rational Expectations Hypothesis." *American Economic Review*, 76, 110–124.

Lucas, Robert E., Jr. 1972. "Expectations and the Neutrality of Money." *Journal of Economic Theory*, 4, 103–124.

Mankiw, N. Gregory. 1990. "A Quick Refresher Course in Macroeconomics," *Journal of Economic Literature*, 28, 1645–1660.

Mansfield, Edwin. 1961. "Technical Change and the Rate of Imitation." *Econometrica*, 29, 741–766.

March, James G., and Herbert A. Simon. 1958. *Organizations*. New York: Wiley.

Meiselman, D. 1962. *The Term Structure of Interest Rates*. Englewood Cliffs, N.J.: Prentice-Hall.

Mills, Edwin S. 1962. *Price, Output, and Inventory Policy*. New York: Wiley.

Modigliani, Franco, and Richard Brumberg. 1954. "Utility Analysis and the Consumption Function: An Interpretation of Cross-Section Data." In Kenneth K. Kurihara, ed., *Post-Keynesian Economics*. New Brunswick, N.J.: Rutgers University Press.

Muth, John F. 1960. "Optimal Properties of Exponentially Weighted Forecasts." *Journal of the American Statistical Association*, 55, 299–306.

———. 1961. "Rational Expectations and the Theory of Price Movements." *Econometrica*, 29, 315–335.

————. 1985. "Properties of Some Short-Run Business Forecasts," *Eastern Economic Journal*, 11, 200–210.

————. 1986. "Search Theory and the Manufacturing Progress Function." *Management Science*, 32, 948–962.

Nelson, Richard R., and Sidney G. Winter. 1982. *An Evolutionary Theory of Economic Change*. Cambridge, Mass.: Belknap Press of Harvard University.

Oi, Walter Y. 1967. "The Neoclassical Foundations of Progress Functions." *Economic Journal*, 77, 579–594.

Phelps, Edmund S. 1968. "Money-Wage Dynamics and Labor Market Equilibrium." *Journal of Political Economy*, 76, 687–711.

Porter, L.W., and E.E. Lawler. 1968. *Managerial Attitudes and Performance*. Homewood, Ill.: Dorsey Press.

Roberts, Peter C. 1983. "A Theory of the Learning Process." *Journal of the Operational Research Society*, 34, 71–79.

Sahal, Devendra. 1979. "A Theory of Progress Functions." *AIIE Transactions*, 11, 23–29.

Samuelson, Paul A. 1947. *Foundations of Economic Analysis*. Cambridge, Mass.: Harvard University Press.

Sargent, Thomas J., and Neil Wallace. 1975. "'Rational' Expectations, the Optimal Monetary Instrument, and the Optimal Money Supply Rule." *Journal of Political Economy*, 83, 241–254.

Shephard, Ronald W. 1970. *Theory of Cost and Production Functions*. Princeton, N.J.: Princeton University Press.

Shiller, Robert. 1978. "Rational Expectations and the Dynamic Structure of Macroeconomic Models: A Critical Review." *Journal of Monetary Economics*, 4, 1–44.

Simon, Herbert A. 1954. "Bandwagon and Underdog Effects of Election Predictions." *Public Opinion Quarterly*, 18, 245–253.

————. 1986. "Rationality in Psychology and Economics," *Journal of Business*, 59, S209–S224. Entire issue reprinted as Robin M. Hogarth and Melvin W. Reder, eds., *Rational Choice*. Chicago: University of Chicago Press. 1987.

Skinner, B.F. 1953. *Science and Human Behavior*. New York: Macmillan.

Smith, V.L. 1957. "Engineering Data and Statistical Techniques in Analysis of Production and Technological Change: Fuel Requirements in the Trucking Industry." *Econometrica*, 25, 281–301.

Solow, Robert M. 1957. 'Technical Change and the Aggregate Production Function." *Review of Economic Statistics*, 39, 312–320.

Taylor, John B. 1985. "Rational Expectations Models in Macroeconomics." In Kenneth J. Arrow and Seppo Honkapohja, eds., *Frontiers of Economics*. Boston: Basil Blackwell.

Telser, L.G. 1982. "A Theory of Innovation and Its Effects." *Bell Journal of Economics*, 13, 69–92.

Tversky, Amos, and Daniel Kahneman. 1974. "Judgement under Uncertainty: Heuristics and Biases." *Science*, 185, 1124–1131.

Venezia, Itzhak. 1985. "On the Statistical Origins of the Learning Curve." *European Journal of Operational Research*, 19, 191–200.

Weibull, E.H.W. 1939. "A Statistical Theory of the Strength of Materials." *Ingeniörs Vetenskaps Akademiens Handlingar, Nr.*, 151.

Will, Clifford M. 1974. "Gravitation Theory." *Scientific American*, 231, 25–33.

Wright, T.P. 1936. "Factors Affecting the Cost of Airplanes." *Journal of Aeronautical Sciences*, 3, 4, 122–128.

Yelle, Louis E. 1979. "The Learning Curve: Historic Review and Comprehensive Survey." *Decision Science*, 10, 302–328.

7 THE MULTIFARIOUS ROLE OF THEORIES IN ECONOMICS: THE CASE OF DIFFERENT KEYNESIANISMS

Andrea Boitani and Andrea Salanti

Abstract

This chapter focuses on today's various Keynesianisms as a case study suited to show how different methodological perspectives, particularly on the proper explanatory role of economic theories, may make some important differences even within approaches that are very akin in many other respects. Post-Keynesians of different persuasions and new Keynesians are surveyed in order to show the relevant consequences of different perspectives concerning the role of economic theorizing and other methodological issues. It emerges that the nature of the links between policy recommendations, theoretical frameworks, and methodological beliefs is more complex than is usually maintained, depending on different points of view about the role of economic theorizing. The plurality of theoretical approaches is to be regarded as legitimate as it stems from largely different conceptions of the role of theories.

Introduction

Our decision to discuss the role of economic theory with reference to the various claimants to Keynes's legacy is dictated by our interest in Keynesian economics and by our conviction that it can provide a case study on the ambiguities surrounding the very notion of the role of economic theory. Keynes undoubtedly thought of the ultimate scope of economic theorizing as eminently practical. Indeed, as one of his most perceptive biographers has rightly observed, "Keynes advocated state intervention to improve the working of economies. He also supplied, and invented, economic theories to justify the interventionist measures he advocated. Ever since the publication of the *General Theory* in 1936, economists have argued about the nature of these theories, and their relationship to Keynes's (and Keynesian) practice" (Skidelsky, 1991, p. 104).

In this sense we might well say that according to Keynes the role of economic theory is to justify economic policies of interventionist kind. We take for granted that the same thing can be said of all the various brands of Keynesianism, in that they share a common distrust in the virtues of laissez-faire (together with a critical attitude toward neoclassical economics, regarded as an apologetic idealization of market functioning) and pay remarkable attention to the issue of the political implications of economic ideas.

As is now becoming widely acknowledged, Keynes had his own particular epistemological convictions, and this may help to explain why he moved in some theoretical directions rather than in others that could have been equally suited to support an interventionist stance concerning economic policy. Undoubtedly, one of the main merits of the new Keynesian fundamentalism is having shown how Keynes's *philosophy of practice* is connected with his early ethical and epistemological beliefs.[1] However, for several reasons with which we are not concerned here, Keynes's epistemology presently appears to be somehow dated, so that it is understandable that each particular Keynesianism has to redefine its own epistemological premises and methodological preferences.

Of course, different methodological justifications do not have the same strength because it may well happen that one kind of argument performs the task of persuading other people better than another. However, what is to be chosen depends, among other things, on the epistemological and methodological contexts implied in the discussion. In this respect, we must note that all Keynesians more or less explicitly advocate some kind of realism.[2] Indeed, it is mainly on such a realist approach (or better, on a plea for more realisticness in economic theory)[3] that most Keynesians rely when they reject Friedman's *as if* methodology or that some Keynesians rely when they reject the assumption of continuous substitutability of inputs as embedded in the notion of neoclassical production function, or Lucas's hypothesis of rational expectations. They also may belittle the utility of too abstract mathematical applications to economics.[4]

As has been repeatedly acknowledged, while it is quite easy to identify the common targets of Keynesians' criticisms, it is far from easy to give a unified picture of their attempts to provide alternative approaches to economic analysis. Harcourt and Hamouda (1988, pp. 230–231), for instance, conclude their discussion of the various strands of post-Keynesians by observing that "The real difficulty arises when attempts are made to synthesize the strands in order to see whether a coherent whole emerges. . . . The important perspective to take away is, we believe, that there is no uniform way of tackling all issues in economics and that the various strands in Post Keynesian economics differ from one another, not least because they are concerned with different issues and often different levels of abstraction of analysis."

We believe that in order to highlight the main differences among today's different Keynesianisms we have to look, among other things, at their different methodological practices. In the following sections we show how different methodological perspectives, particularly on the proper explanatory role of economic theory, may make some important differences in theorizing even within approaches that are very akin in many other respects. This does not mean, however, that we think of this kind of methodological differences as the only ones worthy of discussion. We believe that they may give us a few useful clues about some long-standing discussions within the Keynesian camp.

In a sense this chapter is intended to see if it is possible to give stronger methodological support to Harcourt and Hamouda's conclusion. Note, however, that our definition of Keynesianism is somewhat wider than their account of post-Keynesianism. We include new Keynesians because their attempts to find Keynesian results without rejecting the notions of substantive rationality and general equilibrium are undoubtedly interesting from a methodological point of view.

The chapter is organized as follows. First we consider the methodological basis for the distinction between analyses of the short run and long run in post-Keynesian economics, and we briefly examine the main features of the long-run, or Sraffian, strand in post-Keynesian economics. It will not be difficult to argue that behind the distinction between the short- and long-run approaches one may easily detect different perspectives on the primary role to be assigned to economic theorizing. Then we deal with the second (Marshallian) and third (Kaleckian) strands in post-Keynesian economics. As a great deal of importance is given by the proponents of these two approaches to "realism," an assessment of their methodological tenets requires a somewhat lengthy discussion of the "realisticness" of their theoretical propositions. Finally, we examine the main features of new Keynesian economics and try to evaluate whether the (sometimes implicit) methodological claims of such a new research program in macroeconomics are sufficiently supported by its theoretical results.

The First Strand in Post-Keynesian Economics: Long-Run Keynesianisms

It is somewhat ironic that Keynes — one of the most disenchanted critics of the disproportionately great amount of attention that economists usually pay to long-run equilibrium — has inspired a great deal of analysis of effective demand in the long run. This section is devoted to this apparent paradox. Our thesis is that such a paradox quickly disappears if we look at the conception of the role of economic theorizing that is recognizable in the works of those Keynesians who are mainly, if not exclusively, interested in the long-run features of the functioning of economic systems.

Undoubtedly, the two most prominent names in this respect are those of Pierangelo Garegnani and Luigi Pasinetti. The former starts his discussion of consumption, investment, and effective demand (Garegnani, 1983a, italics added) by announcing that his purpose "is to reconsider the theoretical problems raised by the question of the *long-run influence* of consumption on investment." The latter concludes his interpretation of the theory of effective demand (Pasinetti, 1974, ch. 2) by warning the reader of the necessity of an explicit account of structural change when economic theory has to move from Keynes's short period to longer periods of analysis.

If we look at what lies behind such kind of preoccupations, we may easily realize that in both cases it is the object of inquiry (itself quite different from Keynes's original concern) that justifies a different theoretical approach.

As is well known, for instance, according to Garegnani and his followers[5] the notion of long-period positions should play a fundamental role in economic theory, for a number of reasons:

1. The classical notion of competition, regarded as the fundamental economic force, rests on the existence of some capital mobility between different industries, which drives the system toward the general establishment of a uniform rate of profits.

2. Natural prices — that is those prices corresponding, among other things, to a situation of uniform rate of profits — are "centers of gravitation" for market prices that may happen to be lower or higher than the former whenever the quantity supplied to the market is greater or smaller than the "effectual demand" as defined by Adam Smith.

3. The rationale of focusing attention on natural prices is provided by the assumption that the forces that determine them are the more systematic and persistent and therefore, in the long run, dominate the transitory and unsystematic ones — that is, those responsible for the fluctuations of market prices around their centers of gravitation.

4. The method of long-period positions (that is, the notion of a long-run equilibrium as a sort of benchmark for the actual state of the economy) was not peculiar to classical political economy but was also employed by neoclassical economists such as Walras, Marshall, Wicksell, and so on until the 1940s; subsequently, following Hicks's (1939) seminal work on general equilibrium, the neo-Walrasian approach abandoned that method and progressively focused on temporary equilibria. In doing so, however, this approach loses any relevance precisely because it has to rely on data, including the state of nature and expected prices, which cannot be assumed to remain constant long enough to allow for the economy to reach a meaningful position of equilibrium.[6]

The suggestion that lies behind the points we have outlined above is that of coming back to the "method" of long-period positions in contemporary theorizing. Here we are not interested in a thorough methodological appraisal of a point of view that would have us believe that economic theory should be constructed on the basis of the more dominant, systematic, and persistent forces that are assumed to be at work in the economic system, to be easily detectable by means of some aprioristic argument, and to be able to determine states of the world that tend to be actually established.[7]

Note, however, that what is judged to be meaningful in this context mirrors, on one hand, the Aristotelian distinction between substance and appearance and, on the other hand, presupposes a strong realist interpretation of the notion of causality.

For our present purposes it suffices to note that nothing could be more distant from Keynes's consciousness of the ever-changing conditions of economic activity — which is conditioned by motives, expectations, and psychological uncertainties — than a continual assertion of the notion of long-period positions as the only theoretical tool to be employed in economic theorizing. In a letter to Harrod in 1938 (Keynes, 1973, p. 300) Keynes wrote,

> I also want to emphasize strongly the point about economics being a moral science. I mentioned before that it deals with introspection and with values. I might have added that it deals with motives, expectations, psychological uncertainties. One has to be constantly on guard against treating the material as constant and homogeneous. It is as though the fall of the apple to the ground depended on the apple's motives, on whether it is worth while falling to the ground, on whether the ground wanted the apple to fall, and on mistaken calculations on the part of the apple as how far it was from the centre of the earth.

Though equally deep-rooted in the classical tradition as well as concerned with the typical Keynesian issue of the possibility of unemployment equilibria, Pasinetti's advocacy of the necessity of a sound theory of economic growth comes from different concerns. He is deeply impressed by the enormous effect that technical progress has had on living standards in the industrialized world during the last two centuries (Pasinetti, 1981, p. 21):

> The constantly advancing technology in the modern parts of the world has by now freed entire populations, for the first time in history, from the yoke of hunger and starvation. Technical change has made and is constantly making men less and less dependent on nature and more and more dependent upon themselves. . . . And what is most important to point out is that technical progress is continually going on, so that all these propositions are constantly acquiring a stronger and stronger content. The world of the future is going to become more and more a man-made world.

This judgment on the importance of technical change leads Pasinetti to focus on the dynamic features of production activity rather than on the static properties of consumer's preferences. It also leads him to argue that the proper theoretical framework for Keynes's principle of effective demand puts dynamic production rather than static exchange at the center of the stage (Pasinetti, 1991).

On the other hand, Pasinetti (1992, pp. 7–8) considers the content of his 1981 and 1993 books on structural dynamics due to technical progress in a multisector framework as "a solid, strong skeleton of basic economic relations, which refer to a production economy expanding through time with structural change" and whose main merit is to display a series of natural relations "at a stage of analysis at which behavioral and organizational devices — and therefore institutions — are indeed not considered."

All this emerges from the belief, explicitly stated, that "there is a field of investigation that refers to relations that are so fundamental as to be independent of economic and social institutions."

It goes without saying, therefore, that Pasinetti sees the role of economic theory as that of *discovering* such fundamental relations. Of course, this view of what represents the most important goal of theorizing in economics can be disputed because of the great difficulties facing any attempt to find empirical evidence supporting relations of that kind. What cannot be disputed is that Pasinetti's conception of the role of theory affects the kind of theoretical results that he judges worthy of being pursed.

The following passage (Pasinetti, 1981, p. 25) is revealing of the underlying line of thought:

> Marginal economic theorists have almost always considered efficient positions as the result of specific behavior (maximising behaviour) in a specific institutional set-up (that of an ideally competitive free market economic system). It is my purpose, instead, to develop first of all a theory which remains neutral with respect to the institutional organisation of society. My preoccupation will be that of singling out, to resume Ricardo's terminology, the "primary and natural" feature of a pure production system.

The problem with the classical notion of natural (law), however, is that natural laws, besides being causal laws of a mechanical type (and therefore capable of being discovered), were conceived as beneficial and providentially imposed norms of conduct in an orderly and harmonious state of nature. Indeed, one of the major tenets of naturalist conceptions was the belief that an economic system could evolve according to a natural course and consequently provide its inherent benefits only within a rationally organized society — where *rational* in this context, as opposed to the commonly accepted present meaning of the term, simply means "according to the underlying (natural) order of social phenomena." Given these premises, recommendations intended to foster the establishment of a society according to the dictates of nature are an inescapable corollary.

Taken together, these beliefs and meanings appear to make it difficult to distinguish between the *is* and the *ought* content of most propositions of classical economics. Consequently, the only way of making sense of the classical notion of natural equilibrium is to retain its deterministic component — that is, postulating the existence of some fundamental relation produced by (and productive of) immutable forces that man cannot deflect or impede.

In a sense, it may be said that Pasinetti is interested in the Newtonian laws of motion of the economic system. Discovering such laws, however,

is far from easy. Indeed, it is an old (and still unanswered) question whether
the difference between natural and social sciences is one requiring completely different methods of investigation or whether it is only a matter
of degree. What can be safely said, however, is that physicists' attempts
to find temporally stable correlations appear to have been much more
rewarding than the parallel attempts made from time to time by social
scientists.

The Second and Third Strand in Post-Keynesian Economics

Although the proponents of the second and third strands in post-Keynesian
economics are very critical of mainstream neoclassical theory, they do not
reject all the traditional neoclassical tools. Nor are they willing to leave
aside all sorts of behavioral analysis, as advocated by the proponents of
the first strand discussed above. They actually stress the role played by
expectations and subjective beliefs in any process of decision making that
takes place in an uncertain world and in historical time: "In a world where
uncertainty and surprise are unavoidable, expectations have an unavoidable and significant effect on economic outcomes" (Davidson, 1981, p. 159).

The bug-bear of both strand 2 and strand 3 post-Keynesians is GE
theory, which is seen as "central to neoclassical synthesis and its monetarist relation" (Dow and Earl, 1982, p. 247), while "the essence of the
Keynesian message was that it is not helpful to model the economy as a
GE system" (Dow and Earl, 1982, p. 248). GE is often regarded by post-
Keynesians as conceptually faulty and inevitably devoid of empirical content, hence irrelevant.[8] Even non-Walrasian equilibrium theory (Clower,
1965; Malinvaud, 1977; Benassy, 1982) is looked on with suspicion for
lacking "the distinguishing feature about the role of money in a capitalist
economy" (Minsky, 1975, p. 73), for ignoring historical time and *true
uncertainty* (as opposed to actuarial risk) — for being, in sum, GE.

Both strand 2 and strand 3 post-Keynesians share the Marshallian
realist approach and make wide use of the *ceteris paribus* clauses in order
to capture in their models as much of the economic phenomena that
characterize the "real world" as possible and to stress the relevant causal
connections that are difficult to identify within a GE framework, through
the exogenous versus endogenous variables dichotomy, among those
phenomena.[9]

Marshallian realism comes out also in the strong dismissal on the
part of both strands of post-Keynesianism of the "as if" methodology

propounded by Milton Friedman (1953) in his famous essay on the methodology of positive economics. Economic theory, according to strand 2 and strand 3 post-Keynesians, is relevant as far as it is capable to explain the *stylized facts* of modern capitalist economies. And this is only possible if the assumptions on which economic models are built are as close as possible to the real world, no matter what are the established rules of economic theorizing (individualism, rationality, GE framework, and so on). There is no need to derive macroeconomic propositions from microeconomic first principles, as these are inevitably unrealistic, or else one should start with entirely different first principles.

Besides these common Marshallian methodological underpinnings, there are relevant theoretical differences between the second and the third strands of post-Keynesianism. As noted by Harcourt and Hamouda (1988), the second strand — the most prominent proponents of which are G.L.S. Shackle, Paul Davidson, Sidney Weintraub, Fausto Vicarelli, Jan Kregel, and Victoria Chick — is more strictly Keynesian and Marshallian, while the third strand — comprising Joan Robinson, Nicholas Kaldor, Alfred Eichner, Geoffrey Harcourt, Robin Marris, Adrian Wood, and Tom Asimakopoulos — has a distinct Kaleckian inspiration.[10]

Strand 2: Uncertainty, Money, and Equilibrium

In accordance with their theoretical underpinnings, it comes as no surprise that strand 2 post-Keynesians have greatly contributed to the clarification of Keynes's theory and methodology, which were almost hidden under many coats of neoclassical varnish.

Keynes was convinced that in order to get out of the strictures of Say's law it was necessary to stress the *intertemporal coordination failures* implied by the absence of complete future markets and by the presence of money as a store of value in a "monetary production economy" (Keynes, 1979, pp. 76–92). Following Keynes, the proponents of the second strand of post-Keynesianism place a great deal of importance on the unavoidable uncertainty faced by economic agents in choice making[11] and consequently on the role of monetary factors in the determination of the level of employment and in the process of cyclical growth. One of the post-Keynesians' favorite quotations from Keynes reads as follows: "By 'uncertain' knowledge, let me explain, I do not mean merely to distinguish what known for certain from what is only probable. . . . The sense in which I am using the term is that in which the prospect of a European war is uncertain, or the price of copper and the rate of interest twenty years hence. . . . About these matters there is no scientific basis on which to form any calculable probability whatever. We simply do not know" (Keynes, 1937, pp. 213–214).[12] Keynes maintained that, in such an uncertain world, "the possession of actual money lulls our disquietude; and the premium which we require to make us part with money is the measure of the degree of our disquietude" (Keynes, 1937, p. 216).

Such a premium is the money rate of interest. But money, according to Keynes, has two special characteristics that make its own rate of interest to set a limit to the level of output and employment: (1) money has a zero or very small elasticity of production; and (2) money has an elasticity of substitution equal or nearly equal to zero (see Keynes, 1936, ch. 17). Keynes's conclusion in Chapter 17 of *The General Theory* has been emphasized time and again by Paul Davidson: "in the absence of money and in the absence — we must, of course, also suppose — of any other commodity with the assumed characteristics of money, the rate of interest would only reach equilibrium when there is full employment. Unemployment develops, that is to say, because people want the moon; men cannot be employed when the object of desire (i.e. money) is something which cannot be produced and the demand for which cannot be readily choked off" (Keynes, 1936, p. 235).

An important step toward a full understanding of Keynes's theory and methodology as regards expectations and equilibrium is Kregel's distinction of three models within *The General Theory*, each model being tied to different assumptions about short- and long-term expectations. According to Kregel (1976), the first model offers a static equilibrium framework, where long-term expectations are exogenous and short-term expectations are fulfilled. The equilibrium in such a model is to be interpreted as *virtual* or *notional* at a point in time and thus cannot be observed (see Minsky, 1975; Vicarelli, 1984, 1985). Moreover this equilibrium is transitory, as "long-term expectations, based as they are on conventional factors, may suffer sudden and radical revisions" (Vercelli, 1991, p. 227). Keynes's third model is indeed a shifting equilibrium model, "where disappointment of short period expectations may encourage revision of long period expectations" (Dow, 1985, p. 126).[13]

From this set of observations one is entitled to draw the conclusion that Keynes's and the strand 2 post-Keynesian notion of equilibrium is altogether different from the long-period notion that can be found in the Sraffian strand of post-Keynesianism,[14] besides being different from the neoclassical notion, which implies actual optimization on the part of all economic agents and fulfilled (rational) expectations. Hence Keynes's (and the strand 2 post-Keynesian) notion of equilibrium is under attack by the neo-Ricardians, for being too sensitive to shifts in such subjective elements as expectations, (see, for instance, Garegnani, 1983a; Eatwell and Milgate, 1983, intro- duction) and by the neoclassicals, for being inconsistent with the ration- ality postulates on which economic theory ought to be built and according to which involuntary unemployment equilibrium is a non-intelligible con- cept. (See Lucas, 1977).

Strand 2: Market Structure[15]

The Marshallian underpinnings of the second strand of post-Keynesianism come out clearly in the attempts to give sensible microfoundations to Keynes's aggregate supply function, starting from a Marshallian short- period supply function in a single competitive industry (notably Weintraub, 1959; Davidson and Smolensky, 1964; Davidson, 1978; Chick, 1983).

In *The General Theory* Keynes did not make any explicit assumption about competition and market structure. At most he referred to a "given degree of competition" (Keynes, 1936, p. 245). The reasons why Keynes disregarded imperfect competition as a sensible microfoundation for his theory of unemployment equilibrium have never been satisfactorily ex- plained (see Marris, 1991). Keynes's choice is even more puzzling consid- ering that when he started writing *The General Theory* he had undoubtedly read Kahn's (1929) fellowship dissertation and probably Joan Robinson's *The Economics of Imperfect Competition* (1933) (see Marris, 1992).

Although in the 1939 *Economic Journal* article Keynes appears willing to give up his earlier views on anticyclical real wages, he never realized how much stronger his macro theory would have been if supported by increasing returns and imperfect competition (Kaldor, 1983, p. 14). In contrast, strand 2 post-Keynesians claim (as Kregel does) that "for Keynes, any assumption which explained why entrepreneurs would not expand, even when they could do so under increasing returns at lower costs and prices, and which related to the type of competition would automatically have replaced the explanation based on effective demand" (Kregel, 1987, p. 494).

As already noted, Keynes was not clear on this issue but implicitly assumed — by accepting the first classical postulate — perfect competition with prices equal to marginal costs and real wages equal to the marginal product of labor. Despite several distinguished philological inquires in order to show that Keynes's view of competition is not the same as Walras's perfect competition and that "the first classical postulate can be seen as a layer of Keynes's classical skin that he was reluctant to shed unnecessarily"

(Lawlor, Darity, and Horn, 1987, p. 517),[16] the proponents of strand 2 post-Keynesianism seem to miss the logical requirement of increasing returns and imperfect competition for a consistent theory of involuntary unemployment equilibrium, as stressed by Kaldor (1978, 1983) and — as will be shown below — by many new Keynesians.

It is baffling that, while disregarding imperfect competition (and realism) in the goods market, strand 2 post-Keynesians (resorting to realism) are willing to admit that some imperfection in the labor market is necessary to explain wage stickiness (if not wage rigidity). It is even more surprising that no post-Keynesian is willing to admit that such a labor-market imperfection is central to give a firm foundation to quantity adjustments — that is, to the "principle of effective demand" (Keynes assumed a *given* money wage). Hence the attention paid by this strand of post-Keynesians to some crucial institutional feature of labor markets in the real world (see, in particular, Appelbaum, 1979; Weintraub, 1978–1979). Money wage bargaining in a monetary economy and the role of trade unions and of segmented labor markets are often emphasized, but no coherent model of the labor market featuring the individual or unionized bargaining process has been advanced by strand 2 (or even strand 3) post-Keynesians. Nor have they tried to formalize the dynamic process outlined by Keynes in Chapter 19 of *The General Theory*, where the negative effects of a wage and price deflation on standing real debts are suggested.

It can be maintained that the explicit dismissal of imperfect competition in the goods market (and the lack of a model of the labor market) have severely weakened the strand 2 post-Keynesian claim to be a coherent alternative to the neoclassical economics, the proponents of which have an easy hand in attacking post-Keynesian economics for its lack of sound microfoundations. The attempt to attach some profound methodological reason for such a lack of microfoundations is not convincing, nor can *realism* be advocated easily in this case.

Strand 3: Imperfect Competition, Financial Requirements, and Effective Demand

Strand 3 post-Keynesians are definitely less akin than strand 2 on philological issues and give a broader meaning to the adjective *Keynesian* in order to encompass contributions coming from the Kaleckian and Marxian traditions. Accordingly, for this group of post-Keynesians imperfect competition is the relevant case in real-world capitalism and hence must be used as a cornerstone of any serious theoretical model.

It is in a sense surprising that Joan Robinson, whose *Economics of Imperfect Competition* was published in 1933, was so late in acknowledging the relevance of imperfect competition for Keynesian macroeconomics. It is only after Joan Robinson accepted and started supporting Kalecki's approach to the macrodistribution of income that imperfect competition entered the post-Keynesian camp.

Kalecki, on the other hand, dropped perfect competition as soon as he reckoned that monopoly and oligopoly dominate most industries in a capitalist system. He also dropped the Marshallian increasing average cost curves in favor of horizontal average cost curves up to full-capacity level, and criticized Keynes for his use of U shaped average and marginal cost curves in *The General Theory*.

Kalecki and the post-Keynesian economists following in his footsteps (with the exception of Kaldor and, more recently, of Robin Marris) do not seem to care much about the logical need of imperfect competition for an equilibrium state with unemployed labor and excess capacity. Their principal aim is at providing a consistent macro theory of distribution, based on "realistic" assumptions about microbehavior.

While in his writings from the 1930s Kalecki maintained that imperfectly competitive firms actually maximize profits, in his 1954 *Theory of Economic Dynamics* he assumed that firms set prices according to a mark up over unit prime costs. Kalecki does not say much as an explanation for the size of the mark up. He only argues that the mark up is determined by the competitive structure of each industry — that is, the degree of monopoly of an industry as a whole.

As the competitive structure of industries is assumed to be constant (market demand is isoelastic) in the short run, and nominal wage and labor productivity are also constant by assumption, aggregate demand shocks do not affect prices but the level of output. With the well-known assumptions about the saving propensities of workers and capitalists, it is easy for Kalecki to show that the higher the degree of monopoly (the higher the desired share of profits on income) the lower the investment multiplier.

For any given level of investment, a higher level of aggregate demand and produced output would require a lower mark up and, correspondingly, higher real wages. This conclusion is opposite to Keynes's view in *The General Theory* but is the cornerstone of Kaldor's theory of full-employment steady growth, of Steindl's (1952) theory of stagnation, and of the strand 3 post-Keynesian approach to effective demand.

If the degree of monopoly is rigid, prices are also rigid, and any reduction in nominal wages in the face of unemployment would result in lower real wages and hence in lower aggregate demand and higher unemployment. According to Kalecki, workers' wage resistance is to be regarded as a protection against the spiral of depression, even without taking into account the Fisher effect.[17]

Strand 3 post-Keynesians, who accept Kalecki's theoretical framework, have to face at least two main issues left untackled by Kalecki: (1) what are the determinants of profit margins (that is, the mark up), once profit maximization is abandoned as a sensible explanation of behavior? and (2) why are prices rigid even when nominal wages fall — that is, why should mark ups vary countercyclically?

Inquiry on the determinants of profit margins has attracted some relevant theoretical work. In the 1950s Steindl (1952) and Sylos Labini (1956–1962) developed the well-known normal cost pricing hypothesis, while in the 1960s and 1970s a *pricing-cum-investment* hypothesis was explored (see Ball, 1964; Eichner, 1973, 1976; Wood, 1975; Harcourt and Kenyon, 1976; Shapiro, 1981).[18] Under such an hypothesis the pricing behavior of oligopolistic firms is seen as aimed at generating sufficient cash flows to internally finance planned investment expenditures, since external financing may be expensive or rationed.

Price-leader firms are regarded as being growth maximizers under a minimum profit constraint. Their decisions about future investment are assumed to be based on the relation between the realized and the desired degree of capacity utilization, given the expectations about future demand and the expected profitability of alternative investment projects. With a constant desired gearing ratio, firms choose a mark up that will yield the required level of retained profits. Provided average production costs do not vary over the planning period, prices (and mark ups) are kept constant, and firms respond to demand fluctuations by varying the level of production and the degree of capacity utilization, hence the level of employment.

With this approach to pricing decisions, strand 3 post-Keynesians maintain that price rigidity in the face of demand fluctuations cannot be seen as an ad hoc assumption but as a result of firms' rational behavior. Moreover, such a theory gives a rationale for the low-interest elasticity of aggregate investment, which is an important tenet of orthodox Keynesians. Unfortunately, the pricing-cum-investment theory disregards the kind of strategic interactions that characterize oligopolistic industries, and price leadership is just *assumed* and not derived as an equilibrium outcome of a properly specified game. Again, the plea for realism and the suspicion about analytical tools developed within the mainstream approach contribute to weaken the logical tightness of post-Keynesian microfoundations.

The New Keynesian Research Program

New Keynesian economics is a research program that took shape in the 1980s as a reaction to the new classical macroeconomics and its hands-off precepts. It is not surprising then that classical economists (Smith, Ricardo, and Marx) as well as post-Keynesian economists are entirely ignored by the new Keynesians. They are concerned with the facts and with the theoretical issues that interested Keynes, but they do not really care about "what Keynes really meant," nor do they attempt to tailor Keynes's thought to their own purposes.

The new Keynesians want to take into account the new classical critiques of traditional AD-AS macro models and of non-Walrasian (disequilibrium) fix-price models. Those critiques were directed toward ad hoc hypotheses of irrational behavior (money illusion, less than rational expectation) and lack of proper microfoundations for price and wage rigidities, which can also be found in Keynes and in post-Keynesian models.

As Stiglitz points out, while the new classicals argue "that *all* that one needs to understand macroeconomic activity is the neoclassical model," the new Keynesians attempt "to change microeconomics, to make it possible to derive from 'correct' microeconomic principles commonly observed macroeconomic phenomena" (Stiglitz, 1991, pp. 3–4). What is meant by "correct" microeconomic principles can be understood from the strong hostility toward Friedman's "as if" methodology, which the new Keynesians have in common with the post-Keynesians: "The pseudo-scientific 'as if' methodology promoted by Friedman has been pushed too far: a theory is to be tested not by a selected set of its predictions. Among the testable parts of a theory are those assumptions which are themselves directly testable. . . . We count it a virtue, not a vice, if the assumptions of the model are themselves plausible; if the microfoundations underlying the theory are themselves testable — and tested" (Stiglitz, 1992, p. 276).

This does not necessarily mean that assumptions should immediately reflect the real world. The purpose of economic models is "to give 'pure' illustrations of general principles" (Solow, 1986, p. 313), to show how some relevant stylized macrofacts logically follow from a few reasonable assumptions about microbehavior. New Keynesian research, as we shall see, has taken different routes and a unified theory has still not emerged.[19] However, again in Stiglitz's words, the new Keynesian approach, "to accommodate microeconomics to macroeconomics, introduces doses of imperfect information, imperfect competition and adjustment costs. It looks for a variety of explanations of wage and price rigidities; it seeks to explain both the causes and consequences of these rigidities — consequences that extend beyond the macroeconomic fluctuations to which they may give rise" (Stiglitz, 1991, p. 4, italics in the original).

It should be stressed from the outset that while Keynes's main theoretical contributions were, so to speak, on the "aggregate demand" side of macroeconomics, leaving the "aggregate supply" side largely untouched in its traditional Marshallian structure, the new Keynesian research is mainly directed at the microfoundations of aggregate supply. Aggregate demand, and especially its investment component, is left almost unmodeled.[20] In many new Keynesian models aggregate demand enters as a shift parameter into individual demand functions: in some models we have nominal money, in some others public expenditure, without any substantive change in the results.

Such an agnosticism is reflected in the new Keynesian view about the long-standing monetarist-Keynesian dispute over the relative potency of monetary and fiscal policy. Mankiw and Romer go as far as stating that "an economist can be a monetarist by believing that fluctuations in the money supply are the primary source of fluctuations in aggregate demand and a New Keynesian by believing that microeconomic imperfections lead to macroeconomic price rigidities" (Mankiw and Romer, 1991, p. 3).

Despite these differences, it can be said that the new Keynesian attitude toward the mainstream theory is close to that of Keynes. He took the prevalent orthodoxy of his time — Marshallian and Pigouvian economics — and changed some crucial assumptions in order to explain persistent unemployment and idle capacity. The new Keynesians take the orthodoxy of our time — Walrasian GE theory — and change some crucial assumptions about microbehavior to give new explanations of the same phenomena. Economic theorizing for the new Keynesians means building models that allow predictions that contradict other leading macroeconomic theories (that is, new classical theories), while fitting better than rival theories the stylized facts of actual economies (see Ball, Mankiw, and Romer, 1988; Greenwald and Stiglitz, 1988a; Blanchard and Fischer; 1989, p. 489; Stiglitz, 1991).

Keynes retained much of the Marshallian theoretical and methodological approach in the same way the new Keynesians retain much of the Walrasian approach. General equilibrium is the accepted analytical framework, while economic agents are seen as rational maximizers.[21] Uncertainty is treated within the standard subjective probability framework, and rational expectations are assumed whenever needed, in order to be able to show that Keynesian propositions do not require irrationality or myopic agents or money illusion. The crucial difference is that agents do not act in the standard parametric environment (perfect competition, symmetric information) but in a strategic context, with imperfect competition and asymmetric information.

The consequences, as we shall briefly see, are far reaching. Traditional Keynesian models — either of the neoclassical synthesis brand or of the post-Keynesian brand or of the disequilibrium brand — postulate but do not justify some kind of real or nominal rigidity. However, as Arrow (1959) recognized, price (or wage) rigidity is incompatible with perfect competition and — one may want to add — symmetric information. Once either imperfect competition or asymmetric information, with price or wage setters, is assumed, it makes sense to ask whether agents adjust their prices or wages to a shock, after assessing their private costs and benefits from adjustment. As such, costs depend crucially on the expected behavior of others, conventions and institutions that enable coordination of expectations become extremely relevant.

Imperfect Competition, Externalities, and Strategic Complementarity

By placing imperfect competition and asymmetric information at the center of the stage the new Keynesian economics is able to create a link between the kind of coordination failures stressed by Clower (1965) and Leijonhufvud (1968) and one of the widely acknowledged causes of market failure at the micro level: the existence of reciprocal externalities among economic agents. This leads quite naturally to making extensive use of strategic interactions and to applying the game theoretic notion of Nash equilibrium (and refinements) as the building blocks of Keynesian macroeconomics.

Coordination failures and unemployment cannot logically take place in a perfectly competitive economy with constant returns to scale and representative agents, because in such an economy — as Weitzman (1982) points out — it is always possible for an unemployed worker to set up a minifirm, employ himself, and sell the product on a perfectly competitive market at the going price. There can be no problem of effective demand as, in a balanced expansion, supply creates its own demand. Constant returns to scale are a cornerstone of Walrasian GE under perfect competition but are incompatible with Keynesian economics, if the representative agent assumption is made.[22]

Increasing returns are logically needed to prevent self-employment and Say's law. But increasing returns are incompatible with perfect competition and are the primary cause of imperfect competition. Therefore, as Weitzman puts it, "If you want to build from first principles a broad based microeconomic foundation to a GE theory that will explain involuntary unemployment, you must start with increasing returns and go the route of imperfect competition" (Weitzman, 1982, p. 794).[23] It should also be noticed, in passing, that short-run increasing returns help to explain the stylized fact that output increases more than employment during business upturns.

Under imperfect competition it is possible to show that demand linkages between firms in a multisector economy generate reciprocal positive externalities even if markets are complete.[24] Demand spillovers (due to nonspecialization in consumption) do not result in reciprocal externalities in a Walrasian economy, as under perfect competition agents can sell any amount they choose at the given price. The presence of positive externalities implies that the resulting Nash macroequilibrium is Pareto inefficient.

The existence of reciprocal externalities can also give rise to *macroeconomic externalities* in symmetric equilibrium. That is, for any given value of an exogenous parameter, an equal and coordinated change of all players' strategies will affect the payoffs of each and all players and, under certain hypotheses, social welfare as well. If the exogenous parameter is nominal money and the strategic variable is price, the presence of macroeconomic externalities in equilibrium entails that a coordinated reduction of prices by all firms will induce higher aggregate real output and employment. Macroeconomic externalities show coordination failures that cannot take place under perfect competition and reveal the macroeconomic inefficiency of imperfect competition, as aggregate real output and employment, in equilibrium, are lower than under perfect competition because prices are higher (see Benassy, 1987; Blanchard and Kiyotaki, 1987; Drazen, 1987; Ball, Mankiw, and Romer, 1988).

Another important feature of imperfectly competitive economies, which exhibit reciprocal externalities, is the possibility of *strategic complementarity*. Strategic complementarity arises when changes in one agent's strategy affect the *marginal* payoff of other agents (see Bulow, Geanakopolos, and Klemperer, 1985; Cooper and John, 1988; Milgrom and Roberts, 1990; Vives, 1990; Ball and Romer, 1991). The importance of strategic complementarities lies in their being necessary (though not sufficient) for the existence of multiple Nash equilibria and necessary and sufficient for multiplier effects. Besides, if an economy with positive reciprocal externalities among firms admits multiple Nash equilibria with different levels of employment, such equilibria can be Pareto ranked in the level of employment (see Cooper and John, 1988, pp. 443–449). Hence coordination failures in equilibrium become even more apparent. The economy can be stuck in a Pareto-inferior underemployment equilibrium, although a Pareto-efficient full-employment equilibrium exists. A range of "natural" rates of unemployment can be reached, and the actual level of employment that the economy settles at may depend on the values of the money supply or public expenditure or on agents' state of confidence (see Hart, 1982; Weitzman, 1982; Heller, 1986; Solow, 1986; Dixon, 1988; Frank, 1990; Pagano, 1990; Manning, 1990).[25] The role of conventions and institutions in equilibrium selection becomes extremely relevant.

It is important to stress that strategic complementarity is necessary only for multiple equilibria, though it is necessary and sufficient for multiplier effects. Therefore those models that exhibit strategic complementarity and a unique Nash equilibrium do actually show multipliers but not necessarily Keynesian multipliers. An example is provided by the best-known macro-economic model with imperfect competition: Blanchard and Kiyotaki (1987). Here we find reciprocal externalities, macroeconomic externalities, and strategic complementarity. The macroeconomic (symmetric) Nash equilibrium is unique and shows an inefficiently low level of aggregate output and employment. But nothing can be said about the existence of *involuntary* unemployment, as long as the labor market is assumed to be Walrasian, and equilibrium occurs on the labor supply curve. Moreover, although under imperfect competition a firm's demand depends on *real* aggregate demand, *nominal* money is neutral in this model, and multipliers are just price multipliers (Boitani, Delli Gatti, and Mezzomo, 1992). Some nominal rigidity has to be added to get a Keynesian view of the business cycle and some imperfection in the labor market is needed to obtain involuntary unemployment in equilibrium.

Nominal and Real Rigidities: Policy Effectiveness and Unemployment Equilibrium

Although imperfect competition in the goods market on its own is not sufficient in order to contrast the new classical view of the business cycle, it can be shown that imperfect competition (1) is necessary for "models in which optimizing agents choose to create nominal rigidities" (Ball, Mankiw, and Romer, 1988, p. 2) and (2) can be complemented with asymmetric information or imperfect competition in the labor market to yield equilibria with involuntary unemployment.

While it can be shown that under perfect competition rational agents never choose to create nominal rigidities, even though price adjustments are costly, because the gains from nominal adjustments are large, things look different under imperfect competition, as here "a higher price always implies lower sales. Starting from the profit-maximizing price-quantity combination, the gains from trading off price and sales after a shock are second order" (Ball, Mankiw, and Romer, 1988, p. 13).[26]

If such gains happen to be lower than the small (*menu*) costs of price adjustment, it is rational for firms not to adjust their prices and to react to a nominal shock by changing quantities instead. But the aggregate effect of menu costs is first order, as the economy undertakes large fluctuations. As Ball, Mankiw, and Romer (1988, p. 6) write, "This finding resolves the puzzle of why price setters refuse to incur the small costs of reducing the business cycle through more flexible prices. Despite the large macro-economic effects, the private incentives are small."

It can also be shown that there may be strategic complementarity in price adjustment, as the incentive of a firm to adjust its price rises if its rivals adjust. Thus multiple equilibria in price adjustment arise and nominal rigidity turns out to be another instance of coordination failures when agents behave non cooperatively (Ball and Romer, 1991). Moreover, imperfect competition and menu costs can be jointly used to give sensible microfoundations to models of price and wage staggering (Fischer, 1977; Taylor, 1980; Blanchard, 1986). Models that show that, if firms (workers) set prices (wages) at different times, the adjustment of the price level to nominal shocks is slowed down and the real effects are persistent.[27]

The menu costs approach to nominal rigidities has been criticized by Greenwald and Stiglitz, who argue that the "fixed costs of quantity adjustments (layoffs, etc.) are widely regarded as being greater than the costs of price adjustment," and hence "why, in spite of greater adjustment costs, output and employment are more variable than prices and wages?" (Greenwald and Stiglitz, 1989, p. 364). Greenwald and Stiglitz provide an answer that is based on three hypotheses: (1) firms are risk averse; (2) the greater the change from the status quo the more uncertain are firms about the consequences of their actions; and (3) "there is often greater uncertainty associated with pricing and wage decisions than with output and employment decision."

Unfortunately, the Greenwald-Stiglitz model is better equipped to explain *real* (that is, relative prices) rather than *nominal* rigidities. With real rigidities and nominal flexibility money neutrality still holds. However, some authors have employed risk aversion to get more robust explanations of nominal rigidities (Weinrich and Battinelli, 1992), but much research is still to be carried out to reach a satisfactory and sufficiently simple justification of nominal rigidities along this route.

It can also be argued that with strategic complementarity in price adjustment the Greenwald-Stiglitz critique is less convincing. If firms choose whether to adjust according to their expectations about others' choices, there is no need of ad hoc asymmetries between price and quantity adjustment costs. Quantity-adjustment costs are higher compared to price-adjustment costs when a shock is perceived as nominal — that is, when firms expect others only to adjust prices; the reverse applies when a shock is perceived as real — that is, when firms expect others to adjust quantities.

The multiplicity of self-fulfilling expectations equilibria leaves open the question how the economy can operate the equilibrium selection from among the many possible equilibria. Here the role of conventions, confidence, and institutions once more is seen as potentially relevant. Politics, in a broad sense, becomes an essential ingredient of any description of how the economy works, hence economics and politics can no longer be regarded as sharply separated disciplines. From a methodological point of view this conclusion may have profound consequences on how economists perceive the role and status of economics as a science, besides giving stronger microfoundations to some deep intuitions of Keynes and of the post-Keynesians.

Within the menu costs approach, yet another difficulty is to be faced: for plausible parameter values, small menu costs inhibit adjustment only when nominal shocks are very small (see Ball and Romer, 1990, pp. 189–192). However, if nominal frictions are complemented with real rigidities, the picture changes significantly and small menu costs can yield large nonneutralities, as the incentive to change real prices in the face of a nominal shock is very small or even nonexistent.

Such is the case if real wages are rigid, due to asymmetric information or to imperfect competition in the labor market. It is not by chance that the sources of large nonneutralities coincide, as we shall see below, with the sources of involuntary unemployment. According to the asymmetric information hypothesis, "In the labor market, buyers of labor services are faced with considerable uncertainty concerning many aspects of the productivity of the workers they are hiring. *If lowering the wage they offer significantly lowers the average ability of the job applicants they face, firms may find that lowering their wages makes them worse off*" (Weiss, 1991, p. 3, italics in the original).

As a consequence firms may find that, to certain extent, offering real wages higher than the market clearing wage elicits effort or selects more productive workers. Such an *efficiency wage* will minimize firms' costs in terms of efficiency units; thus it is an equilibrium real wage. As the efficiency wage is above the market clearing level, it will entail unemployment.

Such an unemployment is definitely *involuntary*, since firms are not willing to hire unemployed workers who offer to underbid their employed colleagues, and unemployed workers cannot set up their minifirms and become self-employed because of the increasing returns to scale technology and imperfect competition in the goods market.[28]

Akerlof and Yellen (1985) provide a model in which imperfect competition in the goods market (but not increasing returns) is complemented with a simple efficiency wage model of the labor market and small nominal frictions. In such a way they are able to obtain not only involuntary unemployment but also large real effects of nominal shocks.[29] This can be explained by observing that — with efficiency wages — equilibrium occurs off the labor supply curve and real wages are highly if not entirely acyclical (which is a stylized fact any theory should explain). Hence the private cost of nonadjusting prices "is small because, with nearly acyclical real wages, shifts in aggregate output have little effect on marginal cost, and so firms' desired price adjustments are small" (Ball and Romer, 1990, p. 201).

Similar results can be obtained by combining small menu costs with imperfect competition in the labor market, where unions choose a real wage above the market clearing level,[30] or with insiders-outsiders models of the labor market, such as those propounded in a number of papers by Lindbeck and Snower (1988) or those based on game theoretic bargaining (Hahn, 1987; Solow, 1990).

Interestingly, within the new Keynesian camp there is a revival of interest for the old Keynesian hypothesis according to which workers are concerned with keeping the wage differentials constant. Such an hypothesis has been combined with efficiency wages by Stiglitz (1985) and Summers (1988) and with trade unions by Bhaskar (1990). An appealing feature of this approach is that it yields both real and nominal rigidity at once and allows one to build very simple models with standard Keynesian properties (see Boitani and Mezzomo, 1991; Boitani, Delli Gatti, and Mezzomo, 1992). On the other hand the "indexation puzzle" — that is, the question of why firms and workers do not sign fully indexed contracts (which would eliminate any nominal rigidity) — is still to be solved.[31]

As a conclusion on this point, it can be said that there are a great variety of new Keynesian explanations of both real and nominal rigidities, hence of involuntary unemployment equilibrium and of real effects of nominal shocks. But a unified robust theory has still not emerged. According to Blanchard and Fischer, "whether some unifying principle can be found in the dizzying diversity of explanations, remain to be seen: No doubt some theories that now look promising will turn out to be dead ends and some that now look moribund or already dead will turn out to be important. How does the process work? To some extent the theories that win are those that are more appealing to our professional standards and prejudices. To a greater extent, they will be the theories that succeed in accounting for the macroeconomic facts as well as the microeconomic evidence" (Blanchard and Fischer, 1989, p. 489).

Asymmetric Information and Capital and Credit Market Imperfections

The only attempt to construct a new Keynesian model around a single unifying "first principle" is due to Joseph Stiglitz and his associates (Greenwald and Weiss), who reject the multiplicity of explanatory models (piecemeal approach), apparently accepted as inevitable for the time being by Blanchard and Fischer: "The piecemeal approach is not only unattractive, in requiring a myriad of explanations, but the explanations seem sometimes at odds with one another" (Stiglitz, 1992, p. 276).

The unifying first principle — according to Stiglitz et al. — is asymmetric information, which, as already seen, gives rise to efficiency wages in the labor market. Stiglitz et al. make extensive use of asymmetric information to explain imperfections in the equity and credit markets, regarded by these authors as even more important than goods and labor market imperfections for a consistent theory of the business cycle and of the mechanisms through which policy shocks affect the real economy.[32]

Due to asymmetric information and its consequences — adverse selection and adverse incentives — firms are rationed in the issue of new equity to finance their production and investment decisions. Actually, Stiglitz et al. do not distinguish between investment and production decisions as, in their opinion, both decisions involve risk in the absence of complete future markets. Production takes time, and inputs are to be paid in advance of knowing the value of the output sold.

If the managers of firms are averse to the risk of bankruptcy, their production decisions are strongly affected by the equity base of firms, as the equity base directly affects the incremental risk associated with output decisions: "Thus, the marginal cost of additional output, including the marginal increase in risk borne by the firm's decision-makers, falls when a firm's equity position improves and rises when it deteriorates" (Greenwald and Stiglitz, 1988a, pp. 252–253).

As the firm's demand for labor is derived from the output decision, it follows that, for any given real wage, the demand for labor schedule shifts outward when the equity base improves and inward when it deteriorates.

From the efficiency wage condition the optimum real wage is derived, and employment fluctuates because of the shifts in the demand for labor — that is, because of shocks that affect the financial position of firms.

Equity rationing would suffice to bring about large fluctuations in real output and employment but would not suffice to show money nonneutrality if a monetary transmission mechanism is not added to the model. Stiglitz et al. reject the standard mechanisms based on the real balance effect or on the rate of interest effect on investment. They suggest a mechanism that operates through the credit market, which is characterized by asymmetric information between risk-averse lenders (banks) and risk-averse borrowers (firms).

Asymmetric information entails that "lenders are unable to distinguish among borrowers, that borrowers accept a common fixed loan size and that as the contractual rate of interest charged to borrowers rises the quality of the borrower pool falls" (Greenwald and Stiglitz, 1990, p. 14). As a consequence there is a rate of interest at which expected returns to lenders (banks) reach a maximum. If banks are risk averse and have to choose between investing in safe government bonds or in risky lending to firms, their optimal portfolio entails credit rationing.[33]

Credit rationing becomes tighter when the economy goes into a recession, as the risk associated with the lending activity rises and tends to reinforce equity rationing. But the amount of loans that banks are willing to grant also depends, for any given mean-variance frontier of loan returns, on the assets in the hands of banks that are available for lending (mainly deposits), and on the interest rate on safe government bonds. This means that money supply, in one way or another, affects the amount of loanable funds, which in turn affects investment and production decisions of equity rationed managers.

According to Stiglitz et al., it is through credit, not through standard wealth effects on consumption or interest-rate effects on investment, that monetary policy may influence that real economy, although such an influence may turn out to be very limited in recessions, when banks' willingness to lend is strongly weakened: "The moral of the story is simple: you can lead a horse to water but you can't make it drink. In extreme recessions, it may be extremely difficult to induce the banks to lend more" (Stiglitz, 1992, p. 295).

By allowing for asymmetric information in equity and credit markets a richer picture of firms (and banks) and their decision problems comes out, as well as a greater diversity of possible macroeconomic outcomes after a shock hits the economy. The view of the business cycle that emerges is quite close to that of Keynes, and particularly of some post-Keynesians like Kalecki and Minsky, though the arguments underlying such a view are quite different.[34] Uncertainty and monetary and financial factors, which are absent in the new Keynesian models discussed above, are brought back to the forefront. The crude transaction technology, which gives rise to a quantitative relation between money, real output, and the price level in many models of imperfect competition with Keynesian features, is replaced by a richer and more realistic view of the role of money and credit in modern economies.

The traditional distinction between the supply and the demand side of the economy becomes less clear in Stiglitz et al.'s theory than it was in traditional Keynesian models, or even in new Keynesian models of the imperfect competition variety, as "the variables that affect aggregate demand for investment are precisely the same variables that affect aggregate supply, the amount that firms are willing to produce" (Stiglitz, 1992, p. 289) and as investment is not really distinguished from production. Hence, any shock has partly demand and partly supply effects, which makes comparative statics more complicated but perhaps makes the theory more flexible and more capable of explaining the real world.

So far so good, but there is still an extremely relevant question to be faced by Stiglitz et al.: why should the traditional money neutrality not apply? Or will monetary shocks ever initiate business fluctuations? In Stiglitz's (1992, pp. 295–296) own words, "Is it possible that no matter what the monetary authorities do, only the price level would change, and nothing real would happen?"

Stiglitz et al.'s answer stands on two legs: (1) loan contracts are usually unindexed, which implies that an unforeseen monetary shock has real effects through the real redistribution between creditors and debtors even were prices perfectly flexible; (2) nominal rigidities may result from the common knowledge that the real redistribution effects entail money nonneutrality. Hence any and each firm will be uncertain about the reaction of its competitors and will regard it as risky to act *as if* money were neutral. Since firms are risk averse, they will prefer to adjust quantities rather than prices, as the uncertainties associated with price changes are greater than those associated with quantity changes.

It should be clear that the self-confirming nature of money nonneutrality rests, in Stiglitz et al.'s models, on the assumption that loan contracts are not fully indexed. Although Stiglitz et al. have become increasingly dissatisfied with the menu *costs* approach to price rigidity, they implicitly rely on some unexplained and unmodeled *cost* of writing or monitoring indexed contracts in order to draw their conclusions. Without such indexing costs — that is, without nominal rigidity — initial shocks would be dampened by the working of the price system instead of being amplified through Keynesian feedbacks.

If the above observations are correct, Stiglitz et al.'s claim to have built a theory free from ad hoc-ery and from "piecemeal explanations" seems to be overstated. Nor does a simple appeal to realism (as in Stiglitz, 1992, p. 289 n. 24) seem to be adequate on the part of economists who want to derive their models from a single unifying first principle. A convincing resolution of the indexation puzzle is still missing.

However, one cannot disagree with Stiglitz when he writes that "ad hoc-ery is not the only vice from which a model may suffer: assumptions and conclusions which are counter factual represent far worse sins" (Stiglitz, 1992, p. 298). There is no doubt that Stiglitz et al.'s work has done much for removing implausible assumptions from microeconomics as well as from macroeconomics. The objective of constructing a consistent and complete macro model from a single unifying first principle — such as asymmetric information — may be regarded as too ambitious. But a careful combination of Stiglitz et al.'s views of the financial and labor markets with imperfect competition in the goods market and convincing explanations of nominal rigidities is a task that can not be turned down if new Keynesian economics is to emerge as the leading macroeconomic paradigm in the 1990s, which seems to be the objective of its proponents.

A Final Remark

As shown in the previous sections, what is regarded as sound theoretical work depends, among other things, on the specific role assigned to economic theory. Dealing with similar issues, Dow (1983, p. 44) concludes that "the policy recommendations follow on inevitably from their respective theoretical frameworks which in turns follow on from their respective world-views and methodologies." If we had to summarize in a sentence the conclusion hinted at in this chapter, we would say that Dow's conclusion should be somewhat mitigated in order to acknowledge the more complex nature of the involved links.

Indeed, what emerges from our account of different Keynesianisms is that the nature of the envisaged links between policy recommendations, theoretical frameworks, and methodological beliefs is itself dependent on the underlying (metaphysical?) point of view about the role of economic theories. As the different perspectives we have examined in this chapter clearly show, we cannot take for granted that the proper role of economic theory must perforce be the finding of policy prescriptions.

Those scholars who are primarily interested in the long-run properties of economic systems, for instance, are likely to be either uninterested in policy debates, except for their long-run implications, or else inclined to stress the importance of their preferred fundamental relations as inviolable constraints to be taken into account whatever it might be the particular policy under discussion.

Those scholars — such as the new Keynesians — who are deeply committed to construct theories involving "rational" behavior will not be satisfied with any policy prescription (even if such a recommendation is in keeping with shared value judgments), unless it is strongly supported by sound microeconomic foundations. Moreover, new Keynesians appear to be rather uninterested in disputes about the relative potency of monetary and fiscal policies, while they are much more concerned than any other group of Keynesians with some kind of micropolicy that might improve the working of inherently imperfect markets, by changing the set of private incentives and public institutions on which the actions of rational individuals are based.

In the middle, of course, we find strand 2 and strand 3 post-Keynesians, who are content with theories based on realistic assumptions and leading to the "right" policies (so much the better if somehow left-wing): ranging from demand management to incomes policy, from the regulation of credit and capital markets to some state control over private investment.

Note, however, that the influence of the underlying conceptions of the role of economic theory operates on at least two different levels. The difference between scholars who are mainly interested in the long-run tendencies of economic systems (or, to speak more properly, of capitalism) and those who are concerned with more practical problems arising from the short-run macroeconomic behavior may be traced back to different *epistemological* perspectives on the proper role and goal of social science. Otherwise, differences among the various strands of post- and new Keynesianism can be easily recognized at the (somewhat "lower") level of different research strategies (that is, different *methodological* prescriptions). In this respect, while Kaleckian and Marshallian post-Keynesians are content with empirical generalizations and descriptive behavioral assumptions (the so-called rules of thumb), new Keynesians feel committed to support their macroeconomic analyses with sound microfoundations. It goes without saying that *sound* means based on the notion of rational behavior accepted by mainstream economists.

If we agree on the legitimacy of different points of view on the role of economic theorizing (and we do not see any alternative to this position), then we cannot be surprised by the plurality of theoretical approaches in economics (and in other disciplines, for that matter). Whatever criterion of scientific rationality we have been able to rely on, we could not avoid different theories being prompted by different conceptions of their role.

This seems to leave open only two possibilities. If one accepts living with some form of methodological *and* theoretical pluralism, then one has to confine oneself to "internal" criticism — that is, to appraising the sole inner consistency of each theoretical perspective with its own methodological justification.[35] Otherwise, if one continues to believe that economists should not surrender to the thesis according to which theories are incommensurable, then one must be prepared to embark on (lengthy) methodological discussions on how economic theories (or "models") should be appraised. Along that way, however, one is likely to go through the Duhem-Quine thesis on the impossibility of testing single hypotheses within complex scientific theories. Such an impossibility undercuts all forms of testing, particularly in a discipline like economics, the subject matter of which can hardly be submitted to experiment and is continually changing in historical time.

Acknowledgments

We wish to thank Domenico Delli Gatti, Mauro Gallegati, Philip A. Klein, and the participants in seminars held at the universities of Milan and Perugia for helpful comments. The usual disclaimer applies.

Notes

1. In addition to Carabelli (1988), for two concise and balanced accounts of this kind of study, see Dow (1991a) and Gerard (1992). Further references to such a recent literature may be found in the various contributions to O'Donnell (1991) and Gerard and Hillard (1992, pt. 1).

2. Keynesians' propensity for "realistic" hypotheses and models has been easily detected by all authors who have dealt so far with post-Keynesian methodology: see, for instance, Caldwell (1989), Dow (1991b), and Lavoie (1992). Lavoie's methodological assessment is mainly addressed to the problem of whether and, if so, how it might be possible to define a postclassical research program as a synthesis of post-Keynesianism and neo-Ricardianism. It should be noted that what follows is not meant to be a direct critique of Lavoie's specific arguments or conclusions (a task that would require a very detailed discussion of each of them). Rather, in this connection it may be read as an attempt to call attention on an issue whose importance Lavoie seems to have somehow underestimated. Let us note, by the way, that the same thing could be said of most discussions of the difficult cohabitation of short- and long-run analyses within post-Keynesian economics (see, for instance, Carvalho 1984–1985).

3. This particular terminology has been suggested (and its use convincingly recommended) by Mäki (1989).

4. The referred episodes are so well known that we feel dispensed from providing detailed references. Note, however, that even when the apparent bone of contention is the sole logical consistency of neoclassical theory, a deeper analysis shows that empirical considerations are not completely absent (for more on this, see Salanti, 1989a, 1989b).

5. See, in addition to Garegnani (1976), the following entries in Eatwell, Milgate, and Newman (1987): "Competition: Classical Conceptions" and "Natural and Normal Conditions" by John Eatwell; "Surplus Approach to Value and Distribution" by Pierangelo Garegnani; "Equilibrium: Development of the Concept" by Murray Milgate;" Long-Run and Short-Run" by Carlo Panico and Fabio Petri; and "Natural Price" by Gianni Vaggi.

6. On this last point see also Petri (1978).

7. For a discussion of the methodological adequacy of the notion of long-period position with reference to the two different issues of the correctness of the related interpretation of classical economics and its consistency as a modern methodological perspective, see Salanti (1990).

8. Kaldor (1972) went as far as to extend the attribute of irrelevance to the notion of economic equilibrium as such. See also Joan Robinson (1974).

9. On Marshall's methodological approach see Salanti (1991).

10. An original blend of the two strands can be found in the contributions of Hyman Minsky on the fragility of contemporary financial structures. See Minsky (1975, 1982).

11. "Keynes without uncertainty is something like *Hamlet* without the prince" (Minsky, 1975, p. 57).

12. It should be stressed that Shackle (1974) argued that the 1937 *Quarlterly Journal of Economics* article is the *ultimate* locus of Keynes's monetary theory.

13. For completeness it is to be mentioned that the second model detected by Kregel in *The General Theory* is a stationary equilibrium model, where disappointment of short-term expectations does not affect the state of long-term expectations.

14. Different attempts at reconciling the Sraffian and the strand 2 post-Keynesian views of equilibrium can be found in Caravale (1992) and Sebastiani (1992).

15. This section and the following largely draw from Boitani (1992).

16. See also other contributions to the "Symposium on the Marginal Productivity of Labor", in *Journal of Post Keynesian Economics*, 9(4) (1987), pp. 483–528.

17. See, for instance, Kalecki (1939) and Keynes (1936, ch. 19) for the argument against money-wage flexibility based on the Fisher effect.

18. See also Sawyer (1992a, 1992b) for critical surveys.

19. Good surveys of the new Keynesian economics from different and somewhat idiosyncratic viewpoints are Rotemberg (1987); Ball, Mankiw, and Romer (1988); Greenwald and Stiglitz (1987b, 1988a). See also Gordon (1990) and, for an analytical treatment, Boitani and Mezzomo (1991); Boitani, Delli Gatti, and Mezzomo (1992); and Dixon and Rankin (1991).

20. An exception is Kiyotaki (1988) and, to a certain extent, the contributions by Stiglitz and his associates, which are briefly discussed in the last section.

21. The consequences of small deviations from full substantive rationality are drawn by Akerlof and Yellen (1985).

22. It may be argued that increasing returns are not necessary if heterogeneous agents (workers) are assumed. On the problems raised by the representative individual hypothesis see Kirman (1992).

23. As already noticed one of the most prominent post-Keynesian, Nicholas Kaldor has fully accepted Weitzman's contention (Kaldor, 1983, pp. 11–13). It should also be added that

Kaldor's insistence on increasing returns and imperfect competition as necessary foundations for unemployment and excess capacity dates back to his 1935 *Economica* article.

24. On the role of reciprocal externalities in new Keynesian models see Heller (1986), Drazen (1987), and Cooper and John (1988). For externalities arising from imperfectly informed agents' willingness to participate in the markets see Diamond (1984).

25. The role of animal spirits in equilibrium selection is studied in Kiyotaki (1988) an the role of the state of confidence in Boitani and Delli Gatti (1991).

26. Under imperfect competition the profit function of firms is differentiable in their prices and flat at the top. By taking a Taylor expansion (around the preshock optimum) of the profit lost from nonadjusting, it is easy to see that the first-order term vanishes. Hence the cost of price rigidity is second order (Mankiw, 1985; Blanchard and Kiyotaki, 1987; Rotemberg, 1987; Ball and Romer, 1989; Blanchard and Fischer, 1989, ch. 8). Similar results can be reached by assuming that firms are *near rational* with respect to price adjustment (Akerlof and Yellen, 1985).

27. See Fethke and Policano (1986); Ball and Cecchetti (1988) for a discussion of the conditions under which price asyncronization is a stable equilibrium. For a survey see Blanchard (1990).

28. The most relevant papers on efficiency wages are collected in Akerlof and Yellen (1986). A complete survey can be found in Weiss (1991).

29. It is not difficult to incorporate increasing returns in the Akerlof and Yellen model, in order to avoid the Weitzman critique to constant returns to scale models. See Boitani and Mezzomo (1991); Boitani, Delli Gatti, and Mezzomo (1992).

30. See Dixon and Rankin (1991) for a survey and Calmfors and Driffill (1988) for a discussion of the effect of different union structures on wage determination and employment.

31. A possible explanation has been suggested by Ball (1988), who argues that indexation may be costly because of "the cost of learning about the parameters that determine the optimal degree of indexation, the cost of negotiating the details of the indexation system, and the administrative cost of adjusting nominal wages more frequently" (Ball, 1988, p. 306). Ball (1988, p. 309) shows that if indexation costs (or indexation benefits) vary across firms, and this leads some firms not to index, then indexation does have externalities, as "firms' decision about whether and how much to index affect the behavior of the price level, which in turn affects the variance of employment for non indexed firm." Such an externality from indexation is positive, and in equilibrium there is too little indexation and too much nominal rigidity, only if "changes in real money have larger effects on labor demand than changes in the real wage" (Ball, 1988, pp. 309–310).

Ball's analysis — which is admittedly similar in spirit to the small menu costs literature — is based on the assumption of risk neutrality of firms and does not make use of efficiency wages. His results would be strengthened by either substituting risk aversion for risk neutrality or by adopting an efficiency wage model of the labor market.

32. "Capital is at the heart of capitalism: it is, accordingly, not surprising that we should look to failure in capital markets to account for one of the most important failures of capitalism, the marked fluctuations in output and employment which have characterized capitalism throughout its history" (Stiglitz, 1992, p. 269).

33. A complete model of credit rationing due to asymmetric information can be found in Stiglitz and Weiss (1981).

34. It is therefore surprising that Stiglitz et al. never mention Minsky or even Kalecki, who was, after all, the first propounder of a theory of investment based, through the principle of increasing risk, on the availability of credit. To be honest, it should also be pointed out that Kalecki's paternity is not acknowledged by Minsky either.

35. For a more detailed discussion of the notion of "internal" criticism in economic methodology, see Salanti (1989b).

References

Abramovitz, M., et al., eds. 1959. *The Allocation of Economic Resources: Essays in Honor of B.F. Haley*. Stanford: Stanford University Press.

Akerlof, G.A., and J.L. Yellen. 1985. "A Near Rational Model of the Business Cycle, with Wage and Price Inertia." *Quarterly Journal of Economics*, 100, supp., 823–838.

———, eds. 1986. *Efficiency Wage Models of the Labor Market*. Cambridge: Cambridge University Press.

Appelbaum, E. 1979. "The Labor Market." In A. Eichner, ed., *A Guide to Post Keynesian Economics*. White Plains, N.Y.: Sharpe.

Aretsis, P., and V. Chick, eds. 1992. *Developments in Post Keynesian Economics*. Aldershot: Elgar.

Arrow, K.J. 1959. "Toward a Theory of Price Adjustment." In M. Abramovitz et al., eds., *The Allocation of Economic Resources*: Essays in Honor of B.F. Haley. Stanford: Stanford University Press.

Ball, L. 1988. "Is Equilibrium Indexation Efficient?" *Quarterly Journal of Economics*, 103(2), 299–311.

Ball, L., and S.G. Cecchetti. 1988. "Imperfect Information and Staggered Price Setting." *American Economic Review*, 78(4), 999–1018.

Ball. L., and D. Romer. 1989. "Are Prices too Sticky?" *Quarterly Journal of Economics*, 104(3), 507–524.

———. 1990. "Real Rigidities and the Non-Neutrality of Money." *Review of Economic Studies*, 57(1), 183–203.

———. 1991. "Sticky Prices as Coordination Failures." *American Economic Review*, 81(3), 539–552.

Ball, L., N.G. Mankiw, and D. Romer. 1988. "The New Keynesian Economics and the Output-Inflation Trade-Off." *Brookings Papers on Economic Activity*, 1, 1–65.

Ball, R.J. 1964. *Inflation and the Theory of Money*. London: Macmillan.

Bell, D., and I. Kristol, eds. 1981. *The Crisis in Economic Theory*. New York: Basic Books.

Benassy, J.P. 1982. *The Economics of Market Disequilibrium*. New York: Academic Press.

———. 1987. "Imperfect Competition, Unemployment and Policy." *European Economic Review*, 31(1–2), 417–426.

Bhaskar, V. 1990. "Wage Relativities and the Natural Range of Unemployment." *Economic Journal*, 100, supp., 60–66.

Blanchard, O.J. 1986. "The Wage Price Spiral." *Quarterly Journal of Economics*, 101(3), 543–565.

————. 1990. "Why Does Money Affect Output?" In B.M. Friedman and F.H. Hahn, eds., *Handbook of Monetary Economics*. Amsterdam: North Holland.

Blanchard, O.J., and S. Fischer. 1989. *Lectures on Macroeconomics*. Cambridge Mass.: MIT Press.

Blanchard, O.J., and N. Kiyotaki. 1987. "Monopolistic Competition and the Effects of Aggregate Demand." *American Economic Review*, 77(4), 647–666.

Boitani, A. 1992. "Post Keynesians versus New Keynesians on Imperfect Competition and Unemployment Equilibrium." In M. Sebastiani, ed., *The Notion of Equilibrium in the Keynesian Theory*. London: Macmillan.

Boitani, A., and D. Delli Gatti. 1991. "Equilibrio di sottoccupazione e stato di fiducia in un gioco keynesiano." *Economia Politica*, 8(1), 45–71.

Boitani, A., and L. Mezzomo. 1991. "The New Keynesian Economics: An Analytical Assessment." Mimeo. Università Cattolica, Milan.

Boitani, A., D. Delli Gatti, and L. Mezzomo. 1992. "Concorrenza imperfetta, esternalità e spiegazioni delle rigidità nella Nuova Economia Keynesiana." *Economia Politica*, 9(2), 299–361.

Brunner, K., and A.H. Meltzer, ed. 1977. *Stabilization of the Domestic and International Economy*. Amsterdam: North Holland.

Bulow, J.I., J.D. Geanakopolos, and P.D. Klemperer. 1985. "Multimarket Oligopoly: Strategic Substitutes and Complements." *Journal of Political Economy*, 93(3), 488–511.

Caldwell, B.J. 1989. "Post Keynesian Methodology: An Assessment." *Review of Political Economy*, 1(1), 43–64.

Calmfors, L., and J. Driffill. 1988. "Bargaining Structure, Corporatism and Macroeconomic Performance." *Economic Policy*, 6, 13–61.

Carabelli, A. 1988. *On Keynes's Method*. London: Macmillan.

Caravale, G. 1992. "Keynes and the Concept of Equilibrium." In M. Sebastiani, ed., *The Notion of Equilibrium in the Keynesian Theory*. London: Macmillan.

Carvalho, F. 1984–1985. "Alternative Analyses of Short and Long Run in Post Keynesian Economics." *Journal of Post Keynesian Economics*, 7(2), 214–234.

Chick, V. 1983. *Macroeconomics after Keynes*. Oxford: Philip Allan.

Clower, R.W. 1965. "The Keynesian Counterrevolution." In F. Hahn, and F. Brechling, eds., *The Theory of Interest Rates*. London: Macmillan.

Coddington, A. 1983. *Keynesian Economics: The Search for First Principles*. London: Allen & Unwin.

Cooper, R., and A. John. 1988. "Coordinating Coordination Failures in Keynesian Models." *Quarterly Journal of Economics*, 103(3), 441–463.

Davidson, P. 1977. "Money and General Equilibrium." *Economie Appliquée*, 30(4), 541–563.

————. 1978. *Money and the Real World*. London: Macmillan.

————. 1981. "Post Keynesian Economics." In D. Bell and I. Kristol, eds., *The Crisis in Economic Theory*. New York: Basle Books.

————. 1985. "Liquidity and Not Increasing Returns is the Ultimate Source of Unemployment Equilibrium." *Journal of Post Keynesian Economics*, 7(3), 373–384.

Davidson, P., and J. Smolensky. 1964. *Aggregate Supply and Demand Analysis*. New York: Harper & Row.

Diamond, P. 1984. *A Search Equilibrium Approach to the Microfoundations of Macroeconomics*. Cambridge, Mass.: MIT Press.

Dixon, H. 1988. "Unions, Oligopoly and the Natural Range of Unemployment." *Economic Journal*, 98(4), 1127–1147.

Dixon, H., and J. Rankin 1991. "Imperfect Competition and Macroeconomics: A Survey." *Warwick Economic Research Papers*, 387.

Dow, S. 1983. "Schools of Thought in Macroeconomics: The Method Is the Message." *Australian Economic Papers*, 22(1), 30–47.

———. 1985. *Macroeconomic Thought: A Methodological Approach*. Oxford: Blackwell.

———. 1991a. "Keynes's Epistemology and Economic Methodology." In R.M. O'Donnell, ed., *Keynes as Philosopher-Economist*. London: Macmillan.

———. 1991b. "The Post Keynesian School." In D. Mair and A.G. Miller, eds., *A Modern Guide to Economic Thought*. Aldershot: Elgar.

Dow, S., and P. Earl. 1982. *Money Matters*. Oxfords: Martin Robertson.

Drazen, A. 1987. "Reciprocal Externality Models of Low Employment." *European Economic Review*, 37(1), 436–443.

Eatwell, J., and M. Milgate, eds. 1983. *Keynes's Economics and the Theory of Value and Distribution*. London: Duckworth.

Eatwell, J., M. Milgate, and P. Newman, eds. 1987. *The New Palgrave: A Dictionary of Economics*. London: Macmillan.

Eichner, A. 1973. "A Theory of the Determination of the Mark-up Under Oligopoly." *Economic Journal*, 83(4), 1184–2000.

———. 1976. *The Megacorp and Oligopoly*. Cambridge: Cambridge University Press.

———, ed. 1979. *A Guide to Post Keynesian Economics*. White Plains: Sharpe.

Eichner, A., and J. Kregel. 1975. "An Essay on Post Keynesian Theory: A New Paradigm in Economics." *Journal of Economic Literature*, 13(4), 1293–1314.

Feiwel, G., ed. 1989. *The Economics of Imperfect Competition and Employment: Joan Robinson and Beyond*. London: Macmillan.

Fethke, G., and R. Policano. 1986. "Will Wage Setters Ever Stagger Decisions?" *Quarterly Journal of Economics*, 101(4), 867–877.

Fischer, S. 1977. "Long Term Contracts, Rational Expectations and the Optimal Money Supply Rule." *Journal of Political Economy*, 85(1), 191–205.

Frank, J. 1990. "Monopolistic Competition, Risk Aversion and Equilibrium Recessions." *Quarterly Journal of Economics*, 105(4), 163–190.

Friedman, B.M., and F.H. Hahn, eds. 1990. *Handbook of Monetary Economics*. Amsterdam: North Holland.

Friedman, M. 1953. "The Methodology of Positive Economics." In M. Friedman, *Essays in Positive Economics*. Chicago: University of Chicago Press.

Garegnani, P. 1976. "On a Change in the Notion of Equilibrium in Recent Work on Value and Distribution: A Comment on Samuelson." In M. Brown, K. Sato, and P. Zarembka, eds., *Essays in Modern Capital Theory*. Amsterdam: North Holland.

————. 1983a. "Notes on Consumption, Investment and Effective Demand." In J. Eatwell and M. Milgate, eds., *Keynes's Economics and the Theory of Value and Distribution*. London: Duckworth.

————. 1983b. "The Classical Theory of Wages and the Role of Demand Schedules in the Determination of Relative Prices." *American Economic Review*, Papers and Proceedings, 73(2), 309–313.

Gerard, B. 1992. "From a Treatise on Probability to the General Theory: Continuity or Change in Keynes's Thought?" In B. Gerard and J. Hillard, eds., *The Philosophy and Economics of J. M. Keynes*. Aldershot: Elgar.

Gerard, B., and J. Hillard, eds. 1992. *The Philosophy and Economics of J.M. Keynes*. Aldershot: Elgar.

Gordon, R.J. 1990. "What Is New-Keynesian Economics?" *Journal of Economic Literature*, 28(3), 1115–1171.

Greenwald, B.C., and J.E. Stiglitz. 1987a. "Imperfect Information, Credit Markets and Unemployment." *European Economic Review*, 31(5), 444–456.

————. 1987b. "Keynesian, New Keynesian and New Classical Economics." *Oxford Economic Papers*, 39(1), 119–133.

————. 1988a. "Examining Alternative Macroeconomic Theories." *Brookings Papers on Economic Activity*, 1, 207–260.

————. 1988b. "Financial Market Imperfections and Business Cycles." *NBER Working Paper*, 2494.

————. 1989. "Toward a Theory of Rigidities." *American Economic Review*, 79(2), 364–369.

————. 1990. "Macroeconomic Models with Equity and Credit Rationing." *NBER Working Paper*, 3533.

Hahn, F.H. 1987. "On Involuntary Unemployment." *Economic Journal*, 97, supp., 1–16.

Hahn, F.H., and F. Brechling, eds. 1965. *The Theory of Interest Rates*. London: Macmillan.

Harcourt, G.C. 1992. *On Political Economists and Modern Political Economy*. London: Routledge.

Harcourt, G.C., and O.F. Hamouda. 1988. "Post Keynesianism: From Criticism to Coherence?" In G.C. Harcourt, *On Political Economists and Modern Political Economy*. London: Routledge.

Harcourt, G.C., and P. Kenyon. 1976. "Pricing and the Investment Decision." *Kyklos*, 29(3), 449–477.

Hart, O. 1982. "A Model of Imperfect Competition with Keynesian Features." *Quarterly Journal of Economics*, 97(1), 109–138.

Heller, W.P. 1986. "Coordination Failure Under Complete Markets with Applications to Effective Demand." In W.P. Heller, R.M. Starr, and D.R. Starrett, eds., *Equilibrium Analysis: Essays in Honor of Kenneth J. Arrow*. Cambridge: Cambridge University Press.

Heller, W.P., R.M. Starr, and D.R. Starrett, eds. 1986. *Equilibrium Analysis: Essays in Honor of Kenneth J. Arrow*. Cambridge: Cambridge University Press.

Hicks, J.R. 1939. *Value and Capital*. Oxford: Clarendon Press.

Kahn, R. 1929. *The Economics of the Short Period*. (Published in Italian, Torino: Boringhieri, 1983). London: Macmillan, 1989.

Kaldor, N. 1935. "Market Imperfection and Excess Capacity." *Economica*, 1(1), 33–50.

———. 1972. "The Irrelevance of Equilibrium Economics." *Economic Journal*, 82(4), 1237–1255.

———. 1978. *Further Essays in Economic Theory*. London: Duckworth.

———. 1983. "Keynesian Economics after Fifty Years." In Worswick and Trevithick, eds., *Keynes and the Modern World*. Cambridge: Cambridge University Press.

Kalecki, M. 1939. *Essays on the Theory of Economic Fluctuations*. London: Allen & Unwin.

———. 1954. *The Theory of Economic Dynamics*. London: Allen & Unwin.

Keynes, J.M. 1936. *The General Theory of Employment Interest and Money*. London: Macmillan.

———. 1937. "The General Theory of Employment." *Quarterly Journal of Economics*, 51(2), 209–223.

———. 1939. "Relative Movements in Real Wages and Output." *Economic Journal*, 49(1), 34–51.

———. 1973. *The General Theory and After: Defense and Development. Collected Writings* (vol. 14). London: Macmillan.

———. 1979. *The General Theory and After: A Supplement. Collected Writings* (vol. 29). London: Macmillan.

Kirman, A.P. 1992. "Whom or What Does the Representative Individual Represent?" *Journal of Economic Perspectives*, 6(2), 117–136.

Kiyotaki, N. 1988. "Multiple Expectational Equilibria Under Monopolistic Competition." *Quarterly Journal of Economics*, 102(4), 695–714.

Kregel, J. 1976. "Economic Methodology in the Face of Uncertainty." *Economic Journal*, 86(3), pp. 209–225.

———. 1987. "Keynes's Given Degree of Competition: Comment on Mc Kenna and Zannoni." *Journal of Post Keynesian Economics*, 9(4), 490–495.

———. ed. 1991. *Nuove interpretazioni dell'analisi monetaria di Keynes*. Bologna: Il Mulino.

Lavoie, M. 1992. "Towards a New Research Programme for Post Keynesianism and Neo-Ricardianism." *Review of Political Economy*, 4(1), 37–78.

Lawlor, M.S., W.A. Darity, and B.L. Horn. 1987. "Was Keynes a Chapter Two Keynesian?" *Journal of Post Keynesian Economics*, 9(4), 516–528.

Leijonbutrud, A. 1968. *On Keynesian Economics and the Economics of Keynes*. New York: Oxford University Press.

Lindbeck, A., and D.J. Snower. 1988. *The Insider Outsider Theory of Employment and Unemployment*. Cambridge, Mass.: MIT Press.

Lucas, R.E. 1977. "Understanding Business Cycles." In K. Brunner, and A.H. Meltzer, eds., *Stabilization of the Domestic and International Economy*. Amsterdam: North Holland.

Mair, D., and A.G. Miller, eds. 1991. *A Modern Guide to Economic Thought*. Aldershot: Elgar.

Mäki, U. 1989. "On the Problem of Realism in Economics." *Ricerche Economiche*, 43(1–2), 176–198.

Malinvaud, E. 1977. *The Theory of Unemployment Reconsidered*. Cambridge: Cambridge University Press.

Mankiw, N.G. 1985. "Small Menu Costs and Large Business Cycles: A Macroeconomic Model of Monopoly." *Quarterly Journal of Economics*, 100(2), 529–539.

Mankiw, N.G., and D. Romer. 1991. "Introduction." In N.G. Mankiw, and D. Romer, eds., *New Keynesian Economics*. Cambridge, Mass.: MIT Press.

Manning, A. 1990. "Imperfect Competition, Multiple Equilibria and Unemployment Policy." *Economic Journal*, 100, supp., 151–162.

Marris, R. 1991. *Reconstructing Keynesian Economics with Imperfect Competition*. Aldershot: Elgar.

———. 1992. "R.F. Kahn's Fellowship Dissertation: A Missing Link in the History of Economic Thought." *Economic Journal*, 102(3), 1235–1243.

Milgrom, P., and J. Roberts. 1990. "Rationalizability, Learning and Equilibrium in Games with Strategic Complementarities." *Econometrica*, 58(6), 1255–1278.

Minsky, H. 1975. *John Maynard Keynes*. London: Macmillan.

———. 1982. *Inflation, Recession and Economic Policy*. Brighton: Wheatsheaf.

Mongiovi, G., and C. Ruhl, eds. 1992. *Macroeconomic Theory Diversity and Convergence*. Aldershot: Elgar.

O'Donnell, R.M., ed. 1991. *Keynes as Philosopher-Economist*. London: Macmillan.

Pagano, M. 1990. "Imperfect Competition, Underemployment Equilibria and Fiscal Policy." *Economic Journal*, 100(2), 440–463.

Pasinetti, L.L. 1974. *Growth and Income Distribution: Essays in Economic Theory*. Cambridge: Cambridge University Press.

———. 1981. *Structural Change and Economic Growth*. Cambridge: Cambridge University Press.

———. 1991. "Dal *Treatise on Money* alla *General Theory*: continuità o rottura?" In J. Kregel, ed., *Nuove interpretazioni dell'analisi monetaria di Keynes*. Bologna: Il Mulino.

———. 1992. "Economic Theory and Institutions." Paper presented at the Fourth Annual Conference of EAEPE.

———. 1993. *Structural Economic Dynamics: A Theory of the Economic Consequences of Human Learning*. Cambridge: Cambridge University Press.

Petri, F. 1978. "The Difference Between Long-Period and Short-Period General Equilibrium and the Capital Theory Controversy." *Australian Economic Papers*, 17(2), 246–260.

Roberts, J. 1989. "Involuntary Unemployment and Imperfect Competition: A Game-Theoretic Macromodel." In G. Feiwel, ed., *The Economics of Imperfect Competition and Employment: Joan Robinson and Beyond*. London: Macmillan.

Robinson, J. 1933. *The Economics of Imperfect Competition*. London: Macmillan.

———. 1974. "History Versus Equilibrium." *Thames Papers in Political Economy*.

Rotemberg, J.J. 1987. "The New Keynesian Microfoundations." *NBER Macroeconomic Annual*, 2, 69–104.

Salanti, A. 1989a. " 'Internal' Criticisms in Economic Theory: Are They Really Conclusive?" *Economic Notes*, 19(1), 1–15.

———. 1989b. "Distinguishing 'Internal' from 'External' Criticisms in Economic Methodology." *History of Political Economy*, 21(4), 635–639.

———. 1990. "The Notion of Long-Period Positions: A Useful Abstraction or a 'Platonic Idea'?" *Political Economy: Studies in the Surplus Approach*, 6(1–2), 95–101.

———. 1991. "Marshall's Partial Equilibrium Analysis: A Methodological Note." *Methodus*, 3(2), 73–78.

Sawyer, M.C. 1992a. "Prices and Pricing in the Post Keynesian and Kaleckian Traditions." In G. Mongiovi, and C. Ruhl, eds., *Macroeconomic Theory Diversity and Convergence*. Aldershot: Elgar.

———. 1992b. "On the Origins of Post Keynesian Pricing Theory." In P. Aretsis, and V. Chick, eds., *Developments in Post Keynesian Economics*. Aldershot: Elgar.

Sebastiani, M. 1992. "Keynes and Long Period Positions." In M. Sebastiani, ed., *The Notion of Equilibrium in the Keynesian Theory*. London: Macmillan.

———. ed. 1992. *The Notion of Equilibrium in the Keynesian Theory*. London: Macmillan.

Shackle, G.L.S. 1974. *Keynesian Kaleidics*. Edinburgh: Edinburgh University Press.

Shaked, A., and J. Sutton. 1984. "Involuntary Unemployment as a Perfect Equilibrium in a Bargaining Model." *Econometrica*, 52, 1351–1364.

Shapiro, N. 1981. "Pricing and the Growth of the Firm." *Journal of Post Keynesian Economics*, 4(1), 85–100.

Skidelsky, R. 1991. "Keynes's Philosophy of Practice and Economic Policy." In R.M. O'Donnell ed., *Keynes as Philosopher–Economist*. London: Macmillan.

Solow, R.M. 1986. "Monopolistic Competition and the Multiplier." In W.P. Heller, R.M. Starr, and D.R. Starrett, eds., *Equilibrium Analysis: Essays in Honor of Kenneth J. Arrow*. Cambridge: Cambridge University Press.

———. 1990. *The Labor Market as a Social Institution*. Oxford: Blackwell.

Steindl, J. 1952. *Maturity and Stagnation of American Capitalism*. Oxford: Oxford University Press.

Stiglitz, J.E. 1985. "Equilibrium Wage Distribution." *Economic Journal*, 85(3), 595–618.

———. 1987. "The Causes and Consequences of the Dependence of Quality on Price." *Journal of Economic Literature*, 25(1), 1–48.

———. 1989. "Money, Credit and Business Fluctuations." *NBER Working Paper* 2823.

———. 1991. "Alternative Approaches to Macroeconomics: Methodological Issues and the New Keynesian Economics." *NBER Working Paper* 3580.

———. 1992. "Capital Markets and Economic Fluctuations in Capitalist Economies." *European Economic Review*, 36(2–3), 269–306.

Stiglitz, J.E., and A. Weiss. 1981. "Credit Rationing in Markets with Imperfect Information." *American Economic Review*, 73(3), 912–927.

Summers, L.H. 1988. "Relative Wages, Efficiency Wages and Keynesian Unemployment." *American Economic Review, Papers and Proceedings*, 78, 383–395.

Sylos Labini, P. 1956. *Oligopolio e progresso tecnico*. Milan: Giuttrè. [Engl. trans., *Oligopoly and Technical Progress*. Cambridge, MA: Harvard University Press, 1962].

Taylor, J.B. 1980. "Aggregate Dynamics and Staggered Contracts." *Journal of Political Economy*, 88(1), 1–23.

Vercelli, A. 1991. *Methodological Foundations of Macroeconomics: Keynes and Lucas*. Cambridge: Cambridge University Press.

Vicarelli, F. 1984. *Keynes: The Instability of Capitalism*. Philadelphia: University of Pennsylvania Press.

———. ed. 1985, *Keynes's Relevance Today*. London: Macmillan.

Vives, X. 1990. "Nash Equilibrium with Strategic Complementarities." *Journal of Mathematical Economics*, 19(3), 305–321.

Weinrich, G., and A. Battinelli. 1992. "Price Rigidity Due to Risk Aversion." Mimeo, Università Cattolica, Milan

Weintraub, S. 1959. *A General Theory of the Price Level, Output, Income Distribution and Economic Growth*. London: Chilton.

———. 1978–1979. "The Missing Theory of Money Wages." *Journal of Post Keynesian Economics*, 1(1), 59–78.

Weiss, A. 1991. *Efficiency Wages*. Oxford: Clarendon Press.

Weitzman, M.L. 1982. "Increasing Returns and the Foundations of Unemployment Theory." *Economic Journal*, 92(4), 787–804.

Wood, A. 1975. *A Theory of Profits*. Cambridge: Cambridge University Press.

Worswick, and Trevithick, eds. 1983. *Keynes and the Modern World*. Cambridge: Cambridge University Press.

8 MONETARISM AND ITS RHETORIC

Thomas Mayer

Abstract

Although only a minority of economists call themselves monetarists, monetarism has greatly influenced contemporary macroeconomics. Mainstream macroeconomists now attribute much more importance to changes in the money supply than they did in the mid-1950s when Friedman published his monetarist manifesto, and most now accept the long-run neutrality of money. Monetarism differs sharply from the simplistic doctrine that only money matters, and it does not rely on mere correlations. It is, however, based on a more empirical methodology than is currently popular. Several versions of monetarism exist; this chapter discusses two—the Friedman version and the Brunner-Meltzer version—and deals with both theory and policy.

Introduction

"The quantity theory of money is a term evocative of a general approach rather than a well defined theory." So wrote Milton Friedman in his 1956 quantity-theory manifesto (Friedman, 1956, p. 3). In this spirit I will discuss

159

the quantity theory, and monetarism not as a set of narrow "if . . . then" propositions but as a way of approaching macroeconomic problems. A theory, in this broad sense, has its rhetoric (by which I mean certain methodological presuppositions) and criteria for validating arguments. Such a rhetoric differs from formal methodology by being less self-consciously philosophical, by being inchoate most of the time, and by relating closely to day-to-day practice. In this chapter I pay much attention to these aspects of monetarism but deal only with the American variant, which differs from the British one (see Laidler, 1978).

I will ignore the question whether monetarist theory is "right" and superior to rival theories, in part because a discussion of the "truth" of monetarism might easily give a false impression. It is not just the truth of monetarism that is relevant; what counts is also how useful it proved in advancing our evolving understanding. Monetarism has contributed much to the thinking of many contemporary macrotheorist who are certainly not monetarists. One can tell the following story. Monetarists got hold of some important truths that contemporaneous mainstream economics had ignored. But mainstream macroeconomics was flexible, so it eventually incorporated many of these contributions. Hence, what remain as the distinctive claims of monetarists are those stronger propositions that nowadays only they uphold.

The majority of contemporary economists are not monetarists. But suppose that they were asked to choose between monetarism and the type of Keynesian theory that was current in the early 1950s. It is quite possible that the majority would then declare themselves to be monetarists on many issues. As Steven Sheffrin (1992, p. 266) has remarked, "Early post-war Keynesian thinking tended to downplay the role of monetary factors . . . . More recent Keynesian thinking has tended to emphasize the role and importance of monetary shocks in causing recessions." The Keynesian-monetarist debate is therefore better described as a process of thesis, antithesis, and synthesis than as a struggle of incommensurate paradigms.

To a Keynesian all monetarists may look alike. But not to monetarists themselves. There are at least two major branches of monetarism, Friedman's Chicago version and the Brunner-Meltzer version.[1] They differ, not so much in the conclusions they reach as in their underlying theory. I discuss only these two versions and do not take up the work of other leading monetarists, such Anderson, Bomhoff, Fratianni, Jordan, Kurteweg, Laidler, Poole and Rasche, and of Friedman's students and collaborators. This is not to deny the influential role that Anderson and Jordan's "St. Louis equation" played in the monetarist debate, but by now it is moribund (see Modigliani and Ando, 1976; Benjamin Friedman, 1988b). I first discuss

Milton Friedman's monetary theory and then Brunner and Meltzer's before turning to the monetarists' recommendations for monetary policy.

There are many facets to monetarism. Elsewhere (Mayer, 1990b) I have characterized monetarism by twelve interrelated propositions. Here I discuss only two—the theory of nominal income determination and the theory of central bank behavior—because these are the central issues in the monetarists debate. First, all monetarists obviously believe that changes in the money supply are *the* major determinant of changes in nominal income, while Keynesians consider the money supply to be only *a* major determinant. Second, monetarists are much more skeptical about discretionary monetary policy than is the typical Keynesian.

Some of the disagreement arises from monetarists focusing on a longer run than Keynesians do. This explains why Brunner and Meltzer object that Keynesian theory ignores changes in stocks of assets (which are more important in the long run than the short run), and why Milton Friedman complains that Keynesian theory looks primarily only at the first round effect of changes in money. Moreover, in the long run the economy returns to high employment without government help, and in the long run inflation—about which monetarists show more concern than Keynesians do—has more time to do damage than in the short run. In addition, monetarists believe that we know so little about the short run behavior of the economy that countercyclical policy may be destabilizing.

Do these characteristics of monetarism resemble an ideology rather than a set of scientific propositions? Yes, they do (see Mayer, 1978). Should one therefore dismiss monetarism as "mere ideology"? Definitely not. Ideology can be thought of as the metaphysical core of a social science paradigm, and the rival Keynesian and new classical theories have their ideologies just as much as monetarism does. Ideology is just a belief system, and it is troublesome only if someone sticks to it despite contrary evidence. But there is no reason to think that monetarists are more guilty of this than anyone else. Ideological elements will of necessity play a prominent role wherever it is difficult to debate the issue within the protective belt (see Leijohnhufvud, 1985).

The just-discussed characteristics that monetarists share should not blind one to the differences among monetarists. I therefore discuss separately the rhetoric and theories of Milton Friedman and of Brunner and Meltzer, and then discuss their views on monetary policy. But before turning to the Friedman version, let us look at the rhetoric of macroeconomics both at the time of the monetarist resurgence and at the present. Friedman's monetarism, and to a lesser extent Brunner and Meltzer's, can then be seen as a position intermediate between the older and the newer rhetorics.

Macroeconomics in the Mid-1950s

In 1956, when Milton Friedman published his *Studies in the Quantity Theory of Money*, macroeconomics was very different from the way it is now. Like microeconomics at the time, it paid much less attention to elegant models and to secure microfoundations and much more attention to deriving results that can explain observed economic behavior. Complexity and technical virtuosity were not prized nearly as much as now.[2] Despite its emphasis on practical results, empirical testing in the current sense of the term was not well developed or frequent. Instead, theories were essentially accepted or rejected on the basis of their agreement with more or less casual observation, with the results of introspection and with common sense. At least in macroeconomics realism of assumptions was treated as an important characteristic of sound theories. A telling example is the respect paid to the speculative demand for money. It provided a simple way of showing why the central bank may not be able lower interest rates sufficiently to achieve full employment, and hence it carried an important policy message. Moreover, the idea that speculators hold money if they expect interest rates to rise in the future accords with common sense—with the notion of "that is what I would do if I were a speculator." The question whether the speculative demand for money accounts for a significant proportion or only for a trivial proportion of the total demand for money was left aside.[3]

Standard macroeconomics treated money and monetary policy as unimportant. To illustrate, in the mid-1950s, when I tried to estimate the lag of monetary policy, some colleagues asked me why I wasted my time on such an unimportant issue as the effect of monetary policy. Prices were usually treated as unaffected by the quantity of money. For example, in one of the most influential articles at the time, Tobin (1947) analyzed the effect of changes in the quantity of money on income on the implicit assumption that prices were fixed.

Despite its emphasis on practicality and common sense the prevailing macroeconomics was by present standards naive about politics. The dominant, and almost unchallenged, public-interest theory of government made little, if any, allowance for the self-interest of politicians and bureaucrats or for the effects of pressure groups. A favorite idea of economists was that Congress should authorize the President to change tax rates within limits as he saw fit. Economists, ignorant of political business cycle theory, considered Congress benighted for refusing to accepted such an obviously desirable scheme.

Contemporary Macrotheory

Nowadays macroeconomic theory is largely an exercise in formal modeling from microeconomic foundations. Ad hocery is, rather questionably (see Hands, 1988; Mayer, 1992), treated as a sin. Hypotheses are tested by their regression diagnostics, by seeing if the coefficients are significant with the right signs, or by seeing if the data fail to reject the restrictions implied by the theory. A priori plausibility and concordance with common sense are treated as irrelevant for *scientific* economics. Regardless of what professional methodologists may think of it, extreme "as if" reasoning dominates. Paying attention to the realism of assumptions labels one as belonging to the underworld of post-Keynesian or institutionalist economists. Science is identified with mathematics and formalism. Thus Frank Hahn's in his review of Milton Friedman's *The Optimum Quantity of Money* wrote,

> Friedman neither has, nor claims to have a monetary theory. His strong and influential views are not founded on an understanding of "how money works," but on what his empirical studies have lead him to believe to have been the course of economic history. . . . To justify the dependence of the demand for money on "permanent prices" he is satisfied with the following: "holders of money presumably judge the 'real' amount of cash balances in terms of the quantity of goods and services to which the balances are equivalent." . . . The force of the word "presumably" here is obscure. . . . I simply note the casual theorizing. There are many other instances of this lack of seriousness. . . . I conclude that the "empirical hypothesis" in question [the stability of the money demand function] is nothing more than a claim that empirically established demand functions for money have behaved "better" than empirically established consumption functions. It is puzzling that such a claim should be the basis of a school of economic thought (Hahn, 1971, pp. 51, 52, 57).

Not all mainstream economics is rigorous theory. Despite the trenchant criticisms by James Buchanan, Gordon Tullock, and others, in mainstream macroeconomics the traditional public-interest theory of government has survived, at least in part, the methodological revolution. It is implicit in the policy stance of much macrotheory, particularly that originating in Cambridge, Massachusetts. But in explicit models of government behavior, economists generally employ a simplistic self-interest assumption, and political business-cycle theory has received much attention.

Milton Friedman's Quantity Theory

In his early days Milton Friedman had to contend with the Keynesian rhetoric I described previously, as well as with institutionalist critics who rejected neoclassical price theory. In his later days he had to contend with new classical critics. I first describe Milton Friedman's intermediate position before taking up his substantive work on the quantity theory.

The Rhetoric of Friedman's Quantity Theory

Friedman's quantity theory is embedded in a rhetoric that is in between the older rhetoric and the rhetoric of current journal articles. This is not meant as a value judgment. In many ways the older rhetoric is superior to the modern one; in the absence of effective market discipline change does not necessarily denote progress (see Summers, 1991; Mayer, 1992, ch. 2).

By modern standards Friedman's 1956 discussion of the quantity theory lacks elegance. It is not stated in highly abstract terms and is not even developed as a formal model. Yet compared to the then prevailing macrotheory, Friedman's theory was elegant. It set out equations for the demand for money that subsumed it under the theory of demand for durable goods. By contrast, the prevailing Keynesian theory treated money as something that required its own theory. By treating the demand for money as just a special case of the demand for a durable good, Friedman provided more coherent microfoundations than much of the monetary theory had at that time.

Friedman's theory also differed from contemporaneous macrotheory by its much greater emphasis on empirical testing. If, as Friedman insists, theories are to be evaluated by the validity of their predictions, and not by the realism of their assumptions, or by casual empiricism (a red flag to Chicagoans at the time), then detailed empirical tests are needed.

All of these innovations were well suited to advance the status of the quantity theory.[4] The emphasis on testing provided young economists with a plentiful supply of research topics. Second, the quantity theory now looked like an elegant and polished theory and not as a tiresome reiteration of the $MV = PT$ identity. To be sure much, perhaps most, of the credit here goes to Patinkin, but Friedman allowed empirically minded economists, who were not attracted by Patinkin's austere and abstract formulation, to work with a theory that was sufficiently well explicated for their purpose. Third, Friedman's emphasis on testing the implications of theories provided a powerful way of challenging the dominance of Keynesian theory. If we are to apply a new and different standard in choosing between theories, then the past victory of Keynesian theory over classical theory no longer entitled it to a secure claim to the throne. The crown is now up for contention.

Fourth, the emphasis on testing meant that one has to draw a distinction between the calculus (language) of a theory on the one hand, and its empirical assumptions and implications on other. As a calculus—that is, as a set of "if . . . then" propositions—Keynesian theory is hard to reject. But Friedman did not have to show that Keynesian theory contained logical errors. All he had to do was to show that it was not in agreement with the data. And that was much easier to do. Fifth, by insisting that theories be tested, not by the realism of their assumptions or by introspection and casual empiricism but by the accuracy of their predictions, Friedman sidestepped the argument that intuitively the Keynesian assumption seem more realistic than the quantity theory ones. If it turns out that the assumption of stable velocity predicts income more accurately than does the assumption of stable consumption and investment functions, then I must accept the quantity theory, even if my introspection tells me that my own expenditures depend more on my income than on my money holdings.

Although Friedman thus shifted the rhetoric of macroeconomics some way toward its current position, his rhetoric and aesthetics of science differ sharply from that of the current mainstream. Friedman is a Marshallian. To him a good theory is first and foremost a generalization that explains a wide variety of observed facts. "Abstractness, generality, mathematical elegance—these are all secondary, themselves to be judged by the test of application" (Friedman, 1953, p. 91). He does not aim for the deep type of theory that Hahn is looking for. To him a generalization that explains "the course of economic history" is a good theory, even if it leaves unexplored the question of "how money works," which Hahn treats as a centerpiece of monetary theory. Friedman has never shown much interest in models that derive the demand for money from a set of sufficient and necessary conditions. He is satisfied with the broad statement that since the holding of money economizes on transactions costs, agents want to hold money.

Thus when Friedman responded to the frequent demand that he set out his theoretical framework to facilitate communication, he did not discuss the demand for money in terms of utility functions and production functions, nor did he pay any attention to the then much discussed question whether money should be included as a separate factor in the utility function.[5] Moreover, rather than present a fundamentally monetarist model he adopted and modified the Keynesian IS-LM model.

Similarly, he rejects rational-expectations models in favor of an error-learning model of expectations. Yet Friedman *generally* assumes that agents act rationally. A new classical economist could therefore confront him with the following dilemma. Either you believe that agents act rationally, and then you must accept rational-expectations theory, or you assume that agents do not act rationally, and then you must abandon your neoclassical theory. Friedman would not find that argument compelling because he uses assumptions merely as convenient crutches. An assumption may be valid (or more accurately, helpful) when dealing with one problem and invalid (unhelpful) when dealing with another problem. Assumptions are tools and not axioms. As Abraham Hirsch and Neil de Marchi (1990) have shown with numerous examples, a pragmatic methodology, akin to John Dewey's philosophy of science, pervaded Friedman's work.

Friedman also takes a position intermediate between the old and the new rhetoric in his empirical work. The old rhetoric, at least in its mainstream version, used as empirical tests largely casual observation, while the modern rhetoric relies on applying state-of-the-art econometric techniques to a small set of data usually taken from a data base without much thought about its accuracy or exact meaning. Time is a scarce good, and Friedman, an admirer of Wesley C. Mitchell (see Friedman, 1950), prefers to allocate more of it to analyzing the meaning and quality of the data, and less of it to econometric refinements than do most contemporary macroeconomists. Friedman and Schwartz (1991, p. 39) contrast their procedure with the prevailing one, which is to "start with a collection of numerical data bearing on the question under study, subject them to sophisticated econometric techniques, place great reliance on tests of significance, and end with a single hypothesis (equation), however complex, supposedly 'encompassing' . . . all subhypotheses." Their own approach is

> to examine a wide variety of evidence, quantitative and nonquantitative, bearing on the question under study; test results from one body of evidence on other bodies, using econometric techniques as one tool in this process, and build up a collection of simple hypotheses that may or may not be readily viewed as components of a broader all-embracing hypothesis; and finally, test hypotheses on bodies of data other than those from which they were derived. Both ways [the one just described and the previously described approach]—and no doubt still others as well—have their use. None we believe, can be relied on exclusively (Friedman and Schwartz, 1991, p. 39).

Friedman's Quantity Theory: Some Specifics

The research strategy of the quantity theory is to focus on equilibrium in the money market, since equilibrium in that market is a sufficient and necessary condition for equilibrium in the market for expenditures on goods, services, and securities jointly. The choice between theories that focus on the money market and those that focus on the expenditures market is a choice between research strategies and not a choice between a true theory and a false theory. All the variables that determine income in the Keynesian theory also do so in the quantity theory and converse. Increases in consumption, in the marginal efficiency of investment, in the deficit, and in net exports raise the interest rate, and that, in turn, raises velocity, so that nominal income rises in a quantity theory model just as it does in a Keynesian model.

How then can Friedman come up with different conclusions than, say, James Tobin or Franco Modigliani? Why do they not all agree about what happens to nominal income when the money supply increases? One possibility (for the short run) is a disagreement about the size of the interest elasticities of the demand for money on the one hand, and of investment and consumption on the other. Tobin (1947) treated this as the essence of the dispute.

A second possibility relates to the timing of the response of prices and of expected real interest rates to changes in the other variables, and to the length of the run considered. Suppose the money supply increases. Both theories predict that interest rates initially fall, and then eventually rise. But they differ in how they define *eventually*. According to the quantity theory the interest rate returns to its previous level fairly rapidly, usually within two years or less. By contrast, according to Keynesian theory it may take well over five years before prices have adjusted and the Fisher effect has done its work. This disagreement matters because once the expected real interest rate has returned to its previous level, velocity is back at it previous level too, so that, as the quantity theory predicts, nominal GDP and prices must then have risen proportionately to the increase in the money supply. Hence Keynesians dismiss the quantity theory as applicable only to a long run that is irrelevant for most policy issues. It was in criticizing the quantity theory that Keynes (1924, p. 84) wrote, "In the long run we are all dead." Quantity theorists, on the other hand, dismiss Keynesian theory as relevant only for a period that is too short to matter for most policy issues. The disagreement about the timing of changes in interest rates, in turn, is based on a disagreement about the extent of price flexibility. While quantity theorists take prices to be much less flexible than do new classicals, they consider them to be more flexible than do Keynesians.[6]

A third possibility is disagreement about the relative magnitudes of various exogenous shocks. The relevance of that depends on the type of question asked. It is obviously not relevant if one asks what would happen to interest rates, GDP, and prices *if* a certain shock occurs. But it is relevant if one asks instead why GDP changed during a certain period. Even in an economy with strong Keynesian elasticities and fixed prices nominal GDP still depends primarily on changes in the money supply, *if* the money supply behaves very erratically, while the marginal efficiency of investment, the deficit, exports, and the propensity to consume show little exogenous change.

The relative magnitude of various shocks, the degree of price flexibility, and the interest elasticities of the demand for money and expenditures are, of course, empirical and not theoretical issues. But they help to determine the optimal research strategy; whether one should work with a theory that focuses on the factors determining the demand for and supply of money, or on the factors that account for changes in the marginal efficiency of investment, etc. Indeed, one might look at the quantity theory as a short cut that avoids many of the complexities of Keynesian theory and is useful if certain conditions are met. One of these conditions is that velocity is predictable.

As just mentioned there are two distinct questions to be answered: what happens if a certain exogenous variable changes, and what accounts for the observed behavior of income and interest rates during particular periods? Friedman and his students concentrate on the second of these questions (see, for example, Friedman, 1956; Friedman and Schwartz, 1963a and 1982; Meiselman, 1970). Hence Friedman does not have to spend as much effort as he otherwise would have had to on showing that either the interest elasticities of the demand for money and expenditures imply quantity theory conclusions, or that prices are sufficiently flexible for the interest elasticities to be relatively unimportant, or else that monetary shocks dominate other shocks. Instead, he can argue that since the data show a close correlation between lagged money and prices (with money being causal) at least one of the necessary sets of conditions for the quantity theory must hold. Such a procedure of testing a theory by its central implication rather than by the validity of its assumption is, of course, in line with Friedman's (1953) methodological preference.

Friedman has not discussed in any detail which of the three sets of conditions accounts for the success of the quantity theory. In 1959 he contended that the demand for money can be explained primarily by permanent income with the interest rate playing only a very minor role. This was widely interpreted as saying that the interest elasticity of the demand for money was virtually zero. Friedman (1966) subsequently disavowed this interpretation (which indeed is not a necessary implication of anything in his paper) and argued instead that interest rates quickly returns to their previous levels after an increase in the money supply (Friedman, 1968). However, he did not link this finding about interest rates as closely to the quantity theory as one might have expected.[7] On the third issue, the relative size of the shocks, Friedman and Schwartz documented the magnitude of monetary shocks, particularly during the Great Depression.

With Friedman concentrating on the question of what explains observed changes in income, and looking at the correlation of money and income rather than on the question of how and why changes in the money supply affect income, it is not surprising that he has been accused of crude empiricism. As already described, Hahn, with his formalistic bent, claims that Friedman lacks a monetary theory. Others have accused him of relying on "mere correlations."

Neither of these criticisms is justified. Hahn's criterion for an adequate theory excludes relatively low-level explanations and thus excludes much of what is called "theory" in the empirical sciences. If Friedman succeeds in subsuming many observations under a lawlike generalization, such as the quantity theory, then Friedman has a theory in the sense in which empirical scientists use the term *theory*.

Similarly, the complaint about mere correlations is not compelling because there is much more to Friedman's quantity theory than that. The quantity theory is not an example of an extreme instrumentalism that says, "Money predicts prices. I don't know why and I don't care." The quantity theory is an explanatory theory. On an intuitive level elementary economic theory tells us that when the supply of X (money) decreases, while the supply of Y (goods) is constant, the relative price of Y in terms of X will fall. And if the relative price of Y is sticky, then there will be an excess supply of Y (cf. Friedman and Schwartz, 1982, p. 26). Anyone not satisfied with such an intuitive explanation can always turn to Patinkin's (1965) model. As discussed below, this does not mean that the quantity theory has been sufficiently developed. But it is not a "black box" theory as some critics claim.

What is a much more serious issue than the charge of correlation without theory is whether the observed correlation between money and income should be read as supporting the quantity theory, or the theory that the central bank is accommodative and expands the money supply when income rises. Friedman does not exclude reverse causation (see Friedman and Schwartz, 1963b). Indeed he castigates the Federal Reserve for following procyclical policies. But Friedman and Schwartz (1963b) offer several pieces of evidence for causation running *primarily* from money to income. Their prime evidence is that in a number of specific instances the increase in the money supply was due to a particular event that was clearly exogenous to income, such as a shift in the supply curve of gold.[8] But such clear-cut historical events are rare. For what Friedman and Schwartz call "minor movements"—that is, for the typical business cycle—the evidence on the direction of causality is much less clear: "If the evidence we had were solely for the minor movements, it seems to us most unlikely that we could rule out—or even assign a probability much less than 50 percent to—the possibility that the close relation between money and business reflected primarily the influence of business on money" (Friedman and Schwartz, 1963b, p. 55).

While it may go too far to call the causality issue the Achilles heel of the quantity theory, it is its weakest part. By now the correlation between changes in money and prices is well established. What is disputed is the interpretation of this correlation. Granger causality tests may seem enlightening here. But they are not. Monetarists agree that much of the time the Fed accommodates the demand for money, so that a finding that *on the average*, which is largely what regressions measure, income causes money does not weaken the monetarist position. What is more salient is what happens prior to turning points. Correlations over the entire sample period tell us little about that.

So far I have not discussed a central issue—the predictability of velocity. Over the longer run, M-2 velocity has been stable (Hallman, Porter, and Small, 1989), but to predict short-run changes in M-2 velocity one has to know how interest rates will behave (Hetzel and Mehra, 1989). It is not clear whether this can be done sufficiently well to allow the quantity theory to predict better than a Keynesian model does. Moreover, the experience of the last few years also suggests that the relation between interest rates and velocity may have become unstable (see Carlson and Parrott, 1991).

Another problem relates to the basic theory. There is, if not a gap, at least some terra incognita at the center of Friedman's quantity theory. Friedman separates all assets into two categories—money and nonmoney assets. We are not told why this is the best dichotomy. One possible interpretation is that he is classifying assets by their liquidity. But if liquidity is the touchstone, why is there no role for credit, which is also highly liquid? If the response is that credit is not wealth, then this raises the question why other forms of wealth do not play a similar role to money. And if told that what matters is that money is both wealth *and* liquid, one might ask why this combination of attributes is so critical. Thus Tobin (1972, p. 862) asked, "Is a 'rain' of Treasury bills—promises to pay currency in three months or less—of no consequence for the price level, while a 'rain' of currency inflates prices proportionately?" Friedman (1972, p. 917) replied that

> the evidences of government debt are largely in place of evidences of private debt. . . . The total nominal volume of debt grows by less—and I believe by much less—than the size of the deficit. Moreover, even this growth is offset by two other factors: the increase expected in future tax liabilities accompanying the growth of the government debt . . . and the reduction in the physical volume of assets created because of lowered private productive investment. On the

other hand, the dollar bills are a net addition to the total nominal volume of assets.

Friedman may be correct, but it is strange that on such basic issues he has not presented any detailed analysis. Why should Treasury bills be so much better a substitute for corporate securities than for money? Moreover, since Friedman's reply appeared prior to Barro's paper on Ricardian equivalence, it is surprising that Friedman referred to what had previously been only a rarely and briefly discussed case (see Christ, 1957) without further explanation. Nor does Friedman discuss how long it would take for the substitution of government capital for private capital to reduce output significantly. To be sure, at least some of Friedman's reasoning can be inferred from his other writings. But even so, given the great role that fiscal policy played in Keynesian thinking at the time, one would have expected someone who thought that it contained fundamental flaws to have attacked it head on and not just indirectly. To respond that the empirical evidence shows that it is money and not other highly liquid assets or credit that matter is, for three reasons, not entirely satisfactory. First, while Friedman is right that the correlation between money and income is close, the correlation between liquid assets or credit and income might be just as close or even closer (see Benjamin Friedman, 1988b). Second, there is the problem of reverse causation. Third, even if the empirical evidence unequivocally favors money, we would still like to know *why* money matters so much more than Treasury bills.

Given the amount of empirical evidence for the quantity theory that Friedman provided, and his pathbreaking reformulation of the theory, it would be churlish to blame him for not developing a deeper version of the theory as well. All the same, the absence of a deep version has its costs.[9] Perhaps a deep version of the theory would have sensitized economists to the possibility that changes in monetary institutions, such as the payment of interest on checkable deposits, would raise the demand for money.[10] Perhaps the Fed would then not have adopted such a restrictive policy as it did.

Brunner and Meltzer's Monetarism

The popular tendency to identify monetarism with the work of Friedman and his students is simplistic. Karl Brunner and his former student and frequent collaborator, Allan Meltzer, deserve much of the credit for monetarism.[11] Indeed it was Brunner (1968, 1970) who originated the term *monetarism* and explicated a set of propositions encompassed by that term.

Though Brunner and Meltzer's conclusions and policy recommendations are broadly similar to Friedman's, their analysis differs from Friedman's in salient ways. That it is less well known is, in part, due to their not possessing Friedman's expository talent. Some of their important work is hard to read, in large part because they developed a highly complex theory.

Brunner and Meltzer's Rhetoric

Like Milton Friedman, Brunner and Meltzer reject both the older Keynesian rhetoric and the currently dominant formalist rhetoric. Brunner (1969) published a paper on the methodology of economics that presented a viewpoint similar to Friedman's, the main difference being that while Friedman lacked familiarity with philosophy of science (see Hammond, forthcoming) and thus produced an intuitively brilliant, but technically weak essay, Brunner had studied philosophy of science. All the same, he was deeply influenced by Friedman. He reported that his "encounter with Milton Friedman opened . . . 'new and astounding' vistas" (Brunner, 1980, p. 404).

Brunner rejected the older Keynesian rhetoric. And like Milton Friedman, he distrusted large econometric models, mainly because these models lack clearly specified hypotheses, rely on ad hocery, and confuse forecasting exercises with hypothesis testing. Such criticisms might seem to earn Brunner a commission in the new classical's army. But Brunner rejected the new classical's formalism and their failure to conform to the methodological principles of the empirical sciences. In an interview with Arjo Klamer (1984, p. 195) he remarked,

> The Cartesian tradition insists that all statements be derived from a small set of "first principles." . . . This idea has had a strong influence . . . on the program of the new classical economics. . . . Anything not derived from "first principles" does not count as knowledge. . . . This methodological position is quite untenable and conflicts with the reality of our cognitive progress over history. Science rarely progresses by working "down from first principles"; it progresses and expands the other way. We begin with empirical regularities and go backward to more and more complicated hypotheses and theories. Adherence to the Cartesian principle would condemn science to stagnation.

Brunner and Meltzer therefore place much more emphasis than the new classicals on empirical testing. They do not build an axiomatic system in which elegance and parsimony play a dominating role. Instead, Brunner and Meltzer are unwilling to reject empirically established regularities to preserve a parsimonious theory. As Brunner (1989, p. 217) wrote, "An assertion of empirical regularity remains valid or invalid independently of its logical derivation from a higher level theory. The denial of an established fact because we lack a theory explaining it . . . impoverishes our relevant knowledge."

Brunner and Meltzer are Marshallians in one way, since they aim at concrete results rather than at setting out a menu of possibilities (empty boxes) without determining which one of these possibilities actually occurs. Possibility arguments do not provide the empirically refutable statements that constitute empirical science. Nor do they provide a sufficient guide to policy. And to Brunner and Meltzer economic analysis should be more than an intellectual ornament. Nearly all their own work has important policy implications. At the same time they are Walrasians in the sense of using a general equilibrium approach and in making much greater use of explicit models (including rational expectations models) than Milton Friedman does.

Brunner and Meltzer's Theory of Income Determination

Although Brunner and Meltzer agree with the overall conclusion of the Chicago quantity theory, they reach this conclusion by a different route. Their model investigates the roles of debts, intermediation, and deficits in determining nominal income. They do not draw Milton Friedman's sharp dichotomy between money and everything else and hence have a much richer and more complex theory.[12] Their work on nominal income determination falls into three main parts—early work on the demand for money, a model of income determination, and subsequent work with rational expectations models.

In the 1960s, Brunner and Meltzer, like so many other monetary economists, were busily fitting money-demand functions. One of their contributions was to use as the scale variable (nonhuman) wealth instead of income. Subsequently, in his exhaustive comparison of money-demand functions, Goldfeld (1973) showed that income gives a better fit, so that Brunner and Meltzer's demand function faded from view. But for several reasons their hypothesis that wealth and not income is the appropriate scale variable does not necessarily deserve burial. First, by now Goldfeld's comparison is old, and perhaps an updated version of his test, particularly one that uses recent econometric technology, would result in a different verdict. Second, the superior fit for income might be due to OLS bias. Third, even if income does give a better fit, it is still possible that the demand for money depends more on wealth than on income. Goldfeld's contrary results might be due to our wealth data being less accurate than our income data.[13]

Subsequently Brunner and Meltzer developed a model of income determination that differs substantially from the usual quantity theory model. It deals explicitly with aggregate demand and allows a potentially large role for fiscal policy. Not only does a deficit have the usual short-run multiplier effects, but it also has important long-run effects. Whenever the government runs a deficit, the public's stock of bonds or money increase, which raises aggregate demand. Equilibrium can occur only when income has risen enough to balance the budget, so that the public's stocks of money and bonds no longer grow.[14]

At first glance such a model may seem Keynesian because it provides a major role for fiscal policy. But Brunner and Meltzer argue that their model is not Keynesian. One reason they give is that their model stresses stock equilibrium—the requirement that the stock of money and government debt is constant determines equilibrium. Such stock effects play no role in the Keynesian IS-LM model. This argument is not entirely compelling because the IS-LM model is a simple expository device that hardly represents the frontier of modern Keynesianism. Serious Keynesian models make allowance for stock effects, even if not to the extent that Brunner and Meltzer do.

More persuasive is Brunner and Meltzer's argument that since their model has three assets—money, bonds, and capital—the Keynesian story that the money market is a mirror image of the bond market no longer holds. In their model the interest rate is determined in the market for bonds, and there are separate markets for money and for capital. Brunner and Meltzer present an elaborate analysis of these asset markets, paying much attention to substitution and complementarily. A broad range of assets are substitutes for money, so that, unlike in Keynesian models, the interest rate is not an adequate measure of the effect of changes in the money supply.[15]

More generally, while one might expect that the explicit role assigned to money to be greater in the *theoretical* model of a monetarist than it is in the Brunner-Meltzer model, this need not be the case. What Brunner and Meltzer do is to build a theoretical model in which changes in the money supply, in fiscal policy, in the marginal efficiency of investment, and so on can change income. Which of these factors is responsible for most of the observed changes in income is, as Milton Friedman has so often emphasized, an empirical issue that can be answered only by the empirical evidence. Brunner and Meltzer can therefore legitimately combine an eclectic theoretical framework with an empirical hypothesis, the dominance of monetary shocks, and so produces monetarist results. Thus they state, "For us the propositions now loosely connected under the name 'monetarism' began as a set of empirical observations" (Brunner and Meltzer, 1976, p. 152).

As Laidler (1991, p. 652) points out, in the 1980s Brunner moderated his position that monetary shocks dominate. Toward the end of his life he wrote, presumably with reference to his and Meltzer's branch of monetarism rather than to Friedman's, that

> Keynesians and monetarists seem to have merged together in . . . [rejecting the hypothesis of a single dominant shock]. Both positions recognize . . . the futility of searching for systematic or even dominant impulse patterns. We must expect shifting combinations of nominal or real, aggregate or changing, arrays of specific shocks. These combinations tend to change over time depending on institutional circumstances and the evolution of political processes. This highly eclectic position reflects a major change among some monetarists compared with their views some years ago. . . . [T]his "new view," at least among monetarists . . . does not apply to the persistent inflation rate, which is still recognized to be essentially a monetary phenomenon (Brunner, 1989, p. 220).

The Brunner-Meltzer model never caught on. Subsequently Brunner and Meltzer produced rational expectations models to deal with particular problems. These models sometimes distinguished not only between anticipated and unanticipated shocks, but also between shocks that are expected to be only transitory and those that are expected to persist for a long time. The latter distinction has become an important part of Meltzer's work, who has used Kalman filters for such decompositions.

Monetary Policy

The monetarist account of monetary policy raises the following interrelated issues: (1) the appropriate goal for policy, (2) the need for stabilization policy, (3) the efficacy of such a policy, and (4) the choice of targets, instruments, and indicators of monetary policy.[16] On these issues monetarists have not succeeded in the sense that their views are still those of a minority of economists. But they, or perhaps to a greater extent unfolding events, have changed the profession's consensus substantially, as shown by the widespread objections to what is now called "fine tuning." Here, too, the situation can be described as a process of thesis, antithesis, and synthesis.[17]

In discussing the goals of monetary policy monetarists argue that the natural-rate hypothesis implies that in the long run monetary policy can affect only the price level and not the unemployment rate. This natural-rate hypothesis has received considerable, but by no means universal, acceptance. A survey of economists' opinions (Alston, Kearl, and Vaughan, 1992) found that half the economists in the top ten economics departments and almost one-quarter of other academic economists disagreed with the proposition that "there is a natural rate of unemployment to which the economy tends in the long run," while 31 percent and 41 percent, respectively, agreed only with qualifications.[18]

It is therefore not surprising that although monetarists present the dispute about the goals of policy as a debate between those who recognize long-run constraints and those who don't, some Keynesians describe it differently. Franco Modigliani (Modigliani and Milton Friedman, 1977, p. 10) attributes it to a difference in value judgments: "we value differently the cost of unemployment versus let's say, the cost of inflation." That is questionable. Monetarists who make exactly the same value judgments as Modigliani would still advocate addressing monetary policy to the problem of inflation because they believe that monetary policy cannot reduce unemployment over the longer run. Moreover, even if one were to grant that there does exist a long-run tradeoff between unemployment and inflation, the choice of policy goals would still involve not just a value judgment but also many positive issues, such as the size of the tradeoff, and the effects of unemployment and inflation on the income distribution and on the real growth rate. Whether differences in value judgment unconsciously bias monetarists and Keynesians on these positive issues is a question best left to psychoanalysts.

Another issue relates to the stability of the private sector. Monetarists believe that the private sector is inherently stable and that the fluctuations we experience are largely the result of bad policies. Keynesians disagree. One should not exaggerate this disagreement. Milton Friedman does not claim that a stable growth rate of money would eliminate all fluctuations. And Brunner and Meltzer (1976, pp. 179–178) mean with stability of the private sector only that if it is shocked, it returns to equilibrium. One can agree that the private sector is stable in this dynamic sense and yet argue that the return to full employment is too slow. The stability of the private sector is by itself not a central issue in the monetarist debate.[19] If it were shown that countercyclical policy were efficacious and had no significant costs, monetarists would presumably advocate countercyclical policy, even if the private sector is dynamically stable.

The debate about the efficacy of discretionary monetary policy centers on two other issues. One is whether the Fed can predict GDP and strength and timing of the effects of its policies sufficiently well to be stabilizing.

Early in the debate Friedman (1953, ch. 3) showed that, given forecast errors that do not seem implausibly large, a countercyclical policy might well destabilize rather than stabilize.[20] The data needed to check whether the Fed can forecast well enough to be stabilizing were not available at the time Friedman wrote, so he had to present his case as merely a plausible possibility. Perhaps because it is natural to treat what one cannot measure or analyze as unimportant, Keynesians have generally ignored Friedman's objection and simply assumed without discussion that the Fed has the necessary knowledge.[21]

Monetarists mistrust the efficacy of discretionary policy not only because they doubt that the Fed has the necessary knowledge, but also because they question the Fed's motives and efficiency. They believe that the Fed puts its own interests (such as power and prestige), as well as the interest of its political masters, ahead of its stabilization goal.[22] That is not merely an afterthought, intended to buttress a case based primarily on forecast errors and lags, but represents a commitment to public-choice theory. Milton Friedman (Modigliani and Friedman, 1977, p. 18) stated, "I have increasingly moved to the position that the real argument for a steady rate of monetary growth is at least as much political as it is economic." Similarly, Brunner (1981, p. 37) wrote, "We should not expect that a monetary authority will naturally pursue the optimal social benefit achievable with cleverly designed stabilization policies. . . . They will have incentives to trade off degrees of achievable stabilization for political and personal benefits of various kinds."

It would be hard to deny that the choices that central banks make, like those of other human institutions, are *to some extent* influenced by their self-interest, and by various other shortcomings, such as being unwilling to admit error. The question is the extent to which these factors reduce the efficacy of countercyclical policy. On this issue monetarists can point to the historical evidence in Friedman and Schwartz's (1963a) *Monetary History*, and in Elmus Wicker's (1966) study of Fed policy in the 1920s and 1930s, to the evidence from the FOMC minutes of the 1950s and 1960s that Brunner and Meltzer (1964) presented, as well as to a literature on specific aspects of Fed behavior, such as its penchant for secrecy (such as Borins, 1972; Cukierman and Meltzer, 1986). Keynesians have no comparable ammunition. Instead, they argue that the Fed must surely have learned from experience and can now do better. That *may* be so. But it is far from obvious because the Fed's errors may not be due mainly to ignorance but to the Fed's self-interest and to the absence of a bottom line that would allow the public—and the Fed itself—to evaluate monetary policy (Friedman, 1982). To give a rather obvious example, it is hard to convince a policymaker that the policy he has followed was a mistake, has caused great damage, and should therefore be abandoned (see Mayer, 1990a).

Arguments about such issues are not matters that can be settled rigorously. Much more research is needed, and at present one can do little more than take an informed guess. Perhaps it would help to draw more on the contributions of political science, sociology, and psychology (cf. Mayer, 1990a, ch. 6, 1990b). But economists are reluctant to stray into such company.

The policy implication that monetarists have drawn is that the Fed should abandon, or at least severely constrain, its discretionary policy. What should it do instead? One alternative is Milton Friedman's proposal for a monetary rule that could take several forms. His first choice is to freeze the present size of the monetary base (currency plus reserves), which would leave the Fed with no monetary policy tasks whatsoever. But such a rule would generate secular deflation unless the velocity of the base rises by at least as much as the growth rate of output. Hence Friedman is willing to settle for a policy of a constant growth rate of the base or of the money supply.

A more moderate alternative is a rule, called a semi-rule, that allows the growth rate of a monetary variable to adjust in response to increases in output and to changes in velocity but does not give the central bank discretion. Meltzer (1987) proposed as one possibility that the annual growth rate of the monetary base be set at a three-year moving average of the difference in the growth rates of output and of velocity. Such rules have the great advantage that while they eliminate the Fed's discretion, they still allow policy to adapt, albeit with a lag, to secular changes in output and velocity. Given the instability of M-1 velocity since the early 1980s, it is easy to appreciate the advantage of this adaptability.[23] The debate here centers on whether such a rule would give better results than a discretionary policy that can make faster adjustments and can also allow for some aspects of the economy's behavior that such a rule leaves out of account (see Benjamin Friedman, 1988a; Modigliani, 1988). The Lucas critique poses an obvious difficulty in trying to answer that question.

Turning to some specific aspects of monetary policy, Friedman and Schwartz's (1963a) *Monetary History of the United States* had great influence on the way economists view the Great Depression. Few economists now assert what had previously been standard doctrine—that, on the whole, the Fed had followed a correct policy.[24] Less well known, but also extremely important to specialists in monetary policy, was Brunner and Meltzer's (1964) demonstration that the Fed was operating on the basis of inchoate and muddled ideas. It failed to realize when its policy was expansionary and when it was restrictive, and its operating procedures, such as its focus on free reserves, were destabilizing. For example, it used short-term interest rates and free reserves as an indicator of its policy. During a recession, when falling aggregate demand reduced interest rates, and low interest rates induced banks to hold more free reserves, the Fed thought that it was being expansionary, even though the base and the money supply might be falling. To avoid being too expansionary it would then reduce the growth rate of the base, despite the recession. And conversely during an expansion. At least in principle, most monetary economists seem now to have accepted Brunner and Meltzer's argument that this is a wrong way to gauge policy.[25]

To avoid such confusions Brunner and Meltzer proposed a framework in which the Fed selects certain target variables, such as the money supply or long-term interest rates, that it believes to have a predictable effect on nominal income. Since it does not directly control these target variables, it also selects instrument variables. Those are variables it can control directly, such as total reserves, the base, or the federal funds rate.

This instruments, targets, and goals framework became the standard way of analyzing monetary policy, and a major debate raged over whether the Fed should use as its target the money supply or interest rates. Monetarists also argued for total reserves as the instrumental variable, while the Fed, supported by many Keynesians, stuck with the short-term interest rate. Each side was more adapt at pointing out the defects of the other side's variables, than at showing that its own choices did not also suffer serious defects.

The monetarist position seemed to have won more and more adherents until the early 1980s, when the instability of M-1 velocity and the failure of the so-called monetarist experiment greatly weakened the appeal of the monetarist position.[26] Since then another policy, targeting nominal GDP directly has, rightly or wrongly (see Mayer, 1990b, ch. 9) won great support. This amounts to eschewing any single-target variable in favor of looking at many variables—interest rates, money, credit, and so on. By relying on an eclectic combination of variables that can differ from time to time it essentially abandons the instruments, targets, and goals framework of Brunner and Meltzer. But in an important way it embodies a basic monetarist insight—that to avoid dynamic instability, the Fed must target a nominal variable, such as nominal GDP, and not a real variable, such as real GDP or unemployment. That has, of course, been known since Wicksell but had been forgotten until monetarists brought it up again.

In Conclusion

The upshot of this chapter is first that monetarism is not a doctrine that "only money matters." It is much more subtle and nuanced. Second, it is wrong to say that monetarism has failed because relatively few economists call themselves monetarists. Much of what monetarists have taught has been absorbed into the dominant viewpoint. Whether in subsequent years more will be so absorbed will depend not only on the success of monetarist research, but also on what the unfolding events will show. If M-2 velocity turns out to be predictable, then the debacle of M-1 velocity in the 1980s will eventually be disregarded. If Fed policy appears be stabilizing, the monetarist plea for a fixed growth rate rule or a semirule will fade away. But if the Fed continues to generate destabilizing swings in the monetary growth rate, as it appears to have done in the 1990–1992 period, then monetarist arguments for curbing Fed discretion will garner more support.

Acknowledgments

I am indebted for helpful comments to James Hartley, Philip Klein, Allan Meltzer, Pierre Siklos, and Nancy Wulwick.

Notes

1. I am excluding Patinkin from the monetarist fold because his work is compatible with Keynesian theory as well as with monetarism. He does not make the monetarist claim that changes in the money supply explain the major part of the observed changes in income and in prices. His analysis is compatible with the assumption that shifts in the IS curve account for most of the observed fluctuation in GDP. It is also compatible with an unstable demand function for money, and with the efficacy of countercyclical policy.

2. Patinkin's (1965) monetary theory is much more formal than Friedman's manifesto published the same (1956). But it is quite atypical of monetary theory at that time.

3. It is sometimes said that James Tobin (1947) found empirical evidence for a speculative motive. But what Tobin did was to estimate "idle balances" and not speculative balances. One reason that speculative liquidity is much less discussed now is the proliferation of liquid assets available to investors who do not want to commit to the bond market. Keynes, unlike modern economists, included many (most?) of these in the term *money*.

4. This does not mean that Milton Friedman developed his methodological strictures because they supported the quantity theory. It seems more likely that he espoused the quantity theory because it conforms to his methodology. On the tight fit between Friedman's methodology and his substantive work see Hirsch and de Marchi (1990).

5. Friedman does present his monetarist manifesto as a theoretical discussion, but it is a

simple rather than a deep theory that Friedman employs. Thus in place of a formal derivation from a utility function he relies on the reader's knowledge of price theory.

6. For the relevant interest rate (the expected real after-tax rate) to have returned to its previous level it is prices and not just nominal GDP, that must have adjusted fully to the change in the money supply, because aggregate expenditures can exceed their previous level only as long as the expected real after-tax interest rate is below its previous level.

7. Perhaps this is due to the difficulty of relating the observed interest rate, the nominal rate, to the interest rate that is relevant for the theoretical discussion, the expected after-tax real rate.

8. Other evidence that Friedman and Schwartz cite is the stable relation between variations in money and income, despite the substantial changes in the institutions governing the money supply (for example, the abandonment of the gold standard or the creation of the Federal Reserve) and Cagan's (1965) historical analysis of the determinants of the money supply, as well as the occurrence of turning points in the growth rate of money ahead of business-cycle turning points. On the last of these Friedman was heavily criticized by Culbertson (1960), Tobin and Brainard (1963), and Tobin (1970).

9. Another criticisms of Friedman's quantity theory relates to its paternity Don Patinkin (1971, 1972) has argued that Friedman's theory is not a refurbishment of the traditional quantity theory as taught at Chicago but is basically a Keynesian theory. Thus Patinkin points out that, like Keynes, Friedman employs a portfolio approach to the demand for money, and not a flow approach, as the quantity theory has traditionally done. Friedman (1964, p. 4) does not deny that his "reformulation of the quantity theory . . . [has been] much influenced by the Keynesian liquidity preference analysis." But he objects to Patinkin's procedure of classifying theories by their analytic technique instead of by their empirical assumptions and empirical implications, and to the great emphasis Patinkin places on the neutrality of money (Friedman, 1972, p. 932).

10. In principle everyone would agree that the payment of explicit interest on checkable deposits would raise the demand for money. The issue is how much attention to pay to such an innovation. Barnett's monetary services index, which takes account of such developments, seems like a natural implication of Milton Friedman's formulation of the demand for money, as a special case of the demand for durables, since what Barnett does is to measure the quantity of money demanded more accurately. Yet Friedman and Schwartz (1970, p. 152) mention such a procedure only in passing, calling it an approach "that deserves and will get much more attention than it has so far received. The chief problem with it is how to assign the weights and whether the weights assigned by a particular method will be relatively stable for different periods and places or highly erratic."

11. For an excellent discussion of Brunner's work see Laidler (1991).

12. Thus Meltzer (1992, 1993) wrote, "The whole idea of developing the theory of money, credit and output or money, debt and output was to try to go beyond the quantity theory framework to incorporate intermediation, debt and fiscal policy."

13. But even if demand for money does depend on wealth, if wealth cannot be measured with sufficient accuracy, then for practical purposes income may be a better scale variable than wealth.

14. Brunner and Meltzer's expositions of their model are opaque. It is better to read Dornbusch's (1976) interpretation. Brunner and Meltzer's (1976) rely to Dornbusch and to other critics provides much insight into their thinking.

15. The monetarist credentials of the Brunner-Meltzer have also been challenged because in their model a deficit financed by issuing money *could be* less expansionary than one financed

by issuing bonds. When the government issues bonds, the interest it pays on these bonds adds to next year's expenditures, and with expenditures being larger, income has to rise by more to balance the budget and restore equilibrium. But that does not amount to saying that a bond financed deficit *is* more expansionary than a deficit financed by creating money. Issuing bonds, unlike issuing money *could* raise interest rates, which would have a negative effect on nominal income. Beyond that, it is not legitimate to compare a one time money-financed deficit with a deficit that is financed by bonds and is therefore followed by a continuous stream of additional deficits needed to pay interest. One should compare money financed and debt financed deficits of the same size (see Mayer, 1990b, ch. 11).

16. These issues are interrelated. Thus, if there is no need for stabilization policy, then stabilization should not be a goal, and the same is true if stabilization policy is not efficacious.

17. On the issue of a monetary growth-rate rule the synthesis is represented by Meltzer's advocacy of a semirule discussed below. Moreover, given the behavior of M-1 velocity in the early 1980s, it is likely that a number of economists who previously favored a fixed-growth-rate rule now advocate a policy that is more flexible than that, while avoiding sharp shifts in the growth rate of money. Milton Friedman (1983) considers such a position as consistent with monetarism. The survey by Alston, Kearl, and Vaughn (1992) found that only 12 percent of academic economists agreed that "the Fed should increase the money supply at a fixed rate," while 31 percent agreed with a proviso, and 51 percent disagreed. For the top ten departments the corresponding percentages are 12 percent, 28 percent, and 60 percent.

18. The Alston et al. survey also asked about whether "an economy in short-run equilibrium at a real GNP below potential GNP has a self-correcting mechanism that will eventually return it to potential real GNP." Only 29 percent of all academic economists agreed, and a further 25 percent agreed with a proviso; 44 percent disagreed. The corresponding percentages for the top ten departments are 12 percent, 28 percent, and 60 percent.

19. The stability of the private sector is, however, relevant in an indirect way. Suppose that it were shown that the private sector is highly unstable. Then the relative stability that we experience suggests that stabilization policy has been successful, so that Keynesians are right in advocating such a policy.

20. Milton Friedman was not the only one who raised doubts about whether the central bank has sufficient knowledge to stabilize income. A.W. Phillips (1957), using a more complex model than Friedman's, was also skeptical. Discussions of Friedman's positions often focus on his belief that the lag of monetary policy is long and variable. Friedman's statement that the lag is long should be read in its historical context. At the time Friedman wrote about it, many economists believed that monetary policy has only a very short lag. Hence, an estimate of eighteen month or so seemed long. By contrast, the currently fashionable way of estimating the lag of monetary policy, simulation of an econometric model, usually yields a longer lag than that. The little work that has been done on the variability of the lag suggests that it is highly variable (see Cargill and Meyer, 1978; Tanner, 1979). This variability might well create a problem that is even more serious than the length of the lag.

21. I know of only one attempt—my own (Mayer, 1990b, ch. 5)—to use Friedman's model to estimate the extent to which lags and forecast errors inhibit countercyclical monetary policy. To say that not many people find my results convincing is an understatement.

22. See Friedman (1982). For a collection of much of the public-choice literature bearing on the Federal Reserve, see Toma and Toma (1986). One should not reject the public-choice approach on the argument that Fed officials are decent people. Self-serving biases need not be conscious.

23. One can make an argument that had it not been for Keynesian policies that generated

inflation and for Regulation Q, which monetarists opposed, M-1 velocity would not have changed so much in the early 1980s.

24. Peter Temin's (1976) criticisms of Friedman and Schwartz's analysis of the Great Depression does little to exonerate the Fed. Even if Temin is right in claiming that the Fed does not bear responsibility for the Great Depression, it can still be blamed for not doing its job.

25. Whether this agreement extends to the interpretation of actual events is less clear. During the 1990–1991 recession and the ensuing slow recovery the Fed claimed that it was following an easy policy even though M-2 was growing at a slower rate than before. Few economists seemed to object.

26. During the so-called monetarist experiment from October 1979 to August of September 1982, the Fed let interest rates fluctuate much more than before in a totally unsuccessful attempt to control the money supply better. (For a discussion of what went wrong, see Mayer (1990b, ch. 10). Monetarists strongly reject any responsibility for this policy.

References

Alston, Richard, J.R. Kearl, and Michael Vaughn. 1992. "Consensus Among Economists: The Role of Employment Affiliation." Unpublished manuscript.

Borins, Sanford. 1972. "The Political Economy of the 'Fed'." *Public Policy*, 20 (Spring), 175–198.

Brunner, Karl. 1968. "The Role of Money and Monetary Policy." Federal Reserve Bank of St. Louis *Review*, 50 (July), 8–24.

———. 1969. "'Assumptions' and the Cognitive Quality of Theories." *Synthese*, 20, 501–525.

———. 1970. "The 'Monetarist Revolution' in Monetary Theory." *Weltwirtschaftliches Archiv*, 105 (1), 1–30.

———. 1980. "A Fascination with Economics." Banca Nazionale del Lavoro *Quarterly Review*, 135 (December), 403–426.

———. 1981. "The Case Against Monetary Activism." *Lloyds Bank Review*, 139 (January), 20–39.

———. 1989. "The Disarray in Macroeconomics." In Forrest Capie and Geoffrey Wood, eds., *Monetary Economics in the 1980s*. London: Macmillan.

Brunner, Karl, and Allan Meltzer. 1964. *Some General Features of the Federal Reserve Approach to Policy*. Subcommittee on Domestic Finance, House Committee on Banking and Currency, 88th Cong., 2d Sess.

———. 1972. "Money, Debt and Economic Activity." *Journal of Political Economy*, 80 (September/October), 951–977.

———. 1976. "Reply: Monetarism, the Principle Issues, Areas of Agreement and the Work Remaining." In Jerome Stein, ed., *Monetarism*. Amsterdam: North Holland.

Cagan, Phillip. 1965. *Determinants and Effects of Changes in the Stock of Money, 1875–1960*. New York: Columbia University Press.

Cargill, Thomas, and Robert Meyer. 1978. "The Time Varying Response of Income to Changes in Monetary and Fiscal Policy." *Review of Economics and Statistics*, 60 (February), 1–7.

Carlson, John, and Sharon Parrott. 1991. "The Demand for M2, Opportunity Cost and Financial Change." Federal Reserve Bank of Cleveland *Economic Review*, 27(2), 2–11.

Christ, Carl. 1957. "Patinkin on Money, Interest and Prices." *Journal of Political Economy*, 65 (August), 347–354.

Cukierman, Alex, and Allen Meltzer. 1986. "A Theory of Ambiguity, Credibility, and Inflation under Discretion and Asymmetric Information. *Econometrica*, 54 (September), 1099–1128.

Culbertson, John. 1960. "Friedman on the Lag in Monetary Policy." *Journal of Political Economy*, 68 (December), 617–621.

Dornbusch, Rudiger. 1976. "Comment." In Jerome Stein, ed., *Monetarism*. Amsterdam: North Holland.

Friedman, Benjamin. 1988a. "Conducting Monetary Policy by Controlling Currency plus Noise: A Comment." *Carnegie-Rochester Conference Series on Public Policy*, 29 (Autumn), 205–212.

———. 1988b. "Lessons on Monetary Policy from the 1980s." *Journal of Economic Perspectives*, 2 (Summer), 51–72.

Friedman, Benjamin, and Kenneth Kuttner. 1992. "Money, Income, Prices and Interest Rates." *American Economic Review*, 82 (June), 472–492.

Friedman, Milton. 1950. "Wesley C. Mitchell as an Economic Theorist." *Journal of Political Economy*, 58 (December), 463–495.

———. 1953. *Essays in Positive Economics*. Chicago: University of Chicago Press.

———, ed. 1956. *Studies in the Quantity Theory of Money*. Chicago: University of Chicago Press.

———. 1964. "Postwar Trends in Monetary Theory and Policy." *National Banking Review*, 2 (September), 1–10.

———. 1966. "Interest Rates and the Demand for Money." *Journal of Law and Economics*, 4 (October), 71–85.

———. 1968. "The Role of Monetary Policy." *American Economic Review*, 58 (March), 1–17.

———. 1972. "Comments on the Critics." *Journal of Political Economy*, 80 (September/October), 906–950.

———. 1982. "Monetary Policy: Theory and Practice." *Journal of Money, Credit and Banking*, 14 (February), 98–118.

———. 1983. "Monetarism in Rhetoric and in Practice." *Monetary and Banking Studies*, 1 (October), 1–14.

Friedman, Milton, and Anna Schwartz. 1963a. *A Monetary History of the United States*. Princeton: Princeton University Press.

———. 1963b. "Money and Business Cycles." *Review of Economics and Statistics*, 45 (February), *Supplement*, 32–64.

———. 1970. *Monetary Statistics of the United States*. New York: Columbia University Press.

———. 1982 *Monetary Trends in the United States and the United Kingdom.* Chicago: University of Chicago Press.

———. 1991. "Alternative Approaches to Analyzing Economic Data." *American Economic Review*, 81 (March), 39–49.

Goldfeld, Stephen. 1973. "The Demand for Money Revisited." *Brookings Papers on Economic Activity*, 3(3), 577–638.

Hahn, Frank. 1971. "Professor Friedman's Views on Money." Economica, N.S. 38 (February), 61–80.

Hallman, J., R. Porter, and D. Small. 1989. *M2 per Unit of Potential GNP as an Anchor for Price Level.* Washington, D.C.: Board of Governors, Federal Reserve System.

Hammond, J.D. forthcoming. "An Interview with Milton Friedman on Methodology." *Research in the History of Economic Thought and Methodology.*

Hands, D. Wayne. 1988. 'Ad Hocness in Economics and the Popperian Tradition." In Neil de Marchi, ed., *The Popperian Legacy in Economics.* Cambridge: Cambridge University Press.

Hetzel, Robert, and Yash Mehra. 1989. "The Behavior of Money Demand in the 1980s." *Journal of Money, Credit and Banking*, 21 (November), 455–463.

Hirsch, Abraham, and Neil De Marchi 1990. *Milton Friedman.* New York: Harvester Wheatsheaf.

Keynes, John M. 1924. *A Tract on Monetary Reform.* London: Macmillan.

Klamer, Arjo. 1984. *Conversations with Economists.* Totawa, N.J.: Rowman & Allanheld.

Laidler, David. 1978. "Mayer on Monetarism: Comments from a British Point of View." In Thomas Mayer, *The Structure of Monetarism.* New York: W.W. Norton.

———. 1991. "Karl Brunner's Monetary Economics: An Appreciation." *Journal of Money, Credit and Banking*, 23 (November), 633–658.

McCallum, Bennett. 1988. "Robustness Properties of a Rule for Monetary Policy." *Carnegie-Rochester Conference Series on Public Policy*, 29 (Autumn), 173–204.

Mayer, Thomas. 1978. "Monetarism: Economic Analysis or Weltanschauung?" Banca Nazionale del Lavoro *Quarterly Review*, 126 (September), 233–250.

———. 1990a. "Minimizing Regret: Cognitive Dissonance as an Explanation of Fed Behavior." In Thomas Mayer, ed., *The Political Economy of American Monetary Policy.* New York: Cambridge University Press.

———. 1990b. *Monetarism and Macroeconomic Policy.* Aldershot, Eng.: Edward Elgar.

———. 1992. *Truth Versus Precision in Economics.* Aldershot, Eng.: Edward Elgar.

Meiselman, David, ed. 1970. *Varieties of Monetary Experience.* Chicago: University of Chicago Press.

Meltzer, Allan. 1987. "The Limits of Short-Run Stabilization Policy." *Economic Inquiry*, 25 (January), 1–14.

———. 1992, 1993. Private communication.

Modigliani, Franco. 1988. "The Monetarist Controversy Revisited." *Contemporary Policy Issues*, 6 (October), 3–18.

Modigliani, Franco, and Albert Ando. 1976. "Impacts of Fiscal Actions on Aggregate Income and the Monetarist Controversy." In Jerome Stein, ed., *Monetarism*. Amsterdam: North Holland.

Modigliani, Franco, and Milton Friedman. 1977. "The Monetarist Controversy." Federal Reserve Bank of San Francisco *Economic Review* (Spring).

Patinkin, Don. 1965. *Money, Interest and Prices*. New York: Harper & Row.

———. 1971. "The Chicago Tradition, the Quantity Theory and Friedman." *Journal of Money, Credit and Banking*, 1 (February), 46–70.

———. 1972. "Friedman on the Quantity Theory and Keynesian Economics." *Journal of Political Economy*, 80 (September/October), 883–905.

Phillips, W.A. 1957. "Stabilization Policy and the Time Forms of Lagged Responses." *Economic Journal*, 67 (June), 265–277.

Sheffrin, Stephen. 1992. "Business Cycles." *New Palgrave Dictionary of Economics and Finance*. London: Macmillan.

Summers, Lawrence. 1991. "The Scientific Illusion in Empirical Macroeconomics." *Scandinavian Journal of Economics*, 93 (March), 129–148.

Tanner, J.E. 1979. "Are the Lags in the Effects of Monetary Policy Variable?" *Journal of Monetary Economics*, 5 (January), 105–121.

Temin, Peter. 1976. *Did Monetary Factors Cause the Great Depression?* New York: Norton.

Tobin, James. 1947. "Liquidity Preference and Monetary Policy," *Review of Economics and Statistics*, 29 (May), 124–131.

———. 1970. "Money and Income: Post Hoc Ergo Propter Hoc?" *Quarterly Journal of Economics*, 84 (May), 301–317.

———. 1972 "Friedman's Theoretical Framework." *Journal of Political Economy* (September/October), 852–863.

Tobin, James, and William Brainard. 1963. "Financial Intermediaries and the Effectiveness of Monetary Controls." *American Economic Review*, 53 (May), 383–400.

Toma, Eugenia, and Mark Toma. 1986. *Central Bankers, Bureaucratic Incentives and Monetary Policy*. Dordrecht: Kluwer.

Wicker, Elmus. 1966. *Federal Reserve Monetary Policy, 1917–1933*. New York: Random House.

9 CONCEPTUAL ECONOMIC THEORY

Eric S. Maskin

Abstract

Economic theory is often thought of as being either positive or normative. But this classification scheme is too constraining; there is a large body of theory that does not fall neatly into either category. Much of this is what I would call *conceptual* theory—work that describes the world neither as it is nor as it should be but instead provides us with a set of tools that enable us to answer both positive and normative questions. I illustrate this point of view using two prominent concepts from modern theory—signaling and perfect equilibrium.

Introduction

Economic theory is commonly divided between the *positive*—the study of behavior and institutions as they actually are—and the *normative*—the study of how they should be. Of course, the dichotomy is often a fuzzy one. Is the assertion that equilibrium in a certain market is Pareto efficient a positive or normative claim? Moreover, much economic analysis entails a close interplay between the two perspectives. For example, when considering the various ways in which sellers might auction off an item they have for sale we might be led to investigate optimal auctions—those that maximize the seller's expected revenue (Myerson, 1981; Riley and Samuelson, 1981; Maskin and Riley, 1984). This is a normative enterprise, but any deviation between the theoretical optimum and what we observe in practice immediately prompts the positive question of why there should be a discrepancy.

Despite the practical difficulties in keeping normative and positive economics separate, I do not object to the view that attempting to draw a distinction is methodologically useful. Where I do take exception is in limiting the classification system to a dichotomy. There is, I maintain, a large body of theory that does not fall into either the positive or normative category. Much of this is what I would call *conceptual* theory—work that does not focus on the world (either as it is or as it ought to be) but on abstract concepts, such as equilibrium or expectations. Such concepts are, naturally, useful as tools for answering both positive and normative questions. In fact, it was usually their usefulness that motivated their creation in the first place. But they have become legitimate objects of study in their own right. And this is not simply a matter of abstraction for abstraction's sake. By turning our attention to the tools themselves, we can examine their robustness and see whether they hold up in extreme circumstances. We can refine and polish them to make them more effective lenses in the scrutiny of economic life. We can use them to see the essential connections between what had appeared to be disparate phenomena. We may even discover important positive or normative questions that might not have occurred to us had we not abstracted away all the inessentials.

I will argue by example, taking as my illustrations two abstract concepts from modern economic theory—signaling and perfect equilibrium.

Signaling

The concept of signaling, like many other abstractions, was developed in the first place to help shed light on a specific economic phenomenon—in this case, the common labor-market practice of setting the salary of new employees according to their educational background. Such a practice is, on the face of it, puzzling. After all, as Michael Spence (1974) noted, the lessons taught in classrooms often seem to have little to do with a job's demands. It is unlikely, for example, that bank tellers' marginal products are so greatly enhanced by university training to account for the salary differential between those who are and are not college-educated. Spence argued, however, that even if education has no effect on an employee's productivity (nor even any other worthwhile effect), it may still serve as a signal of a worker's innate talent and therefore of his marginal product.

To see why, suppose that a new worker's ability cannot be readily gauged by an employer, but that this ability is the main determinant of how productive he will be. Assume, moreover, that the worker himself knows how talented he is. Suppose, finally, that graduating from college confers no benefits in and of itself but imposes lower costs on those with higher ability. (Even if people of limited ability manage to get through, their psychic and financial sacrifices are likely to be substantial.) Under these circumstances, a college graduate may be able to command a substantially higher salary than someone without a degree. The reasoning works as follows. A relatively untalented person will not go to college because, even if college graduates are paid more, this does not outweigh the substantial cost of getting through. A talented individual, however, *will* choose to get a degree if the consequent salary is high, since for him the cost of college is relatively slight. Finally, an employer is prepared to pay a high salary to a college graduate since she knows that only able people choose to go to college. Thus, the behaviors of the three actors—talented worker, untalented worker, and employer—are mutually self-sustaining and form an equilibrium. Notice, moreover, that in this equilibrium the talented individual in effect *signals* his ability by choosing to go to college (just as the less able person signals his lack of talent by refraining from doing so).[1]

I have sketched a simple model designed to explain salary differentials linked to education level. But the driving force behind the model—signaling—is quite pervasive in economic life. For example, think of an industry in which there is an incumbent monopolist and a potential entrant. It may well be the case that entry is profitable for the latter only if the incumbent's costs of production are relatively high (in which case, the incumbent's output would be low were entry to occur, implying high residual demand for the entrant). As Milgrom and Roberts (1982) showed, the incumbent, should its cost actually be low, may be able to signal that fact (and thereby deter entry) by producing at a high level before the entrant has a chance to come in. Such a signal would be successful provided that the same strategy is unprofitable in the case where its costs are high. To take another common situation, imagine individuals with inside information about the value of an asset they are selling. Such individuals may be able to signal that the asset has high value by offering it at a high price. This is something they would not do if the value were actually low since a high price entails a high risk of no sale, and this risk matters more if the seller could get stuck with an asset having low value (see Laffont and Maskin (1989)).

I have mentioned just three examples of signaling, but there are probably hundreds of such models in the literature. Virtually all of them, however, have the same basic structure. Agent 1 but not agent 2 knows the value of a parameter θ that enters both their utility functions. Agent 1 acts first and chooses an action a_1. After noting agent 1's choice, agent 2 chooses a_2. The payoff functions are $u_1 (a_1, a_2, \theta)$ and $u_2 (a_1, a_2, \theta)$. In the education model, a_1 corresponds to the education level, a_2 to the salary offer, and θ to the ability of the worker.

Although the notion of signaling was introduced to explain a particular economic phenomenon, and although most papers on the subject are devoted to specific applications, there is a considerable literature devoted to the pure theory of signaling—to studying the properties of the abstract model of the preceding paragraph. A brief (and far from exhaustive) list includes Cho and Kreps (1987), Cho and Sobel (1987), Engers (1987), Crawford and Sobel (1982), Farrell (1985), Maskin and Tirole (1992), and Ramey (1988). Such work is precisely the sort of conceptual theory— neither positive nor normative—that I referred to in the introduction.

There are several considerable advantages that this pure theory confers. First, as I mentioned, most of the applied models share the same basic structure, and so there is a clearly an economy of scale entailed in being able to appeal to a general framework rather than setting up the model from scratch each time around. More important, the nature of the equilibrium set in signaling models is complicated (Note 1 points out two equilibria, one pooling and one separating, but there is a continuum of others as well), and so repeating the characterization of equilibrium each time around would be extremely wasteful.

Second, the abstract model pares the signaling structure down to the bone, whereas any good model of a real economic situation normally injects a multitude of special features peculiar to that specific situation. By comparing the specific model to the general model it becomes possible to see which of these features make an essential difference and which do not. Reconciling differences between the predictions of particular models is also facilitated. For example, Spence's model allows for a separating equilibrium, but the model due to Crawford and Sobel (1982) does not. Before the development of a more general model of which these two are special cases, it was not possible to reach a full understanding of the reasons for the discrepancy (see Laffont and Maskin (1988)).

Third, working with a general model enables researchers to investigate the *robustness* of the properties of signaling equilibria, to elucidate the weakest possible conditions under which they can occur. Thus, for instance, Engers (1987) showed that equilibria are relatively unaffected if we generalize the model to make signaling multidimensional (suppose, for example, that a worker has a choice of where she goes to college as well as how much higher education to get). As another example, Maskin and Tirole (1992) showed that the conclusions of the standard model remain more or less intact if a_1 and a_2 are negotiated together between agents 1 and 2 rather than being chosen sequentially.

Signaling models, as I have mentioned, typically have a plethora of equilibria. This makes their predictive or explanatory power problematic unless we can single out a small number of equilibria as being particularly likely. A final reason for treating signaling models in the abstract, therefore, is to deal with this equilibrium selection issue. There are two principal lines that have been explored. One is to study the implications of *stable* equilibrium (a strengthening of Nash equilibrium due to Kohlberg and Mertens, 1986) for models with signaling (see Cho and Kreps (1987)). The other is to imagine that agent 1—the agent with private information—can communicate with agent 2 using a sufficiently rich language (Farrell, 1985). Both lines achieved some success in reducing the set of equilibria to a manageable number—in some cases just one separating equilibrium.

I would like to make two points about equilibrium selection. First, the idea that the richness of language—how many different things we can say—can be relevant to the issue of signaling was something quite unexpected before Farrell's work, and probably would not have been discovered had the similarities between a large number of signaling models already been well elucidated at the general level. Second, equilibrium selection is itself a general concept—just as signaling is—and it is therefore appropriate to consider it generally, without worrying too much about particular applications.

Perfect Equilibrium

An important issue in many dynamic economic models is how to capture the idea of a credible promise or threat. When can an agent who claims that he will follow a particular strategy be believed? This is a question that arises in settings ranging from monetary policy (see Kydland and Prescott, 1977) to entry-deterrence (see Dixit, 1980).

My argument here for the value of abstraction is rather different from before. It is that the very difficulties we face in even adequately formalizing

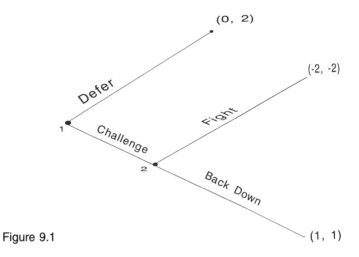

Figure 9.1

the concept of credible commitment call for a general approach. By focusing on commitment, we can try out alternative formalizations in a large
variety of circumstances.

One important attempt to capture the notion of a credible strategy is
through the concept of a subgame-perfect equilibrium (SPE) (see Selten,
1965). An SPE in a game is a vector of strategies that form a Nash
equilibrium not just at the beginning of the game but at all subsequent
points (subgames) as well. To see that an SPE lends credibility to strategies,
consider the game in Figure 9.1. In this game, player 1 moves first and
chooses to defer or challenge. If player 1 defers, her payoff is 0 and that
of player 2 is 2. If player 2 is challenged, then she fights (in which case,
both players' payoffs are –2) or backs down (both players get 1). Notice
at the point where 2 has already been challenged, it is optimal for him to
back down (his payoff is 1 rather than –2). Thus, the unique SPE is for
player 1 to challenge and for player 2 to back down. There is, however,
another Nash (but not perfect) equilibrium in which player 1 defers because of the threat that player 2 will fight. The threat to fight is optimal for
player 2 to make as long as player 1 actually defers. However, it is not
credible, in the sense that, if player 2 is actually put to the test (that is, if
player 1 goes ahead and challenges), he would back down.

Although SPE has merit as a formulation of credibility, it also has weaknesses. To see one difficulty, suppose that we add an additional choice to
the beginning of the game in Figure 9.1 (see Figure 9.2). Specifically, we
now permit player 2 to decide between bribing player 1 to go away (in
which case the payoffs are $(\frac{1}{2}, \frac{3}{2})$) or not doing so, in which case the game

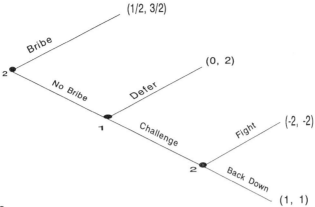

Figure 9.2

of Figure 9.1 is played. I claim that there is a unique SPE in Figure 9.2. As we already saw, given a choice between fighting and backing down, player 2 will back down. Thus, player 1 will challenge rather than defer since she prefers the payoff 1 to 0. This implies that, should player 2 fail to bribe, he can expect a payoff of 1 (from 1's challenging and then 2's backing down). But if he bribes, his payoff is $\frac{3}{2}$. Thus, in SPE, player 2 will indeed bribe.

But what if player 2 does not bribe? Notice that player 1's decision to challenge in the above argument was predicated on his forecast that player 2 would back down. But player 2, by failing to bribe, may call his own rationality into question. After all, he has a sure payoff of $\frac{3}{2}$ by bribing, whereas otherwise, according to player 1's forecast, his payoff is only 1. Player 1 might well worry about this seemingly perverse behavior and, in particular, about the risk entailed in challenging: if player 2 was erratic enough not to bribe, perhaps he cannot be counted on to back down. Indeed, player 1 may well decide that challenging, with a possible payoff of −2, is too dangerous and elect to play it safe by deferring.

All this calls into question the plausibility of SPE as the outcome of the game. Indeed, we have, in effect, argued in favor of the imperfect Nash equilibrium in which player 2 chooses not to bribe, and player 1 then defers for fear that 2 will fight. Clearly, this is neither a positive nor a normative argument. We have simply been exploring the implications of a particular concept—subgame-perfect equilibrium—to see how well they accord with the idea of credible commitment. But this is precisely the style of analysis to which a great deal of theoretical research is devoted. Indeed the vast literature on the refinement or strengthening of Nash equilibrium (of which subgame-perfect equilibrium is just one example) is largely an exercise in trying out concepts in many different contexts—sometimes rather contrived contexts—to see whether they do what they are supposed to (see, for example, Selten, 1975; Kreps and Wilson, 1982; Myerson, 1978; Kohlberg and Mertens, 1986).

Conclusion

Economics is a science, at least a would-be science, and any concept will ultimately prove of little value unless it helps us explain the economic world or improve it. Nevertheless, my point here, to use a carpentry analogy, is that to build a good cabinet one needs good tools. Let us tend to the tool kit as well as to the cabinet.

Note

1. It should be pointed out, however, that despite the virtue of distinguishing between the two types of workers (which makes this a *separating* equilibrium), this equilibrium is wasteful: the able individual goes to college—a costly activity—*only* because of its signaling value. There is, in fact, another more efficient equilibrium of the model in which neither the able nor the untalented worker goes to college (so that they are indistinguishable to the employer), and both types of worker receive a wage that is an average of the high and low wages in the separating equilibrium. This is called a *pooling* equilibrium because the workers are treated the same.

References

Cho, I.K., and D. Kreps. 1987. "Signaling Games and Stable Equilibria." *Quarterly Journal of Economics*, 102, 179–221.

Cho, I.K., and J. Sobel. 1987. "Strategic Stability and Uniqueness in Signaling Games." Mimeo. University of Chicago.

Crawford, V., and J. Sobel. 1982. "Strategic Information Transmission." *Econometrica*, 50, 1431–1452.

Dixit, A. 1980. "The Role of Investment in Entry Deterrence." *Economic Journal*, 90, 95–106.

Engers, M. 1987. "Signaling with Many Signals." *Econometrica*, 55, 663–674.

Farrell, J. 1985. "Credible Neologisms in Games of Communication." Mimeo. Massachusetts Institute of Technology.

Kohlberg, E., and J.F. Mertens. 1986. "On the Strategic Stabiligy of Equilibria." *Econometrica*, 54, 1003–1038.

Kreps, D., and R. Wilson. 1982. "Sequential Equilibria." *Econometrica*, 50, 863–894.

Kydland, F., and E. Prescott. 1977. "Rules Rather Than Discretion: The Inconsistency of Optimal Plans." *Journal of Political Economy*, 85, 473–491.

Laffont. J.-J., and E. Maskin. 1988. "Signaling and Efficiency." Mimeo.

———. 1989. "The Efficient Market Hypothesis and Insider Trading on the Stock Market." *Journal of Political Economy*, 98, 70–93.

Maskin, E., and J. Riley. 1984. "Optimal Auctions with Risk-Averse Buyers." *Econometrica*, 52, 1473–1518.

Maskin, E., and J. Tirole. 1992. "The Principal-Agent Relationship with an Informed Principal, II." *Econometrica*, 60, 1–42.

Milgrom, P., and J. Roberts. 1982. "Limit Pricing and Entry Under Incomplete Information." *Econometrica*, 50, 443–460.

Myerson, R. 1978. "Refinements of the Nash Equilibrium Concept." *International Journal of Game Theory*, 7, 73–80.

———. 1981. "Optimal Auction Design." *Mathematics of Operations Research*, 6, 58–73.

Ramey, G. 1988. "Intuitive Signaling Equilibria with Multiple Signals and a Continuum of Types." Mimeo. University of California, San Diego.

Riley, J., and W. Samuelson. 1981. "Optimal Auctions." *American Economic Review*, 71, 381–392.

Selten, R. 1965. "Spieltheoretische Behandlung eines Oligopolmodells mit Nachfrageträgheit." *Zeitschrift fur die gesante Staatswissenschart*, 12, 301–324.

Selten R. 1975. "Re-examination of the Perfectness Concept of Equilibrium Points in Extensive Games." *International Journal of Game Theory*, 4, 25–55.

Spence, A.M. 1974. Market Signaling. Cambridge, Mass.: Harvard University Press.

10 AN INSTITUTIONALIST MODE OF INQUIRY: LIMITATIONS OF ORTHODOXY

Marc R. Tool

Abstract

This chapter presents and applies a pragmatic instrumentalist mode of social inquiry, widely utilized by institutional economists, to analysis in economics. First, it offers an introduction to, and exploration of, John Dewey's theory of social inquiry. Consideration is given to purposes, context, scope, character, and outcomes of instrumental inquiry. Second, this instrumental mode of inquiry is then used as a standard with which to assess basic theoretical and methodological elements of inquiry in neoclassical economics. Third, a comparative discussion suggests the implications for economics of dependence on the neoclassical mode of inquiry versus dependence upon a pragmatic instrumental mode of inquiry. It necessarily explores the significance of impaired and obstructive theorizing in economic inquiry (misspecified problems, inadequate explanations, denial of creative institutional options).

Introduction

Who can deny that the discipline of economics is in vigorous ferment? Scholars both within and outside the mainstream tradition recognize that the fundamental neoclassical methodology and its theoretical applications are in important respects inadequate and inappropriate.

Scholars within the orthodox tradition seek more pertinent explanations and greater relevance: Arthur Okun (1981) analyzes an economy of price setters, not price takers, in labor and commodity markets; Herbert Simon (1979) addresses "bounded rationality" as a behavioral approach to economic choicemaking; Douglass North (1990) wishes to imbed a theory of institutions, combining behavioral and transaction cost analyses, in neoclassical theory; Oliver Williamson (1986) joins law, economics, and organization theory to enhance understanding of corporate decisionmaking; and Frank Hahn (1991) expects to see more historical and evolutionary elements in conventional analysis.[1]

Heterodox scholars outside the orthodox tradition offer alternative approaches to neoclassical scholarship: Philip Klein (1980, 1987) explains why institutionalists insist that power as discretion must be a part of economic inquiry; Harry Trebing (1984, 1987, 1994) explores the impact of orthodoxy on regulatory theory and offers institutionalist alternatives on pricing and control; Thomas DeGregori (1985; see also Lower, 1988) rejects the endowment theory of resources and includes technological determination of resources in analyses of development; Randall Wray (1990) provides a post-Keynesian theoretical explanation of an endogenous money supply; and Alfred Eichner (1976) provides a pertinent theory of administered pricing in oligopolies, among others.

Horrendous problems of malperformance and restructuring in both rich and poor countries are forcing beds for yet other agonizing reappraisals of how scholars and policy framers "do" economics (Murrell, 1991; Etzioni, 1991). A remark of Paul Homan's (1932, p. 15) concerning institutionalists, made more than half a century ago, has contemporary relevance: "They caused the whole structure of economic theory to be subjected to searching and critical scrutiny." Now the challengers extend well beyond institutionalists. Contemporary economists—as they are called on by governments to frame policy on questions of accelerating growth, alternative pricing systems, resource creation, technological development, macroeconomic stability, budgetary management, investment strategies, environmental impacts, and the like—must also give contemporary orthodoxy "searching and critical scrutiny" and self-consciously redefine and assess its relevance for policy guidance, if problem amelioration or resolution is to occur.

At issue here is the character of the process of inquiry that will generate applicable theory. What model or approach to inquiry should be employed? How do and should economists generate causal explanations as relevant theory? How does one distinguish good theory from bad theory? What are the tests of relevance? It is my purpose here to explore such questions.

The chapter consists of three sections. In the first part I present an institutionalist view of an instrumentally warranted theory-building process. In particular, I examine, and in the main accept, John Dewey's theory of inquiry, developed primarily in his *Logic: The Theory of Inquiry*, as the most credible and functionally useful mode of inquiry available for economists and social scientists. In the second section, I then use this model as a standard with which to appraise orthodox constructs that contrast with and depart from warranted instrumental inquiry. Given present constraints, these considerations are limited to examples drawn from neoclassical economics, although a similar exercise could be undertaken for other paradigmatic formulations in political economy. The final section is addressed briefly to the significance of impaired and obstructive theorizing in the process of inquiry. I suggest that flawed neoclassical theorizing leads to irrelevant definitions of economic problems, to inadequate explanations of phenomena examined, and to a denial of creative institutional options for problem resolutions.

The fundamental purpose of this discussion, of course, is not to formulate ultimate solutions. It is rather to help keep inquiry into inquiry as a topic of high priority in the continuing quest for more pertinent and sophisticated economic theory.

Dewey's Theory of Pragmatic Instrumental Inquiry[2]

Following Dewey, I consider in turn the purposes, context, scope, character, and outcomes of instrumental logic as a model of inquiry.[3] What Dewey contributes regarding social inquiry applies generally and directly to economic inquiry.

For Dewey, the *purposes* of social inquiry derive directly from the continuum of human experience. Inquiry is invoked to remove doubts that arise about how to think and behave in particular settings. More specifically, "Inquiry is the controlled or directed transformation of an indeterminate situation ['uncertain, unsettled, disturbed'] into one that is so determinate in its constitutent distinctions and relations as to convert the elements of the original situation into a unified whole" (Dewey, 1938, p. 105). Doubt prompts questions. Inquiry is set in motion by the effort to answer the question of why.

For Dewey, the logical attributes of inquiry emerge in the course of its conduct: "Logical forms accrue to subject-matter when the latter is subject to controlled inquiry" (Dewey, 1938, p. 101). Social inquiry is a quest to create or restore coherence and order, to recorrelate and reintegrate concept and conduct. Successful inquiry reduces or removes doubt, although in the process new doubts and questions most often arise.

Social inquiry, for Dewey (1938, p. 107), is addressed to problem solving: "The indeterminate situation becomes problematic in the very process of being subjected to inquiry." It is a continuing effort to gain understanding of causally related phenomena in order to perceive the origin and nature of problems. It is a quest for comprehension of the determinants of problems as breakdowns, impairments, terminations, disorders, conflicts, and disrapport in and among the functions and structures comprising the social process, including, in particular, the production and distribution of real income in the economy and the determination and administration of public policy in the polity. "Inquiry is a progressive determination of a problem and its possible solution" (Dewey, 1938, p. 110). Inquiry is purposive; its relevance is derived from its applicability to real problems affecting real people.

Dewey attempted to formulate a model of social inquiry that would generate levels of causal explanation and understanding comparable to levels achieved in the physical sciences. But he did not seek to develop a physics-mimicking, mechanistic approach (Dewey, 1938, p. 438) as has evolved in neoclassical thought in the last century or so (Mirowski, 1989). His mode of inquiry shows none of these attributes. Because the subject matter of social inquiry is human beliefs and conduct, with all their complexities, motivations, and judgmental dimensions, Dewey thought that social inquiry was more difficult that physical inquiry. His drawing of parallels with physics is not fueled by concerns of status or dominion; he is simply seeking comparable explanatory capacity in quest for problem-solving capabilities for theory.

Dewey's central concern was to contribute philosophic undergirdings for a *social* science. The subject matter is person-to-person relations—behavioral patterns and reflections thereon. Individuals are both products and creators of culture. The object of social inquiry is the social process, the universe of person and culture interdependencies. Inquiry is addressed to this universe of emergent organisms and their cultural conditioning. Accordingly, it is concerned with cognitive and analytical perceptions of persons in these human relationships. Such inquiry encompasses theoretical constructs, existential materials, demonstrable connections, evidential grounding, and reflective assessments. Conspicuously absent from this contextual frame of inquiry is any deference to extrasensory, extraexperiential, or teleological sources or relations of conduct. It is inquiry into real-world problematic relations among persons.

Dewey believed that people generally have the inherent developmental capacity to perceive means and consequence connections. The institutionalist meaning of rationality is rooted in this generalized capacity. But such capacity develops and is enhanced only through interaction of persons and culture. Cognitive, linguistic, motivational, and behavioral capabilities are acquired through this interaction. People are both creatures of habit and discretionary agents. They are educable. They are tool-designing and tool-using organisms. They create conceptual and material tools as instruments with which to facilitate and expand both understanding and participation in a problem-solving context. All wants, tastes, and preferences are acquired: unconsciously through conditioning and adaptation and consciously as chosen and learned attributes. Many, if not most, become habitual.

People in their daily lives routinely engage in problem-solving reflections and actions: they convert doubts and concerns into questions; they explore the factual context in which questions arise; they review their own experience for clues and ideas about what is going on and how to proceed; they create modest conceptual and manipulative tools with which to extend their understanding and control; they consider alternative scenarios to account for what they experience and expect; they focus in on what seems to be the most plausible explanation among competing accounts; they select a course of action or response that attempts to answer the question raised and adjust conduct as seems necessary or desirable. Such activity is not an unfamiliar experience; it is commonplace. For Dewey, scientific social inquiry is mainly an effort to deal with more intricate and complex realms of causal connections than can be addressed through commonplace levels of understanding. As he put it, "Scientific subject-matter and procedures grow out of the direct problems and methods of common sense, of practical uses and enjoyments, and . . . react into the latter in a way that enormously refines, expands and liberates the contents and the agencies at the disposal of common sense." (Dewey, 1938, p. 66).

The *scope* of scientific social inquiry for Dewey is broad and open-ended. Boundaries are not set a priori; dimensions are not prepackaged. The scope is not set by forces or determinants anterior or external to the inquiry process itself. On the contrary, the scope of pragmatic instrumental inquiry is set and reset in the context of carrying on the inquiry process itself. Inquiry must encompass whatever is found through inquiry to be pertinent as significantly determining the conditions or problems brought under critical scrutiny. Inquiry is delimited by the identification and tracing out of causal determinants of problematic conditions, not by disciplinary boundaries.

By implication then, social science for Dewey is not compatible with or or accommodative to nihilism, fatalism, or any of a variety of determinisms that generate a priori monocausal accounts (such as psychological, environmental, geographical, historical, cultural, and racial deterministic formulations). Neither is there inclusion of special, intuitive, and private knowledge, which is beyond the reach of communication or demonstration.[4] With Dewey (1938, p. 103), "logical theory is liberated from the unobservable, transcendental and 'intuitional' " ways of knowing.

The foregoing, of course, is only a prologue to comments on the *character* of Dewey's mode of inquiry, a pragmatic instrumental theory of knowledge. Dewey saw inquiry as a collective endeavor, a discretionary continuum, into which individual inquirers move and from which they emerge. Inquiry is a conjoint process of truth *seeking*. It is evolutionary, incremental, cumulative, instrumental, and indeed, even self-corrective in considerable measure. Dewey characterized the process as he perceived it to be actually engaged in by inquirers. He sought to characterize how thinkers actually respond to reflective doubts and behavioral questions that become matters of conscious and substantive concern.

Inquiry is a quest for causal comprehension. Observable linkages and regularities of experience, exhibiting complexities of causal relations, are the object of the search. One may well begin with conceptual material, relate it to evidential material, and emerge with revised conceptual material. However, the central concern is not the sequential ordering of conceptual and evidential material; it is the disclosure of their interdependence that has explanatory significance. Inquiry is a search for conjugate correlation between concept and conduct, between theory and fact, between explanatory constructs and evidence.

Dewey was not constrained by the conventional distinction between inductive and deductive constructs and materials. Dewey did not *impose* a reductionistic deductive-inductive construct as a template. In social inquiry there is a necessary, continuing, and interdependent moving of the mind between theoretical formulations and observed evidence in search for increased understanding. Does the theory explain what it purports to explain? To elevate *either* the rational (deductive) or the empirical (inductive) aspect into a preeminent role is to abort the inquiry process. Inquiry demands operations of data acquisition and of conceptual analysis. The control of the process of inquiry requires that each of these operations be *formed with reference to the other*. Dewey (1938, p. 103) argues that "the distinction between induction and deduction does not lie [then] in the processes of inquiry but in the *direction* which the processes take—according as the objective is determination of relevant and effective existential data or relevant and effective interrelated conceptions."

Dewey's model of inquiry, moreover, encompasses substantial and continuing creativity. His particular, but by no means exclusive, locus of creativity in the inquiry process, reflecting the influence of Charles Sanders Peirce, is in the formulation of hypotheses, an abductive exercise. As Peirce explains, "Abduction is the process of forming an explanatory hypothesis. It is the only logical operation which introduces any new idea; for induction does nothing but determine a value, and deduction merely evolves the necessary consequences of a pure hypothesis" (quoted in Mirowski, 1988, p. 62). Hypotheses are tentative, usually preliminary, formulations in ideational form of what a plausible, possible, even probable causal accounting of observable relations could be. The creation of hypotheses calls for the most imaginative and perceptive *re*casting of prior knowledge and experience, analytical capabilities, and anticipatory insights that can be marshalled. What is called for is an evocative and judicious distillation of insight and understanding, an abductive creation, applied in a novel but demanding context.

Illustratively, consider the role and function of a medical diagnostician confronting a complex and difficult array of symptoms in a patient.[5] The habitual diagnostic characterization appears not to apply; it does not fit or serve; the condition of physical impairment continues. Inquiry is invoked. New tools of disclosure may be employed. These new tests may themselves alter conditions and modify the causal complexities. Possible alternative explanations are conceptually passed in review. New diagnostic insights generate need for a fresh selection and ordering of evidences. The process of juxtaposing hypotheses and observed reality continues. Each recasting is tested for its explanatory capacity. The diagnostic responsibility is concurrently to create and sensitively to explore more definitive explanations and more confirming factual information. Ultimately, but provisionally, the diagnostician selects the hypothetical explanation that most completely accounts for the observed impairment and treats the condition so diagnosed. Creativity is thus invoked *internal* to the inquiry process and leavens that process. It is reflective of the continuously evolving experiental and ideational acquisitions in the diagnostician's mind.

Finally, Dewey (1938, p. 112) saw that the creation of hypotheses was of special significance in inquiry: "An hypothesis, once suggested and entertained, is developed in relation to other conceptual structures until it receives a form in which it can instigate and direct an experiment that will disclose precisely those conditions which have the maximum possible force in determining whether the hypothesis should be accepted or rejected." While the opportunity to conduct a controlled "experiment" of the kind implied here may not be all that frequent in social and economic inquiry, the more *general insight* is crucial. For Dewey (1938, pp. 112, 519), *hypotheses guide and direct inquiry*; they set and revise the questions invoking inquiry. They contribute directly to the identification of relevant evidence, help arrange it for analysis, and offer implications of correspondence and significance. They must often be modified to establish and retain their applicability and suitability "to interpret and organize the facts of the case." "As a broad statement, no important scientific hypothesis has ever been verified in the form in which it was originally presented nor without very considerable revisions and modifications. The justification of such hypotheses has lain in their power to direct new orders of experimental observation and to open up new problems and new fields of subject-matter."

But the character of Dewey's theory of inquiry does not, as the foregoing might mistakenly imply, dismiss traditional and formal logics as being irrelevant or of no consequence. He correctly challenged claims of these logics to superiority and sufficiency. He did dispute their often accorded status as creators of eternal truths. For Dewey, logical forms and models were tools of inquiry; they were conceptual constructs to be used, as is any tool, in the operational tasks appropriate to their design and function. As conceptual tools, they are products of human invention in various times and places. Their usefulness is a function of their capacity to contribute to the coherent ordering and causal comprehension of phenomena under review. Dewey was not unmindful of, nor insensitive to, such formal logical concerns as internal consistency, dichotomous or dualistic relations, and the warrantability of deductive and inductive inferences. But the question of relevance and significance of these logical constructions relates to their instrumental role in the conduct of inquiry. Relevance of logical forms does not derive from or relate to their ancestry, authorship, longevity, elegance, simplicity, aesthetic appeal, or rigor. Neither does it relate to the numbers who concur in support or the status of originators of such defining constructs. When perceived as potential instruments for ordering and relating of subject matter to enhance understanding of causal connections, formal logics may have an important instrumental contribution to make. Dewey used conventional logical forms when the circumstances of characterization and analysis made their use appropriate.

In Dewey's view, the *outcomes* of inquiry reflect the character of inquiry from which they emerge. All truths, for Dewey, are tentative in the sense that subsequent inquiry may require their modification or abandonment. There are, in social scientific inquiry, no absolute truths—truths that have standing and credibility apart from the process from which they emerge and of which they are determined to be a part. Truth status requires the placement of the item in the continuum of which it is determined to be a part, as J. Fagg Foster often insisted in his lectures.[6] References to anterior truths, a priori truths, revealed truths, deductively derived truths, intuitive truths, and the like, because they exhibit a detached, out-of-process status, are not admissible as definitive subject matter in the continuum of social inquiry.

Outcomes of inquiry, following Dewey's theory of the generation of knowledge, are captioned in his own words as generalizations having "warranted assertibility." That is, one can demonstrate warrant for asserting that the causal determinants of the observed phenomena are as hypothetically formulated. Such knowledge is reliable even though tentative. The capacity to assert with evidential warrant means that sufficient confidence has been generated, in establishing conjugate correlation between theory and fact, to permit and justify the incorporation of such warranted assertions into subsequent research. It constitutes knowledge reliable enough to be used analytically in further inquiry, even though subsequent experience and theoretical investigation may invalidate a part or even the whole of what earlier was warrantably assertable.

Finally, Dewey's (1939, passim) theory of inquiry incorporates a running recognition that normative assessments and judgments are an inherent and continuing part of the process of inquiry. This demonstration is reflected in part in Dewey's rejection of the normative-positive dualism. This dualism posits an allegedly necessary and given excluded middle (mutually exclusive) relationship between, for example, ends and means, ethics and economics, ought and is, value and fact, ideal and real, and art and science. Dewey rejects this *dualism* on the grounds that it blocks the path of inquiry. But a dichotomy is not a dualism. To invoke inquiry with the emergence of doubt or the perception of a problem (especially about social relations or institutions) compels the use of a dichotomous *distinction* between "what ought to be" and "what is." And *both* the *is* and the *ought* are an integral part of the inquiry process. To conceive of a social problem is inescapably to apply social value criteria. If inquiry is purposive, in its application to problem solving, it is and must be value-laden. And for Dewey the relevant criteria are imbedded in and derive from the inquiry process itself and what is required to keep it viable and pertinent.

Dewey's (1939, pp. 40–50) rejection of the normative-positive dualism and the inclusion of value tenets in inquiry evidently originates with his recognition of the processual, developmental character of inquiry. This recognition takes cognizance of the fact that means determine consequences; the latter in turn become means to further consequences. Processual inquiry is an evolutionary continuum. As the means are chosen, so are the outcomes determined. But the captioning of what are "means" and what are "consequences" is a judgmental act of the inquirer. No item is per se either a cause or effect or a means or consequence; its placement in inquiry defines its role and consequences. Means and consequences have the standing in inquiry of relational, temporal, and causal connections. Consequences *do not* have the standing of ends antecedently given from outside the inquiry process. As integral elements within the inquiry process, Dewey called them "ends-in-view." They are consequences sought as outcomes of a kind or character that permits further inquiry about, and continuity in, the social process itself.[7] Those ends-in-view (consequences) that enhance the capacity for further inquiry or that provide for the continuity of the social process are termed *instrumental*; they are essential as means in generating further consequences. The continuing development and application of reliable knowledge—identified here as what is *warrantably assertible* —are required for the identification and resolution of economic problems.

The use of reliable knowledge reflects the employment of the pragmatic instrumental theory of social value. Such knowledge is used to restore and enhance the provision of the material means of life—that is, to improve efficiency and rapport among institutions coordinating production, to ensure noninvidious economic participation, to restore adequacy and continuity in flows of real income, to provide for the fullest intellectual and social development of individuals, and the like. The social-value principle imbedded in instrumental-value theory as formulated by J. Fagg Foster (1981) is "the continuity and instrumental efficiency of the social process," or more simply, "instrumental efficiency." I have revised and elaborated on Foster's value principle in my own work as follows: do or choose what provides for "the continuity of human life and the noninvidious recreation of community through the instrumental use of knowledge" (Tool, 1985, pp. 291–314). When institutionalists, following Dewey, attribute *purposiveness* to economic inquiry as making a contribution to problem solving, it is my observation that, implicitly or explicitly, they are employing instrumental social-value theory and the criteria embedded therein.

Accordingly, for institutionalists, criteria for the choosing among alternative institutional options in problem solving cannot be drawn from antecedently given idealistic ends, ideological utopias, absolute truths, or other nonevidential sources. Such inquiry outcomes may be characterized as ethically absolute; they are criteria that are anterior, given, matters of faith, and unexaminable. Neither can institutionalists accept the ethical relativism embedded in utility-based criteria such as consumer equilibrium or the Paretian optimum: they are criteria based on personal tastes and preferences and are presumed to be unexaminable. Instrumental criteria, as an inherent part of the Deweyian mode of social inquiry, function to facilitate inquiry and identify and resolve economic problems.

Competing Views of Economic Inquiry: Applying Instrumental Logic and Value as a Standard

I now contrast an institutionalist view of inquiry with that of aspects, elements, or applications of neoclassical approaches to inquiry. In so doing, I will use attributes of Dewey's theory of pragmatic instrumental inquiry, as introduced above, as ordering topics.

At the outset, a caveat may help clarify matters: I am fully aware that the materials offered and views attributed will not apply to some or all orthodox neoclassical scholars. The spread of orthodox positions on some issues addressed may well be quite broad. Whether I have chosen "representative" positions to address is certainly arguable and is an important concern, but it cannot be pursued here. Since my purpose is to stimulate inquiry, not finally to settle methodological debates, the pertinent question is whether the examples chosen illuminate the issues addressed. Moreover, it is my intent to view the character of economic theory inclusively, as through a wide-angle lens, but a definitive or comprehensive treatment is not attempted.

Purposes of Inquiry

Institutionalists engage in inquiry to extend the substance and range of warrantable economic knowledge, to facilitate social and economic problem solving, and to aid and abet the initiation or restoration of instrumental functions in the institutional fabric of the political economy.

Neoclassical theorists, particularly in the tradition of Milton Friedman, purport to be concerned primarily with predicting economic behavior. Given a covey of conjectural assumptions, they seem less concerned to generate a causal understanding or explanation of observed behavior than to acquire the capacity to predict economic behavior. In M. Friedman's (1953, p. 7) words, the "ultimate goal of a positive science is the development of a 'theory' or 'hypothesis' that yields valid and meaningful (i.e., not truistic) predictions about phenomena not yet observed."

This neoclassical presumption suggests that deductive inferences will generate behavioral predictions. Their basic assumptions include the following: (1) that tastes and preferences, technology, and capitalistic institutional structure are given; (2) that the singular motivation of individual participants is to maximize utility (in cardinal utility theory) or to prefer more to less (in ordinal utility theory); (3) that entrepreneurs will seek to maximize profits; and (4) that workers will seek real wages to offset the also assumed disutility of work (in cardinal theory) or loss of leisure (in ordinal theory). Given these assumptions, one can predict that an inverse relation between price and quantity will obtain for the demand function, and that a direct relation between price and quantity will obtain for the supply function. One might, additionally, predict that the alleged contending market forces would generate movement toward an equilibrium position, that, in the absence of disturbing influences, would remain stable. Employing the technique of deductive inference, the predictive purpose appears to be served; if A and B and C obtain, then one can predict D; given the elaborate assumptions, price-quantity relationships can be predicted.[8]

All of this provides nothing more than the logical foundation for the primacy of certain types of prediction. There is no derivation of an *explanation* in complex interactive causal terms, of how the economic process correlates behavior, how motivations are acquired, how institutions evolve, how relevant knowledge is generated and applied to economic experience as technology. Predictive inferences, even if rigorous, do not constitute explanation.

But other purposes are also served by the economic theory of many neoclassicists. Their theory raises few questions about institutional malfunction, technological inadequacy, or the presence and use of economic power. Historically, they have had no history-based theory of institutional adjustment, although Douglass North (1990, pt. 2) now seeks to provide one; the growth of warranted knowledge and its application as technology is mostly outside their perview; manifestations of economic power and its use are treated as abberational and pathological. Even their consideration of "market failures" is typically couched in the deductivistic language of "barriors to entry," "externalities," and "internalities" (Spulber, 1989, pp. 8–10). One implication is that, with rare exceptions, little serious threat is posed by their theory to existent concentrations of power by megacorps, privately organized interest groups, or international consortia. Designedly or tacitly, theoretical contributions of neoclassicists do not point to restructuring and institutional reform. They appear, rather, to support the status quo—the existing structure and power systems of the political economy.

Contemporary rational expectations theory, for example, generates a modern defense of laissez-faire; Say's law is resurrected. Doing nothing about instability is superior to using governmental interventionist policy—fiscal, monetary, or incomes—to cope with instability. Rational economic agents with full information (expectations) act predictably and promptly enough to modify their behavior to thwart and defeat any such interventionist strategy: "There is an implicit, and often explicit belief that the market economy, left to its own devices, would perform more adequately than when intruded upon." Announced, but "inappropriate," fiscal and monetary policies "will be discounted *ex ante*" (Klein, 1986, pp. 16–17).

Contestable market theory, as another example, argues that even in highly concentrated markets, in the absence of sunk costs, the simple elimination of entry and exit barriers will bring monopolist or oligopolist behavior into conformity with competitive standards. The absence of barriers to entry will intimidate incumbent providers and lead them to forego supranormal profits in order to avoid the attraction of new entrants. The presence of this "potential competition" leads monopolists to act "as if" actual competitive conditions prevailed. The elimination of legal barriers to entry through deregulation is all that is required. The *theory* is blind to the presence and use of economic power. In the words of its advocates, "A wide difference in appearance between a particular market and the form of perfect competition need not deprive the invisible hand of its power to protect the public interest. . . . We can no longer accept as *per se* indicators of poor market performance evidence such as a concentration, price discrimination, conglomerate mergers, nor vertical or horizontal integration. . . . [Such] phenomena . . . can be desirable and should indeed be presumed so" (Baumol, Panzar, and Willig, 1982, p. 477, cited in Klein, 1987, pp. 1351–1352). What is good for megacorps—the telecommunications industry—is good for the country. Interventionist antitrust or other regulatory action is viewed as counterproductive. Regulation is, in such circumstances, unnecessary and pernicious. In effect, an ideological apologia is employed to defend an existing power system. Is the public interest served thereby?[9]

There is another and related implication of neoclassical theory relating to the purposiveness of inquiry. The use of the capitalist model, undergirded and validated by neoclassical theory, as the standard with which to judge existing economies or to define the route of restructuring from socialism shapes the purpose of inquiry. It is the roadmap; it identifies which direction is forward. Here inquiry becomes a tunnel vision exploration of the extent to which an economy is moving *toward* or *away* from the competitive market model. Inquiry is pursued in order to demonstrate the a priori contention that a capitalist system is a superior ordering and coordinating arrangement for economic activity.

This affirmation of superiority derives from the natural law tradition of the 17th and 18th centuries. As Veblen (1961, p. 61) put it, "Natural law is felt to exercise some sort of a coercive surveillance over the sequence of events, and to give a spiritual stability and consistence to the causal relation at any given juncture. . . . [A] sequence . . . must be apprehended in terms of a consistent propensity tending to some spiritually legitimate end." This teleological rootedness undergirds the conviction that capitalism is the natural system and that what is natural is good. In a world devoid of interdictions to natural impulse and arrangement, this natural system autogenetically appears; its inherent law-like propensities function; it automatically generates allocative efficiency. Departures from the capitalist model are "unnatural" and "inefficient." *Problems* then are defined as departures from or shortfalls in the emergence of that system; they are "disturbing factors." The search for routes to the achievement of the closest approximation to the competitive model defines the purposes of inquiry and policy. Its realization, presumably, would constitute a "solution" for problems and a vindication of neoclassicists' theoretical purpose.

This normative use of the competitive model—extolling the price system as the only efficient allocative instrument—truncates inquiry, seals off other plausible options, and constrains inquiry to the reaffirmation of prior orthodox "truths" (see also Tool, 1986, pp. 104–125). For neoclassicists, problem solving through institutional adjustment does not drive the process of inquiry. For institutionalists, this is the fundamental reason for engaging in economic inquiry.

The Human Focus and Context of Inquiry

For *institutionalists* economic inquiry is pursued as a social science. The object of inquiry is the social process in which institutional structures organize and implement continuing functions of the provisioning process. In the social sciences generally, with the exception of mainstream economics, there is now common agreement that people in this social process are at once creators of culture and conditioned products of their culture. Although most patterns of their reflection and behavior are or become habitual, they are rational, discretionary agents engaged in transforming themselves coincident with the transformation of their cultural fabric. They perceive causal-effect or means-consequence relations; they understand if-then propositions. They are rational in *this* sense. All of their tastes, preferences, motivations, and behavior are culturally acquired, although basic drives may prompt their formation.

For *neoclassicists*, the singular human agent, as with sides of a coin, has two facets, each an expression of the other. Man is rational; man is a maximizer. *And each defines the other*. In their view, an economic agent who determines the net benefits of every act and elects the one that best maximizes his or her satisfactions, is rational. To exhibit inherent rationality *means* to maximize utility in any form. This characterization is a given psychological attribution, not a distilled product of reflective inquiry. It is acultural and asocial. I will argue that it is reductionistic and without demonstrable evidential grounding.[10]

Their model of man is *acultural* because it encompasses no concern with the evolutionary emergence of individuals who are both contributors to and conditioned products of their respective environmental settings. The rational agent of neoclassical analysis has no history; there is no analytical consideration of acquired habit, custom, or behavior of which account must be taken except as it becomes manifest in market behavior. There is no analytical account taken of growth in perception, of transformation of choices, of maturation of capacities through cultural interdependencies. He or she simply *is* a utility maximizing organism. This attribute is given; it is a *natural* characteristic of people. Bentham's pleasure-pain calculus is converted into a utility-based benefit-cost calculation. We are offered an archaic posture of "metaphysical individualism" as a theory of human behavior (Dewey, 1939, p. 64).

The neoclassical premises are *asocial* in their continuing myopic stress on the individual agent whose character, motivations, and behavioral traits, other than as a rational maximizer, are without analytical interest. "Greed is enough." Neoclassicists do not grant that the whole of human experience is that of *interaction* with others in consequence of which people reason, articulate, learn, organize, direct, assess, and participate. The economic agent is a social agent; his or her individual judgments and actions are an emerging product of interaction with others.

The neoclassical view of human nature is *reductionistic* in the singular focus on maximization, on individual gain, on self-serving motives, on insensitivity to the concerns of others. "The idea of utility grows out of the attempt to understand all of an individuals' choices in terms of a single thing he is trying to maximize—happiness, pleasure, or something similar. We call this utility" (D. Friedman, 1990, p. 68). But the substance of what constitutes "utility" can not be explored; it is an asserted feeling-state that is beyond inquiry. In consequence, orthodox theory is unable to accommodate the complexity, the continuing transformation of purpose and motive, of action and appraisal, that is the common character of economic participation at any level.

Finally, claims of utility maximization are nondemonstrable and inde-fensible. An alleged universal characterization is used to affirm any eco-nomic behavior whatsoever. Whatever the act, whatever the judgment, the presumption is that the individual *must* have been maximizing utility or he or she would have acted otherwise. *It is a universal account that explains nothing.* All behavior—any behavior—is maximizing behavior. The circu-larity is inescapable. It strips the maximization premise of all *analytical* significance whatsoever. As a conceptual tool it cannot discriminate; it is analytically sterile.

To continue with the utility maximizing premise, as the core attribute of the rational economic agent, is to distort and misdirect the inquiry process at its very core.

The Scope of Inquiry

In *institutional* analysis, what is included in any particular inquiry—its perimeters and parameters—is set and reset in the course of conducting inquiry. Since the purpose of inquiry is to generate causal understanding of what is observed and to utilize such analytical insights to contribute to problem resolution, there can be no given *anterior* delineation of scope that constrains and inhibits the inquiry process. Doubt is the forcing bed for questions; questions invoke inquiry. The investigator cannot know in ad-vance of inquiry which determinants of an indeterminant situation will be identified as significant, which subject matters will have to be tapped, which theoretical tools and constructs will prove instrumentally useful, which hypotheses may show plausible promise and effectually guide the inquiry process itself. Inquiry is open-ended but directed by initial questions and preliminary hypotheses, focused but amenable to being refocused, crea-tive, and interconnected but still evolving in the universe of concern. Theory building is demanding, frustrating, and untidy; it continues as a search for coherence and causal understanding.

In *neoclassical* analysis, ironically, the scope of inquiry is both remark-ably narrow and exceedingly broad. Its analytical focus is narrow in the sense that its practitioners have generated a remarkably elaborate and sophisticated system of analytical models of a very limited facet of the economic provisioning process—"the price system." As any orthodox col-lege-level intermediate theory text will confirm, to explain price is pur-portedly to explain the whole of what is significant in the economic process. The price-theory core, undergirded by the logic of constrained maxi-mization, is set off early on; the remaining chapters extend, refine, and purportedly apply that core theory (for example, see D. Friedman, 1990, passim). Whatever can be made to fall within that delineation is economics; whatever cannot be accommodated in that model is something other than economics. The model defines the discipline.

This model of inquiry is exceedingly broad in the imperialistic sense. Having conquered economics, its practitioners have moved on purportedly to explain how this rationalistic maximizing model, or derivatives therefrom, can explain, with only minor amendments, the political process (Downs, 1957), operation of households (Becker, 1976), governmental operations (Buchanan and Tullock, 1962), economic history (North, 1990), corporate power systems (Williamson, 1986), and economic development (Baner and Yamey, 1957), among topical areas. This allegedly pan-cultural and pan-temporal model converts reductionistic price theory into a universal model of social analysis. No one questions the instrumental need for abstraction and selectivity in addressing ideas in inquiry. But with price theory, aspects of the real world are massaged, compressed, selectively ignored, and manipulated in order to wrap this conceptual cloak around any chosen subject matter.

Consider more directly what is excluded from consideration in this model—its claims to breadth and relevance notwithstanding. As noted, the "givens" of orthodoxy—including wants, tastes and preferences, technology, institutions of a capitalist systems, character of motivation are all largely assumed; they are not often themselves objects of analysis in the neoclassical paradigm. Also generally outside the pale of consideration are such areas as the possession and use of economic power (including administered pricing), the nature and significance of corporations, the role of education for economic growth, and the cultural, political, technological, and social determinants of economic development.

Even more significantly, neoclassicists, in their claims to positivist analysis, eschew any serious consideration of criteria of social value in exercising discretion in the provisioning process. Embracing the normative-positive dualism, they are content to perceive utility as the meaning, and price as the measure of value. The exercise of discretion in markets is guided by individualistic and unexaminable preferences. The ought is *implicitly* realized if behavior follows price-theory directives. No value theory to guide choices among or between institutions is required; the facilitating structure for price determination, through which utility choices are made, is not at issue in their inquiry.

There are, to be sure, "in-house" responses to perceived limitations in the foregoing. In order to provide an approach thought to be of greater relevance to the real world, neoclassicists sometimes push out the self-imposed constraints on the scope of economic inquiry: Ramsey pricing (the inverse elasticity rule) provides for the use of power, in regulated utilities, to place expansion costs on buyers of basic services whose purchases are inelastic. Transaction-cost economics acknowledges the intracorporate need to choose between markets and hierarchies in making judgments on costs. Human-capital-formation theory acknowledges the significance of the growth of skills and knowledge to provide for more effective market participation. The stages theory of economic growth acknowledges the presence and importance of cultural influences on the capacity to become productive over time.

A case-by-case examination would disclose some limited departures from the neoclassical paradigm in the foregoing, but there is no intention in these departures to challenge the fundamental claims to near universal relevance of neoclassical orthodoxy as defining the scope of economic inquiry. Scholars who accede to neoclassical constraints on the scope of inquiry risk loss of significance for their inquiry generally.

The Character of Inquiry

Institutionalists view inquiry as a conjoint process of truth seeking in which deductive, inductive, and abductive procedures are interrelated elements of an evolving and processual quest for causal understanding of the experiential phenomena under scrutiny. Its creative dimensions are reflected in the posing of questions for inquiry, creation, and application of tools of inquiry, formulation, and continuing assessment of hypotheses that guide inquiry, and the use of instrumental judgments to direct and pattern the inquiry process in pursuit of theoretically coherent and evidentially grounded comprehension. The inquiry process is purposive, evolutionary, judgmental, and provisional. It seeks conjugate correspondence of theoretical and evidential material.

That *neoclassical* inquiry has, in the last half century, become predominantly formal, particularly in the mathematical sense, needs no elaboration here.[11] A few minutes spent with the most recent issue of the *American Economic Review*, for example, will disclose little else. Complaints of Wassily Leontiff (1971), Robert A. Gordon (1976), and others about this formalistic refocusing of economics since World War II has had little discernible effect on the character of mainstream economic inquiry.[12] In explaining this "mathematization of economic theory," Gerard Debreu candidly acknowledges that values "are imprinted on an economist by his study of mathematics." Indeed, "the very choice of the questions to which he tries to find answers is influenced by his mathematical background. Thus, the danger is ever present that the part of economics will become secondary, if not marginal, in that judgment" (Debreu, 1991, p. 5).

As Ken Dennis (1994) sees it, neoclassicists "seek above all else a precise, orderly, simple, and rigorous version of economic truth, a version that offers full scope for the exercise of predictive powers, based upon the projection of measured uniformities derived from the recorded past." To pursue this kind of inquiry, they must assume that in all matters of economic substance, the basic analytical constructs are all reducible to and can be expressed in mathematical symbolistic terms, and can and should be subjected to mathematical deductivistic reasoning (Lawson, 1994). Mathematical symbolism is not just a form of logic, but "a full-blown and self-contained language by which to 'formulate' (i.e., express) the propositions of economic theory" (Lawson, 1994).

This concern is amplified in Philip Mirowski's (1986, pp. 192–194) assessment of how a "system of obscure symbols" can be responsible for "the maintenance of orthodoxy." His explanation draws attention to the following attributes of mathematics as reflected in neoclassical economics: mathematics is "a restricted language. . . . It possesses a certain ritual efficacy over and above its content"; it is a "discourse where the assertion of the discreteness of intellectual constructs is pushed to its extreme"; "mathematics fosters the impression that the actors who are the subject of analysis are determined by alien extraneous forces"; "the discrete character of mathematics encourages . . . 'the norm of closure' . . . the creation of a system restricted in time and in space"; "the penetration of mathematics induces a particular form of hierarchy within a discipline. . . . Theorists become separated from a lower class of researchers. . . . Mathematics frees the theorist from having to create a context of justification."

The problems with this focus are many; only a skeletal capsulization can be provided here:

1. While the statistical assembling of pertinent information and the summaries drawn therefrom do sometimes constitute significant data in evidential grounding of hypotheses or behavior, their usefulness may be impaired by the conceptual frame that specifies and guides their acquisition. After all, as Fagg Foster often admonished his students, it is theory that tells us which facts to gather and how to arrange them for analysis. Mathematical expression, per se, says nothing about the significance of the acquisition; that must be determined by theoretical analysis *external to* the mathematical reasoning process itself.

2. The comprehensive effort to translate economic propositions into mathematical formulas denies to inquiry constructs and propositions that cannot be so translated. Indeed, as noted, the discipline has increasingly been more narrowly defined to include only material and constructs that are amenable to mathematical formulation and expression (Watkins, 1992).

3. The alleged "explicitness, precision and rigor" claimed for this methodology is illusory: "The deductive validity of any logical argument that passes from one language or symbolism into another language or symbolism depends as much upon the adequacy of the translation linking the two symbolisms together as it does upon the validity of any deductive inference that is expressed entirely by means of either one of those symbolisms" (Watkins, 1992). And the adequacy or appropriateness of those translations from mathematics to economics, imposing law-like orderings given simplistic assumptions, are rarely considered. As Dennis observes, "Most of the standard assumptions of economic theory are propositions about human behavior (actions) or human dispositions (beliefs, preferences and intentions, as well as capabilities), propositions such as 'economic actors possess perfect knowledge'; and 'economic actors prefer to maximize their utility,' and yet these receive no formally explicit expression. . . . Their role in assuring deductive validity is totally gratuitous" (1994 (A-K) p. 254).

4. The character of neoclassical inquiry, to the extent that its major analytical mode is converted to mathematical formalism, symbolism, and deductivistic reasoning, exhibits a reductionism that leaves most of the major analytical questions unaddressed: determination and revisions in economic structure, negotiational policy making, motives other than greed for participation, locus and use of economic power, technological determinants of production, acquisition of skills, among others. Mathematical models, econometric regressions, and the like may at times be pertinent tools or instructive exercises, but their analytical significance and contribution can be identified only through recourse to pragmatic instrumental inquiry. As Kenneth Boulding (1986, cited in Watkins, 1992, p. 3) observes, mathematical reasoning is very useful, but its language structure has so few verbs: "It is hard to think of more than four: is equal to, is greater than, less than, or is a function of." That is, such symbolism and reasoning may at times be useful, but it is incidental to, not the defining character of, economic analysis.

The narrowing of scholarly focus in neoclassical economics to what can be conceived, analyzed, and predicted through mathematical symbolism, deductivistic reasoning, and economic regressions constitutes a major impediment to the inquiry process. The pursuit of more pertinent modes of inquiry is left underdeveloped and undersupported.

The Outcomes of Inquiry

For *institutionalists*, pragmatic instrumental inquiry culminates provisionally in tentative truths, with what Dewey called "warranted assertions." With the establishment of conjugate correlation between ideational hypotheses and evidential grounding, sufficient confidence is generated in the outcomes of inquiry to warrant their tentative inclusion in subsequent inquiry and in provisional problem solving. This continuously emerging fund of evidentially warranted knowledge is derived from a deliberative, processual, cumulative, and self-corrective inquiry activity.

The tentatively concluding query in institutionalist inquiry is this: Will the proposed alterations in institutional structure, based on reliable knowledge derived from pragmatic instrumental inquiry, enhance the provisioning process? That is, as noted above, do they improve efficiency and rapport among coordinating institutions, ensure noninvidious participation, maintain flows of real income, provide for full development of individuals, ensure a healthy and sustainable environment, and the like?

Neoclassicists, in contrast, generally perceive economic inquiry to culminate with a reaffirmation of that with which their inquiry began, albeit with modest refinements or addenda. What is reaffirmed is a deductivisticly conceived economic model with ungrounded assumptions about human agency, given structure, market phenomena, and naturalistic tendencies that provides movement toward allocative efficiency (identified as Paretian optimality), equilibria, and the reaffirmation of the competitive model. Indeed, the outcomes identified, as perceived by the orthodox, are *conjointly* realized: Given "competitive markets . . . every conceivable Pareto condition of economic efficiency would tend to be fulfilled if profit-maximizing firms and utility-maximizing households were to determine the optimum quantities they wished to trade with the help of equililbrium prices established in such markets" (Kohler, 1990, p. 291).

This approach to inquiry does rest on a priori truths—deductively derived truths that become constructs that serve as bases for mathematical truths. Nowhere is this inquiry activity genuinely processual, cumulative, or self-corrective. Tests of deductivistic inference, cogency, elegance, and simplicity are, by themselves, insufficient to establish reliable knowledge. In orthodoxy, the inquiry givens are derived anterior to and outside the inquiry process itself. Although claims are sometimes made that these assumptions are tentative or hypothetical, in text and classroom they remain remarkably constant and unmodified.

Claims to allocative efficiency appear as conjectural and inhibitive. The outcome of allocative efficiency is presumed to result from the unhibited workings out of the competitive market system. The attributes of this resultant are that profits are "normal"; real wages equal the marginal productivity of labor; pricing power is zero; innovative incentives are present; maximal product is generated at minimal cost; consumers maximize utility. The achievement of allocative efficiency in the private sector *constitutes* the public's economic interest. Few neoclassical economists believe in the *descriptive* merits or adequacy of this characterization, but its quest defines the direction and character of much of their inquiry. It is conjectural because of its flawed descriptive capacities; it is inhibitive because it tends to foreclose alternative approaches.

Corollary claims are made that the Paretian optimum serves as a primary criterion of allocative efficiency, a major stipulation of a analytically desired outcome, and an effectual and employable judgmental premise. Such claims are also conjectural and inhibitive. Neoclassicists, when compelled to abandon their positivism in judgmental contexts, consider the Paretian optimum to be a quite acceptable principle of social value. It is a criterion of judgment that permits an "ought to be" choice to be made without the need for comparative assessment of preferences or their cardinally measured utility. Indeed, it is the only principle of normative assessment that most neoclassicists will acknowledge. (The Kaldor-Hicks extension/revision is cut of the same conceptual cloth.) The Paretian optimum serves as a welfare index in its stipulation of technical marginal conditions of economic efficiency that, if fulfilled simultaneously, indicate that no reallocation could make anyone better off (in their own judgment) without making someone else worse off (in their own judgment). It is not surprising that these Paretian conditions are best met in an unfettered competitive economy (Kohler, 1990, pp. 484 ff). The "better off–worse off" judgments are referenced back into the given wants, tastes, and preferences of individuals. Wants *ought* to be fully met, but the origin and character of wants is unexamined. The inherent ethical relativism is inescapable. As Edythe Miller (1990, p. 729) put it, "The preoccupation of orthodox economics with Pareto efficiency flaws perspective.... It portends the existence of a precise set of solutions to any given set of economic problems. But, Pareto efficiency lacks operational content and cannot be measured by independent criteria. It is ambiguous and esoteric and, at bottom, metaphorical. A Pareto optimum turns out at any time to be 'what is,' for if what is were not optimal, individuals would not have negotiated in order to achieve it."

Claims to the inherent emergence of equilibriums as a desired outcome are conjectural and inhibitive. As most are aware, the construct of "equilibrium" lies at the heart of orthodoxy[13] both as a descriptive characterization of economic phenomena and, notwithstanding vigorous contentions to the contrary (Robbins, 1952, p. 143), as a normative quest or condition that ought to prevail. Equilibrium plays a linchpin role; withdraw the construct and much of orthodox analysis comes apart; a major organizing premise disappears.

The construct of equilibrium presents a stasis view of reality instead of an evolutionary one. Even a limited survey suggests that contemporary inquiry in sociobiology (Wilson, 1978), bioeconomics (Georgescu-Roegen, 1971; Dragan and Demetrescu, 1991), biopolitics (Thorson, 1970), welfare economics (Hahnel and Albert, 1990), chaos theory (Goodwin, 1990), as well as evolutionary economics (Hodgson, 1993), points to a processual reality of continuous, not necessarily regular, change. Incessant change involves creation, mutation, displacement, abandonment, reconstruction, readjustment; it will reflect cumulative and, at times, circular causation.

However, economic change does not necessarily exhibit cyclical or rhythmic patterns in which previously established conditions are restored. Rates of change do vary, of course, but the fact of change is a constant. Critical here is the recognition that change is *not* inherently or characteristically a movement toward or away from an equilibrium state—a place or point from which there is no directional movement.

Setting economics as inquiry-examining movements toward or away from equilibrium misconceives the nature of economic change, in my view. In its more rigid form, movement is mistakenly conceived as episodic: from an original quiescent state, to a disturbance of quiescent state, then to a restoration or return to quiescent state—an equilibrium condition, and the episode is completed. Whether this essentially static focus is intended merely to provide a conjectural construct for inquiry or to characterize reality, it ill serves either intent. As a construct, it tempts inquirers to misspecify determinants of change; as a description in social analysis, it is inadequate and misleading.

Observable reality, as noted, is processual, unexceptionally so: causal linkages tie the past and the present; conscious choices shape the character of the future; even approximate replications of previous conditions are exceedingly rare. Perhaps the most obtrusive fact is that all social and economic systems are in a state of flux. Rates of institutional change vary from minimal to rapid; the character of institutional change may be modest or convulsive. But structural change is continuous. Growth in knowledge, meaning, and understanding generate capacity for change; emergence and recognition of major impairments in the flow of real income activate interest in change. But all such change is processual; it is neither episodic nor inherently equilibrium-seeking.

Conventional economic instruction, disclaimers notwithstanding, does tend to attribute normative significance to equilibrium outcomes. The workings of alleged free, unfettered markets *ought* to culminate in consumer equilibrium—a state or condition in which the "rational greedy economic agent" (Hahn, 1973, p. 40) cannot alter his or her purchasing behavior in any way to increase his or her total utility; it is the consummate resultant, desired and preferred. Equilibria are normatively better than disequilibria.

What will be obvious on reflection, however, is that the neoclassical construct of equilibrium, as such, is normatively barren; it has no evaluative content. Its claim to relevance as in consumer equilibrium reflecting maximized utility, producer equilibrium as maximized profits, and general equilibrium (via Walras) as the above with fully cleared markets, is wholly conjectural. Even if equilibrium could be demonstrated in some way, the question of the character and significance of the emergent consequences must be determined by other than *ethically relative* criteria. Such criteria, as noted, reflect the insistence that all ethical norms are relative to the individuals and cultures that exhibit them. No interpersonal comparisons of preferences or cross-cultural assessments of choices are permitted. Criteria of choice may not *themselves* be subjected to social and ethical inquiry. A frequent outcome, then, is simply to contend that "what is, is right." The status quo is reinforced.

The neoclassical outcome of inquiry that emerges as a reaffirmation of the competitive model is, in another sense, an *ethical absolute*. Not only is there an inherent circularity in the reaffirmation of that with which inquiry began, the virtues and alleged merits of the competitive model, there is a continuing insistence on the normative use of this competitive model.[14] Although there have been many refinements and extensions over the years, it is not an exaggeration to contend that the *fundamental* character of that model has not been significantly modified over the last half-century through scholarship of orthodox economists. The mathematical revolution in economics, the development of axiomatic theory, rational expectations formulations, cost-benefit analysis, and contestable market theory, for example, all leave the main corpus intact. The basic market model has become a Platonic ideal—always to be sought but never to be realized. Its substance, its role as an analytical construct, and its normative guidance are given; they are not suffuciently admitted into the inquiry process.

Consequences of Dependence of Neoclassical Model of Inquiry

In these concluding comments, I note three implications of reliance on this mainstream approach. First, the *neoclassical* model of inquiry tends to stress predictablity rather than causal understanding and, in so doing, truncates inquiry in a manner that leaves the real problems of institutional breakdown largely ignored. The neoclassical conception of an "economic problem" is specified by the deductivistic mode of inquiry to which it is committed and by its ideological commitment to the institutional structure of free and equilibrating markets. The inquiry constraint delimits by discarding as noneconomic all approaches save those that are derived from or accommodative to the price-theory model. The institutional constraint is imposed by the absence of a credible theory of institutional change or adjustment. Neoclassical theory simply does not encompass or address as such the myriad prescriptive and proscriptive patterns of correlated behavior that organize the provisioning process. Accordingly, they cannot identify a "problem" of malfunction within that structural fabric.

An *institutionalist* asks how and to what degree correlated patterns of behavior and attitudes, institutional forms and the values on which they rest, operate to impair the provisioning process. Institutionalists focus their analyses on the institutional malfunctions that generate inefficient production, involuntary unemployment, macroinstability, inequality of income distribution, environmental deterioration, discriminatory denial of participation, deprivation of medical care, and the like. Impairments in the provisioning process constitute the universe of "problems." An institutionalist asks where in the structural fabric are invidious or ceremonial patterns of judgment and behavior impeding or distorting the continuous and adequate provision of real income; these patterns constitute regressive forces. An institutionalist asks how instrumentally warranted knowledge and value can be brought to bear to guide the restructuring of the institutional fabric in a progressive fashion.[15]

Second, the *neoclassical* mode of inquiry does not provide an adequate explanation of economic phenomena: its predictive purposes are sometimes pertinent but quite insufficient; its views of human nature, rationality, and motivation are truncated and in some measure archaic; its scope of inquiry does not extend to include the demonstrable determinants of real break-downs in the provisioning process; its shift in character, in recent decades, to mathematical formulations has permitted concern with method to overtake and subvert substance; its answers for institutional breakdowns, in recommending the institution of free markets, deregulation, and so on have exacerbated, not resolved, fundamental distortions and obstructions in the flow of real income.

Institutionalists, building on Dewey, try to implement a mode of analysis that pursues an open-ended, causal accounting of institutional malfunction that neither encompasses nor recommends any prepackaged ideological answers as policy. It does continuously pose significant and answerable questions. The test of the adequacy of their theory is whether or not it explains what it purports to explain; the test of the relevance of their theory is whether it is diagnostically significant and creative in identifying and resolving real problems, as identified above.

Third, when *neoclassicists* are compelled to employ their model of inquiry and generate policy recommendations derived therefrom, they discover that their model deprives them of creative institutional options in their quest for relevance. As an extension of both the first and second observations above, I note that the creation of *new* institutions can scarcely be brought on the agenda. The invention, recasting, and reinvigoration of correlated patterns of behavior is foreign to their perspective. Their options are limited to the "givens" of their model. Consider the following example:

Neoclassical recommendations concerning the provision of medical care would typically call for privatization of services, "market" allocation by providers of medical care, termination of "impure" price administration by organized hospitals or other care providers, pecuniary incentives to alter behavior, minimization of governmental involvement or supervision out of deference to market surveillance and fears of bureaucratic dominion, and rationing of access to care via market constraints. Compliance with this ethically reductionistic market model might well take precedence, for example, over concern about inequitable availability of care. These policy considerations derive from the price-theory model.

When an *institutionalist* is asked what kind of a medical delivery system should be generated, the answer would derive fundamentally from a Dewey-based model calling for a meticulous examination of causal phenomena observable in the existing structure, belief systems, health industry power systems, government's role, and the like, in an effort to identify where the obstructions and short falls are to be found. Administered prices paid, negotiated costs incurred, conflicts among organized power groups, quality of care actually available, professional and political control over the development and use of new knowledge, adequacy of supply of skilled personnel, and the like, would all enter the inquiry process as subject matter. But it is their causal interdependencies, linkages, and determinants that would be the object of analysis. What regressive beliefs and behaviors invoke the consequences observed? Hypotheses are created and cast against emerging evidences in search of understanding. Once attained, this understanding can then undergird a tentative but relevant progressive program of institutional creation, revamping and adjustment intended to extend and enhance the health care provisioning process. This increasing *understanding* of actual causal determinants of the malfunctioning of medical institutions undergirds the formulation of credible policy recommendations as institutional adjustments.

In sum, the pragmatic instrumentalist mode of inquiry provides philosophic bases for the creation of institutional economic theory. This model of inquiry supports and guides policymaking. Its normative dimensions serve neither relativistic nor absolutist goals or interests; they serve only the furtherance of inquiry and problem solving. This perspective serves no ideological enclave; it invites pluralistic explorations. Its character, use and relevance are under constant scrutiny. It does not generate new forms of impairment; it fosters open inquiry and creative applications.

Acknowledgments

The author wishes especially to thank Paul D. Bush and Edythe S. Miller for most helpful comments on an earlier draft.

Notes

1. In the future, he says, "there will be an increasing realization by theorists that rather radical change in questions and methods are required if they are to deliver, not practical, but theoretically useful results" (Hahn, 1991, p. 47). Also, for a brief overview of departures from orthodoxy, see Hodgson (1994).

2. The caption "pragmatic instrumentalism" has recently been reintroduced from Dewey's early work by Paul D. Bush (1993) to distinguish Dewey's version of instrumentalism from various other contemporary usages including those of Milton Friedman and Imre Lakatos.

3. The primary source for this model of inquiry is Dewey (1938).

4. This topic was the subject of an interesting exchange between Dewey and Philip Blair

Rice. See Dewey (1946, pp. 250–272). See also Dewey (1938, pp. 139–158), on "immediate knowledge."

5. A similar account will be found in Dewey (1938, p. 318).

6. J. Fagg Foster was professor of economics at the University of Denver from the mid-1940s until the mid-1970s.

7. On these and related matters, see Dewey (1938, pp. 496–497, 502–503).

8. Insightful comments of Paul D. Bush were incorporated into the preceding paragraph.

9. Insightful comments from Edythe Miller were incorported into the foregoing paragraph.

10. For an extensive critique along these lines, see Hodgson (1988, pp. 51–144).

11. For a characterization of this transformation see Debreu, (1991, pp. 1–7).

12. For a somewhat vigorous consideration of this, and related, matters, see Wiles and Routh (1984, pp. 1–77, 293–325).

13. Frank H. Hahn argues that the construct of "equilibrium" has significance for economic inquiry even if it is not perceived as having normative implications or of describing "a sequence of actual economic states [that] will terminate in an equilibrium state." The term is given a role in delineating the meaning and significance of agent rationality in the mainstream abstract model of a market economy. He writes, "an economy is in equilibrium when it generates messages which do not cause agents to change the theories which they hold or the policies which they pursue." The sense of quiescence remains. See Hahn (1973, pp. 4–5).

14. For examples and a critique, see Tool (1986, pp. 104–125).

15. On the distinction between "progressive" and "regressive" change, see Bush (1988, pp. 125–166).

References

Bauer, P.T., and B.S. Yamey. 1957. *The Economics of Under-developed Countries.* Chicago: University of Chicago Press.

Baumol, William J., John C. Panzar, and Robert D. Willig. 1982. *Contestable Markets and the Theory of Industry Structure.* New York: Harcourt Brace Jovanovich.

Becker, Gary S. 1976. *The Economic Approach to Human Behavior.* Chicago: University of Chicago.

Boulding, Kenneth. 1986. "What Went Wrong with Economics?" *American Economic*, 30 (Spring), 5–12.

Buchanan, James M., and Gordon Tullock. 1962. *The Calculus of Consent.* Ann Arbor: University of Michigan.

Bush, Paul D. 1988. "The Theory of Institutional Change." In M.R. Tool, ed., *Evolutionary Economics, Vol. 1, Foundations of Institutional Thought.* Armonk, N.Y.: Sharpe.

———. 1993. "Methodology of Institutional Economics." In Marc R. Tool, *Institutional Economics: Theory, Method, Policy.* Dordrecht: Kluwer.

Debreu, Gerard. 1991. "The Mathematization of Economic Theory." *American Economic Review*, 81 (March), 1–7.

DeGregori, Thomas R. 1985. *A Theory of Technology.* Ames: Iowa State University.

Dennis, Ken. 1994. "Formalism in Economics. In Geoffrey M. Hodgson, Warren J. Samuels, and Marc R. Tool, eds., *The Elgar Companion to Institutional and Evolutionary Economics*. Aldershot: Edward Elgar.

Dewey, John. 1938. *Logic: The Theory of Inquiry*. New York: Holt.

———. 1939. *Theory of Valuation*. Chicago: University of Chicago.

———. 1946. *Problems of Men*. New York: Philosophical Library.

Downs, Anthony. 1957. *An Economic Theory of Democracy*. New York: Harpers.

Dragan, J.C., and M.C. Demetrescu. 1991. *Entropy and Bioeconomics: The New Paradigm of Nicholas Georgescu-Roegen* (2nd ed.). Rome: Nagard.

Eichner, Alfred S. 1976. *The Megacorp and Oligopoly*. White Plains, N.Y.: Sharpe.

Etzioni, Amitai. 1991. "Eastern Europe: The Wealth of Lessons." *Challenge*, 34 (July/August), 4–10.

Foster, J. Fagg. 1981. "The Relation Between the Theory of Value and Economic Analysis." *Journal of Economic Issues*, 15 (December), 899–905.

Friedman, David D. 1990. *Price Theory*. Cincinnati: South-Western.

Friedman, Milton. 1953. *Essays in Positive Economics*. Chicago: University of Chicago.

Georgescu-Roegen, Nicholas. 1971. *The Entropy Law and the Economic Process*. Cambridge, Mass.: Harvard University.

Goodwin, Richard M. 1990. *Chaotic Economic Dynamics*. Oxford: Clarendon Press.

Hahn, Frank. 1973. *On the Notion of Equilibrium in Economics*. Cambridge: Cambridge University Press.

———. 1991. "The Next 100 Years." *Economic Journal*, 101 (January), 47–50.

Hahnel, Robin, and Michael Albert. 1990. *Quiet Revolution in Welfare Economics*. Princeton: Princeton University.

Hodgson, Geoffrey M. 1988. *Economics and Institutions*. Cambridge: Polity Press.

———. 1994. "Critique of Neoclassical Microeconomic Theory." In Geoffrey M. Hodgson, Warren J. Samuels, and Marc R. Tool, eds., *The Elgar Companion to Institutional and Evolutionary Economics*. Aldershot: Edward Elgar.

———. 1993. *Economics and Evolution*. Cambridge: Polity Press.

Homan, Paul T. 1932. "An Appraisal of Institutional Economics." *American Economic Review*, 22 (March), 15.

Klein, Philip A. 1980. "Confronting Power in Economics: A Programatic Evaluation." *Journal of Economic Issues*, 14 (December), 871–896.

———. 1986. "Reinventing the Square Wheel." In Philip A. Klein, *Handbook of Behavioral Economics*. New York: JAI Press.

———. 1987. "Power and Economic Performance: The Institutionalist View." *Journal of Economic Issues*, 21 (September), 1341–1377.

Kohler, Heinz. 1990. *Intermediate Microeconomics: Theory and Applications* (3rd ed.). Glenview, Ill.: Scott, Foresman.

Lawson, Tony. 1994. "The Limits of Econometrics." In Geoffrey M. Hodgson, Warren J. Samuels, and Marc R. Tool, eds., *The Elgar Companion to Institutional and Evolutionary Economics*. Aldershot: Edward Elgar.

Leontief, Wassily. 1971. "Theoretical Assumptions and Nonobserved Facts." *American Economic Review*, 61 (March).

Lower, Milton D. 1988. "The Concept of Technology Within the Institutionalist Perspective." In Marc R. Tool, ed., *Evolutionary Economics, Vol. 1, Foundations of Institutional Thought*. Armonk, N.Y.: Sharpe.

Miller, Edythe S. 1990. "Economic Efficiency." *Journal of Economic Issues*, 24 (September), 729.

———. 1994. "Theory of Economic Regulation." In Geoffrey M. Hodgson, Warren J. Samuels, and Marc R. Tool, eds. *The Elgar Companion to Institutional and Evolutionary Economics*. Aldershot: Edward Elgar.

Mirowski, Philip. 1986. "Mathematical Formalism and Economic Explanation." In Philip Mirowski, ed., *The Reconstruction of Economic Theory*. Boston: Kluwer-Nijhoff.

———. 1988. "The Philosophical Bases of Institutional Economics." In M. R. Tool, ed., *Evolutionary Economics, Vol. 1, Foundations of Institutional Thought*. Armonk, N.Y.: Sharpe.

———. 1989. *More Heat Than Light: Economics as Social Physics, Physics as Nature's Economics*. New York: Cambridge University.

Murrell, Peter. 1991. "Symposium on Economic Transition in the Soviet Union and Eastern Europe." *Journal of Economic Perspectives*, 5 (Fall), 3–161.

North, Douglass C. 1990. *Institutions, Institutional Change and Economic Performance*. Cambridge: Cambridge University.

Okun, Arthur M. 1981. *Prices and Quantities*. Washington, D.C.: Brookings Institution.

Robbins, Lionel. 1952. *On the Nature and Significance of Economic Science* (2nd ed.). London: Macmillan.

Simon, Herbert A. 1979. "Rational Decision Making in Business Organizations." *American Economic Review*, 69 (September), 493–513.

Spulber, Daniel F. 1989. *Regulation and Markets*. Cambridge, Mass.: MIT Press.

Thorson, Thomas Landon. 1970. *Biopolitics*. New York: Holt, Rinehart.

Tool, Marc R. 1985. *The Discretionary Economy*. Boulder: Westview Press.

———. 1986. *Essays in Social Value Theory*. Armonk, N.Y.: Sharpe.

———. 1993. *Institutional Economics: Theory, Method, Policy*. Dordrecht: Kluwer.

Trebing, Harry M. 1984. "Public Control of Enterprise: Neoclassical Assault and Neoinstitutional Reform." Journal of Economic Issues, 18 (June), 353–368.

———. 1987. "Regulation of Industry: An Institutionalist Approach." *Journal of Economic Issues*, 21 (December), 1707–1738.

———. 1994. "The Networks as Infrastructure: The Reestablishment of Market Power." *Journal of Economic Issues*, 28 (June).

Veblen, Thorstein B. 1961 *The Place of Science in Modern Civilization*. New York: Russell and Russell.

Watkins, John. 1992. "Neoclassical Economics as an Exercise in Ceremonialism: Economics as Physics Envy." Paper presented at meetings of the Association for Institutional Thought, Denver, Colorado, April.

Wiles, Peter, and Guy Rouths, eds. 1984. *Economics in Disarray*. Oxford: Basil Blackwell.

Williamson, Oliver. 1986. *Economic Organization: Firms, Markets, and Policy Control*. Brighton: Wheatsheaf.

Wilson, Edward O. 1978. *On Human Nature*. Cambridge: Harvard University.

Wray, L. Randall. 1990. *Money and Credit in Capitalist Economies: The Endogeneous Money Approach*. Aldershot: Edward Elgar.

11 AN ASSESSMENT

Philip A. Klein

Introduction

A careful reading of the essays in this volume offers much food for thought. As expected, the contributors have their own way of delineating both what they mean by *economic theory* and what role they envisage for theory. Beyond this, however, their discussions shed light on the factors that influence economists to espouse the views they hold.

No economist, no matter how dispassionate or objective, could react to all these essays which equal sympathy. Thus the present chapter should be seen as what it is—merely one reader's reactions to what has gone before. Having said that, it may be worth adding that this reader finds all of the essays—in various ways, to be sure—instructive and insightful, whether in the end the position is one he can support or not.

Indeed, it is useful to be reminded of what one can learn from people with whom one disagrees. More than this, of course, the essays reflect the current state of economics, particularly economic theory, with its great divide both in micro- and macroeconomics between interventionists and noninterventionists. Clearly the automatic assumption that the task of theory is to illumine policy debates is no longer (was it ever?) universally shared.

229

That there are other tasks that economic theory can perform is illuminated neatly in the introductory essay by Warren Samuels. Reflecting his heterodox orientation Samuels suggests that an economy is part ideology and so separation of the positive from the normative in the developing of economic theory is usually impossible. The "what is" usually acquires at least a patina of the normative by virtue of mere existence in an ideologically oriented world.

Mainly, Samuels does us a service by reminding us that there is a vast variety of types of theory in economics, differing in level of generality, structure, character, and rigor, although this by no means exhausts the sources of diversity in theory. Some theories find their justification in an appeal to reality, and others in their appeal to logic, easy quantification, and so on. It is helpful to recall that insofar as Samuels finds a justification for theory in "understanding" the economy or part of the economy, he invokes a group of justifications for theory that many diverse economists can share and that indeed, are quite independent of policy development. All economists—both those who look at that functioning admiringly and those who would offer various interventions to alter its performance— would presumably wish to understand the functioning of the economy better. As such, theory provides attractive possibilities for those who seek ways to legitimize existing aspects of the economy, aspire to greater scientific status for economics, and so forth. These roles for theory clearly venture into the second question raised at the outset: What factors influence the kind of theory to which economists are drawn? Viewed from this vantage point, the discussion serves to underscore that even the most positive and rigorous of economists can be influenced by normative or other factors into developing certain types of theory that presumably they might not have developed but for the special circumstances surrounding their own early schooling.

Samuels has, in sum, offered a useful introduction to the essays to follow by characterizing theory generally, suggesting the inherent limitations of theory, and only then considering the roles theory can play. His approach is, of course, encyclopedic: he puts down on paper virtually every possible role that could be assigned to economic theory.

Buchanan suggests that a "scientifically superior" way to view the economy and its functioning would be as a "spontaneous order." If I interpret this correctly, asking, "What are the objectives of such an economy?" is not unlike asking, "What are the objectives of any aspect of daily existence that operates "naturally"—that is, is found more or less in nature?" This is, we noted earlier, the essence of the noninterventionist position.

They argue that despite some problems, the market works remarkably

well. For this group, the problems interventionists are fixated on are short run and self-correcting. No doubt, interventionists would argue that non-interventionists regard as "tolerable" unemployment levels and inflation rates which interventionists would regard as intolerable. (We discuss this further below.) Non-interventionists, of course, would argue further that even if performance borders on the unacceptable, intervention is as likely—or more likely—to make things worse as to improve things. In any case, however, non-interventionists like Buchanan insist that the emphasis should be on how well free markets allocate resources.

Lawrence Klein, on the other hand, has chosen, as Keynesians of many stripes do, to focus on the recurring failure of the macroeconomy in many industrial market economies to provide for adequate stable growth without either unduly high rates of inflation or unemployment. Like many economists who are not in the orthodox mainstream, Klein, as we have seen, insists that much theory is normative. For Klein the ultimate test is the ability to predict. Prediction is important mostly if one wishes to monitor performance so as to modify it through interventionist policy. For Klein the Keynesian approach has been, as we have seen, vindicated by empirical tests and so has been able to provide the world with useful "Keynesian medicine."

It would be hard to imagine, in sum, two more diametrically opposed analyses or conclusions than those of Lawrence Klein and Buchanan. Buchanan would no doubt reply that there is no need to offer any medicine at all to so healthy a patient. Part of the explanation for the divergence between interventionists and noninterventionists in general may lie in a variant of the very old tendency to compare one system in ideal form with another as it actually operates. The more important part of the explanation for the differences noted here is that each of these economists looks at a different body of evidence and with different selective notions of what is important. These two papers do not really compare two ideals or two actual systems. Buchanan stresses the success of "the market" (that is, Western economies in actual operation) compared to centrally planned economies and compares the results to what in fact occurred in Eastern Europe. Klein, as was just noted, considers the failures of the market as reflected in unemployment and inflation rates and compares it not to a centrally planned ideal but to the implicit promise many see in a Keynesian model.

The differences observed, therefore, necessarily reflect divergent reactions to a basic question about economic performance. How much unemployment, inflation, or other divergence from current estimates of our economy's potential performance are we prepared to live with?

As such it is not easy to predict what the authors would conclude were they forced to compare the same two possibilities. Klein would no doubt grant that rigidly planned systems don't work but would nonetheless advocate interventionism to offset gross market failures (defined as unemployment rates, inflation rates, growth rates, and so on of the sort that all too often Western market economies now exhibit)—an alternative he regards as feasible. Buchanan would (and does) grant that the market has "warts" but would insist that efforts to remove them would lead to worse performance than living with the "warts." A critical difference, therefore, revolves around the critical reaction to the size and nature of the market's "warts." Buchanan, speaking for most noninterventionists, argues implicitly that "we" (all of us) can live with them. Indeed, Buchanan, with his view of the economy as a spontaneous order, would not describe the current blemishes as "warts" at all, if by "warts" one means departures from the ideal requiring activist policy. Klein, speaking for most interventionists would, I would guess, insist that the price in human misery of a noninterventionist course is too high.

In short, both Buchanan and Klein assure us that they believe in economic theory that is empirically based. Both believe they have formulated or endorsed economic theory that is consistent with the main facts of recent economic history. The "main facts" to which they point, of course, differ. Nonetheless they embrace radically different economic theory coming to radically different conclusions and with radically different policy implications. In the final analysis what is involved is a judgment call. In developing economic policy for the future (say, the next fifty years) and "learning from the past," what is most important? Should the failure of virtually all rigidly planned economies or the sometimes large deviations from the ideal in the inadequacies of the market in actual operation govern one's thinking? Arguably, both should. Klein doubtless distinguishes careful intervention from rigid planning. Buchanan would grant that there are failures in the performance of the market, but he regards them as more trivial than does Klein, and he thinks we can live with them more comfortably. He probably would not rule out all intervention (although he distrusts the policy makers), but he is undoubtedly comfortable with—and advocates far less—than Klein. The objective fact of, say, a 7 percent unemployment rate is, we have seen, one with which Buchanan can probably live more easily than Klein. (And we will see that other noninterventionists have other ways of explaining market results leading to noninterventionist policy implications.) The possibility that bringing down unemployment might take some central intervention and might entail an inflation rate greater than zero is one Klein can probably live with better than can Buchanan.

We have dwelled on the contrasts between Buchanan and Klein because they illustrate quite clearly the basic differences in the perspective of interventionists and noninterventionists. The other contributors to the volume can be broadly classified in one or another of these two groups.

In the end, we see, the economic theory embraced must be one that fits the normative perspective of the theorist. This institutionalist statement—that positive and normative cannot be separated—seems clear from the comparison just made but is one that neoclassical economists would deny.

One who would not deny it, of course, is Howard Sherman. In his essay he attempts, we have seen, to stake out the views of what he calls "critical Marxism." The principal difficulty that I find with his position is that in the end, critical Marxism appears to differ from institutionalism—and indeed from the Keynesianism (where they treat similar phenomena) exemplified by economists like Lawrence Klein—principally in the role they assign "class." The problem is that try as one can, it is, in my judgment, difficult to fathom the way in which critical Marxists use this term. In the two-class system of Marx, class was relatively easily defined. One either owned or one worked the means of production. It was easy to distinguish workers from capitalists. In contrast, at one point Sherman speaks of "a multitude of classes" but gives not a clue as to how these (many) classes are to be distinguished from each other.

Sherman repeatedly uses the phrase, "workers, women, and minorities." This phrase certainly covers a multitude of contemporary societal fissures, but whether all three groups can be lumped together as one class is questionable. The women's movement, for example, (which, of course, is by no means monolithic) has always attached great importance to "breaking the glass ceiling." Presumably a disproportionate effort (numerically) has been put into getting a relatively few women into the corporate managerial class. Shall we argue that once there, women suffer internal confusion because their sex and their class roles are in conflict? Is the notion of class conflict, basic in Marx, to be abandoned? Similarly, a significant effort has been made to establish an African American entrepreneurial class. Is this because the "true" interests of African Americans are bound up in having significant representation in the "capitalist" class? Or is this an illustration of how the prevailing capitalist culture is hoodwinking African American, into thinking this? Sherman does not comment on these questions, but by consistently referring to "workers, minorities, and women," he glosses over these problems and produces a system of categories, all presumably revolving around "class," which is not easy to comprehend, except that this is one (overlapping) way to refer to groups of people who have been exploited or disallowed from reaching their economic potential.

In short, Sherman appears to be trying to salvage something from Marx that is relevant to current economic and social organization, and for him that something must seemingly necessarily revolve around the distinctive position that critical Marxists give to class. But in the process class is divorced from the means of production, many people don't apparently know their "true" class interests, and there are "multitudes" of classes. The basis on which they may be identified and distinguished from other social or economic groups is nowhere explained. In the end enough other categories (gender, the attitude toward the environment, race, and so on) are introduced to cover the principal observable conflicts, but how critical Marxists are to be distinguished from other groups whose policy pre- scriptions critical Marxists endorse has been lost in the shuffle. In general, how we are to differentiate the "critical Marxist" view of theory from other interventionists view of theory remains ambiguous. At least this is one reader's assessment.

One school that looks askance on most intervention, on grounds that such efforts are not very likely to improve economic performance, is the rational-expectations approach. It is espoused here by its founder, John F. Muth. His essay, we have earlier noted, is built around his view of a number of recent contributions to the development of economic models. Much of modern mainstream theorizing is designed to be a contribution to modeling techniques rather than directly to the solution of economic problems. This is no doubt the origin of the charge that such contributions are not much help in improving economic policy. Its practitioners would reply that better modeling will in itself lead ultimately to analyses that can produce better policy, even though, as is the case with rational expectations, the ultimate efficacy of interventionist policy is called into question.

In economic expectations Muth largely dismisses both moving averages and the leading-indicator system. Of the latter he comments that the "system appeals to the intuition of many but has some limitations." No one denies this, of course, but he concludes, "Why is it important to predict an event that is difficult to determine after the fact?" Without claiming more than is appropriate for leading indicators, one may still reply that no system has yet produced better or more useful results. The Department of Commerce, for example, still reports monthly on the condition of the leading indica- tors. As such it is a principal forecasting method. No such regularly pub- lished monitoring technique has yet emanated from the debate about rational expectations. Another assessment, not from a disinterested observer to be sure, is that of Geoffrey, H. Moore (1983, p. 340): "The leading indicators have a noteworthy record. The composite index of twelve leading indicators . . . has turned down before every business cycle peak and turned up before every business cycle trough since 1948." The reliability of leading indicators has been tracked back in our economic history a good deal further than 1948.

Moving averages have never been utilized as anything more than smoothing devices. As such, they have limitations depending on what one is striving to do. But they have been far from displaced.

A fundamental question to be put to any analysis leading to the conclusion that public policy is ineffective is, "What is the objective of such analysis?" Muth comes to a conclusion that is distinctive. For Muth theory is not required for public policy because "empirical laws" will suffice. What he means by empirical laws is not clear. Muth's contention may be compared, for example, with Wesley Clair Mitchell's assertion that a necessary precursor to any theory is to ascertain the "main facts of economic history." To me this means empirical laws. For Mitchell, empirical regularities (often, of course, in the form of complex patterns of interrelationships among time series that he teased laboriously from the empirical record) become the basis for the hypotheses that, when confirmed, become economic theories. It would appear, therefore, that Muth is merely arguing that empirical regularities when established and confirmed (when they can be regarded as "laws") can be the basis of theory. But what he does not say is that historically confirmed empirical regularities undergird realistic theory. What the latter adds is explanatory in nature.

To argue that empirical regularities alone can form the basis of sound public policy is to argue that in medicine empirical regularities (pulse, respiration, temperature) can form the basis of sound medicine. These processes do indeed customarily exhibit a regular record that can be traced. (From observation of regular breathing one derives a "law" of respiration.) A malfunctioning of the body can and often does produce irregularities in these processes. But only by knowing how and why the processes become irregular (which means knowing how their regularity is related to health) can physicians use the regularities in treating patients. A long record of empirical regularities without any insight into why they exist (that is, without a theory) is one that can scarcely be reliably used for interventionist policy because one has no clues as to conditions under which the regularities become irregular.

In connection with the leading indicators, which Muth does not think much of, one has confidence in them not alone because they exhibit empirical regularities but because by now there is theory related to every leading indicator detailing why it leads. It is precisely because the indicator system, far from representing "measurement without theory," is indeed measurement *with* theory that it is persuasive and impressive. Measurement merely preceded theory.

Muth asserts that "inaccurate empirical information can be tolerated," an assertion that would no doubt cause Mitchell to turn over in his grave. Inaccurate information for Mitchell could be tolerated only if one did not wish to develop sound theory. (Muth notes that inaccurate empirical information was tolerated through most of the nineteenth century. Heterodox and mainstream economists would differ about the quality and reliability of the theory that emerged in the nineteenth century. Certainly the former would argue that economics paid—and perhaps is still paying—a very high price for inaccurate empirical information in the nineteenth century.) We may perhaps be in the throes of a semantic conflict here. If Muth means that historically accurate empirical laws can be the basis of public policy, then he is saying that to develop sound policy we must do all the work required to devise sound theory except actually articulate the theory that emerges. His last admonition is that policy requires experimentation and testing to ensure that the assumptions on which it is based are indeed appropriate to the task at hand. But this is precisely what realistic theory must reflect.

Despite these caveats, Muth has made a genuine contribution. For one thing, he has suggested weaknesses and limitations to rational expectations that its most enthusiastic champions tend to drown out. His words are worth listening to, both by rational-expectations advocates and by its critics. For another, he is deserving of attention because it is clear that he is very much concerned with whether or not models lead to "conclusions wildly different from the facts." The rational-expectations movement is not customarily credited with injecting greater concern for the facts into the construction of economic theory. (Some adherents to this approach would argue, for example, that if a model leads to conclusions that enable the analyst to make judgments that are appropriate, this is justification enough for the model, regardless of its accuracy in reflecting "the real world.") The most conventional of Marshallian models may be based on assumptions widely at variance with the facts and may indeed be subject to criticism on the grounds that the conclusions one draws from it are at variance with oligopoly theory, although the latter has never been regarded as satisfying or satisfactory. It is refreshing to learn that Muth criticizes models that are merely descriptive or lead to conclusions that cannot be drawn from the facts. This suggests that there is indeed a common ground on which economic theory can be debated—namely, relevance. This adds a new dimension to the old debate about rigor or relevance by suggesting that significant elements in the debate would agree now that rigor may be admirable and useful from a number of view points, but is cannot be regarded as a substitute for relevance.

In the end Muth has advanced areas of agreement among theorists of all shades by suggesting that relevance is critical, concern for change and growth cannot be bypassed, and expectations are a principal component linking the present state of economic activity with the future state. While rational expectations is customarily discussed as a viewpoint that leads to policy irrelevance, Muth appears to put the movement he launched on a quite different path. The only reason that it should matter whether a model leads to conclusions at variance with the facts or not would appear to be if the model is to be applied to changing the system. Otherwise, failure of conclusions to conform to reality would be a relatively unimportant footnote to consideration of economic models.

Boitani and Salanti take a different tack, focusing as they do on the several current descendants of Keynes's approach among macro theorists. They are, of course, in my judgment, entirely correct in echoing Samuels's view that the relationships among methodology, theoretical frameworks, and policy recommendations are more complex than is often assumed. The conclude that "the envisaged links between policy recommendations, theoretical frameworks, and methodological beliefs are dependent on the underlying (metaphysical?) point of view about the role of economic theories." I interpret this to mean that they would agree with Samuels that one's view of the role of theory is influenced by psychology, sociology, and perhaps pedagogical objectives quite as much as by the logic driving one's economics.

Boitani and Salanti make an interesting observation in suggesting that economists interested in "the long-run properties of economic systems" are probably less interested in policy debates. They suggest that policy tends to focus on short-run disturbances. Whether this view can be justified is open to question. Howard Sherman, who certainly qualifies as one whose interests involve the long-run tendencies of capitalist systems, is nonetheless one who argues that the proper role of economic theory is to change the way the system operates—and by change he means affecting what might be characterized as short-run stability.

Their view that all who delve in economic theory are not necessarily concerned with policy questions is certainly in line with some of the views of other contributors (e.g., Samuels and Muth) who argue that a role for theory may be simple to understand the operation of the system.

It seems to me that Boitani and Salanti have done a service in reminding us that the differences among theories can revolve not so much around the question of rigor or relevance as in how much of "reality" the theorists attempt to encompass in setting the parameters of the world to which they wish their theory to apply. Thus the differences among varieties of current Keynesian theorists can be explained by the way they handle expectations, uncertainty, market imperfections, rationality, and a host of other variables—all of which may never be incorporated simultaneously into a single theory. Theories can differ not only by their relation to potential public-policy debate, but by which aspects of reality they attempt to shed light on. As such, two theories may, in principle, differ in their treatment of a group of variables but be equally useful in policy formation. A priori it is difficult to say that a theory assuming dynamic properties derived from technological change is more or less crucial than a model that includes uncertainly on the part of economic agents or market imperfections. (And one could argue that such efforts could facilitate subsequent efforts to develop a model including all or a number of such variables.) Hence, different theories may be based on different groups of assumptions that illuminate different facets of that complex entity we call "reality."

In the end, they give some support to the view that overall perspective colors the approach that economists take toward theory. Thus economists who think in terms of perfecting the market might focus on, say, incentives and be predisposed to dismiss macropolicy even before they begin to develop theory. The relationship between the *weltanschauung* of the theorist and the ultimate theory produced is, therefore, one more strand to the heterodox assertion that separating the normative from the positive is at one level virtually impossible.

While Boitani and Salanti choose to discuss the role or roles for economic theory by focusing on varieties of Keynesian theory, Thomas Mayer chooses to focus on the light to be shed on the topic by consideration of varieties of monetarism. In particular, as we have seen, he finds two broad schools of thought within monetarism—the well-known position of Milton Friedman and a somewhat less well-known approach to monetarism associated with the work of Karl Brunner and Alan Meltzer.

Overall, monetarism as a theory clearly regards itself as having policy implications. It is true that Friedman distrusts discretionary policy. Monetarism in general can be formulated with some variation in these policy implications. Thus there is a role for theory in considering the effectiveness of discretionary policy even for a theory that in general finds little or no role for such policy. (Brunner and Meltzer, Mayer reminds us, are more flexible in this regard than Friedman.) One implication of the Mayer essay (with which at least Samuels, Tool, and Sherman would probably agree) is that "theory" can make a contribution, even when it is not accepted *in toto*, if it enlightens adherents of other schools or causes modifications in how such economists treat critical factors—in this case money and related monetary aggregates.

In general, Mayer's essay is useful because it illustrates how a discussion presumably focused rather narrowly on two contrasting schools of monetarist thought can have interesting implications for the broader questions on which this volume as a whole was designed to focus.

These views in turn may be contrasted with Eric Maskin's view that much theory is neither normative nor positive but rather concerned with providing a set of tools with which both normative and positive questions can be answered. He calls such theory "conceptual theory." Maskin's view is provocative. For one thing he is an economist who might be classified as a noninterventionist (although how he might be classified is not entirely clear from his paper) but who nonetheless agrees with many heterodox and Keynesian economists about the impossibility of separating the normative and positive. More generally, his approach takes us back to the "scientific method" perspective from which explanation and analysis can be separated from all normative matters. But it is important to remember that the normative-positive debate finds its origins in the classical efforts to develop theoretical models based on simplifying assumptions that made it easier to answer questions about how the economy operated. The debates of the past 150 years have revolved around how much simplification of reality can be justified in model building, recognizing that short of mere description, some simplifying is required if theory is to live up to its intrinsic requirement to have any capability of applying to more than one case. But here precisely has come the "controversy." Many would argue that economics has gone entirely too far in justifying precise and rigorous models, derived from excessive simplification of reality via "grossly" oversimplified assumptions. (We have already noted, in connection with the consideration of Boitani and Salanti's essay, that a critical aspect of theory construction is determing which aspects of reality to include.) Justifications of some recent models fairly simplified have not been long in coming. Types of models fairly far removed from reality have been vigorously defended, including "as if" models, models purporting to address only "stylized facts," simulations, models that are tested by their conformity to different aspects of "reality"—but never all of reality.

Of Maskin then, the question that must be asked is, "Are there normative implications involved in how the tool is constructed?" Institutionalists have always argued that the difficulty with the normative-positive distinction is that the assumptions that accompany "what is" involve acceptance of "what is"—at least for the purposes of the immediate analysis—and this is itself a normative position. It is not clear to me that Maskin avoids this problem. Both Buchanan and L.R. Klein would no doubt argue, for example, that they are making contributions to the economist's tool kit. Their theories are incompatible, and coherent policy cannot conform to the implications of both sets of analysis.

Marc Tool has written an essay squarely in the institutionalist tradition.

Tool takes it as given that there are "horrendous problems of malperformance" and therefore wastes no time in discussion of "the miracle of
the market." Nor does he question whether the role of theory is to "generate applicable theory" with which to cope with this malperformance.
Thus from the outset, the task he sets for himself is to consider how best
"the process of inquiry should be employed" to develop better (more
relevant) public policy. It seems to me that an economist who wished to
disagree with this approach would necessarily have to dispute the underlying premises: are there "horrendous problems of malperformance?"
(Buchanan for one would say no.) Is there a need for better theory with
which to address what malperformance is agreed to? Joining Buchanan
in saying no to this would perhaps be Muth and Maskin (for different
reasons).

We are left with an interesting question. If the other contributors would
not disagree with Tool's major premises, why are they not institutionalists? To the extent that institutionalism is indeed grounded in the logic of
John Dewey, it is possible to argue that there are theorists who would not
disagree with the thrust of the Dewey position summarized by Tool but
feel it is unnecessary to base interventionist policy on this bedrock. I would
argue that Tool has done a splendid job of setting out clearly and succinctly
a perspective that can be associated with Dewey: the continuity of human
experience, social inquiry as problem-solving activity, the critical importance
of viewing problems in any social science as being embedded in a specific
culture, the essential nontechnological and abductive nature of such inquiry,
and so on. All this requires of dissenters that they say wherein the reasoning has gone wrong and what should or could be placed in its stead. For
the rest, however, Dewey has been controversial. Institutionalists may
regard the Dewey assertion that theory have "warranted assertibility" as
convincing, and this is Dewey's way of grounding theory in reality. There
are counterassertions, represented in some of the essays in this volume,
that theory need not be linked in reality if it helps in understanding reality.
Institutionalists, moreover, are in agreement on their insistence on the
rejection of the normative-positive duality. They have not yet convinced
many mainstream economists of the truth of this position. Why have they
failed to do this?

For the rest, Tool lays out carefully the institutionalist alternative to
mainstream inquiry. It is fair to assert that the mainstream response in the
past quarter century has been to ignore this line of attack and not to
respond to it. There are disputes among mainstream economists on such
questions as how and if utilities are to be regulated, how a hundred years
later to view the antitrust laws, and in what way (if at all) they should be

enforced. More generally mainstream economists ignore the Debreu assertion to which Tool calls our attention that "values are imprinted on the economist by his study of mathematics." Tool is on target, in my judgment, in reminding us that a critical question with which economics should contend is, "Which questions need to be asked?" Do economists in general wrestle with the most critical questions, the ones to which the tools they favor can be most readily applied, or is there no difference? Are the differences in the tools economists prefer to work on and with, or with the problems with which we ought to contend, or both?

When Tool quotes Foster's view that "it is theory that tells us which facts to gather and how to arrange them for analysis," it is clear that Foster was only echoing Mitchell's assertion of many years ago that the initial task in developing theory is "to get the facts." A major controversy among economists is over the correctness of that ancient Mitchell maxim.

Finally, Tool states the controversy between mainstream economists and many heterodox economists—that for the heterodox with their avowedly normative approach the task of economists, and hence the role of its theory, must be to conduct inquiry into how to "enhance the provisioning process" whereas mainstream economists, sufficiently comfortable with the status quo to be comfortable as well with positive analysis, are content to let the discipline revolve around understanding the allocation that is the assumed heart of any capitalist economy. The assumptions back of this allocation they assert are not only convenient but need not be questioned.

A Perspective on the Role of Theory

What we see, of course, is that different economists holding different views look at the same historic record and come to radically different conclusions with radically different implications for the efficacy of different economic theories.

What finally are we to conclude from our review of diverse economists and their respective views of the role of economic theory? One conclusion would appear to be that the exercise we have conducted confirms some of Samuels's views of the various roles economic theory plays. It is difficult to find an economic theorist whose dispassionate study of economic theory, however defined, comes to conclusions with which the economist is personally very uncomfortable. We are talking about what can be called the sociology of knowledge, á la Karl Mannheim, applied to economic theorists. What does the expression "This is an idea whose time has come" mean when applied to economic theory? Partly it means pertinence to current problems.

The views of mercantilists made it appropriate that Smith would try to dispute their "erroneous" ideas about the origins of the wealth of nations. The acceptance of Smith's world, including his paradigm with its basic assumptions, made Ricardo's concentration on distribution seem appropriate. The advent of the Great Depression made continued emphasis on distribution seem misguided in view of the crying need to reask Smith's question, "What determines national income and output?" The persistence of serious problems with inflation in the 1970s made the questioning of the adequacy of Keynes to answer the questions that needed asking seemed appropriate as well.

In the historical sense, then, economic theory does not appear in a vacuum, unrelated to the questions that have arisen. But beyond this economists are very much the product of their background, their training, their *weltanschauung*—of the things that produce their value system. This is as true of economists who insist theory toils in the service of a "positive" science as it is for those who would grant that theory toils in an admittedly normative discipline. (This view will perhaps be more readily accepted by heterodox economists than by orthodox economists.) In a real sense, we would assert the contributors to this volume have, therefore, inadvertently but collectively reconfirmed a view of economic theory that was expressed many years ago by Leo Rogin (1956, pp. 1–3):

> Economics is a science of fact. The validity of a system of economic theory ... depends upon the adequacy of its correspondence with fact. This test has been applied by the protagonists of contending systems of economic theory, and by critics and historians of economic thought. Yet it has persistently failed to resolve fundamental disagreement as to what should constitute the principles of economics.
>
> Mere correspondence between the premises of a theory and the complex and devious flux of historical experience is hardly the criterion of a theory's pretensions to validity.... There remains the alternative ... that the selective appeal expressed in the premises relates to, and is in some sense adequate to, relevant facts. Relevant to what? To the guidance of policy ... even the original progenitor of a theory may be unaware of the extent of its historical and practical contingence.... This merely points to the circumstance that the selective appeal to fact is subordinated to the theorist's sense of values.

In short, we may presume that all economists pursue the scientific method, and we may presume that most are honest scholars trying to derive if not scientific truth, at least greater genuine insight (ultimately if not necessarily immediately) into the operation of the real economy. But evidence that one economist finds convincing another does not. An unemployment rate of 7 percent may be acceptable to one and a signal for vigorous intervention to another. If, therefore, we return to our basic division of the economic theorists into interventionists and noninterventionists, we may see the accuracy of Rogin's analysis. The two groups may be distinguished by their reaction to identical macroevidence. Interventionists would be those who conclude from their theoretical work that the performance of the economy can be improved by interventions (either, micro, macro, or external) and, on the other hand, noninterventionists, who on the same basis conclude the contrary—that "leaving it to the market," however painful this may be, is in the long run the best "policy" to pursue. It is highly unusual—almost unheard of—for an adherent to one position to conclude after a spate of analytical work that his findings have forced him or her to the contrary conclusion. The most famous exception is the transition from the Keynes of the *Treatise on Money* to the Keynes of the *General Theory*. In more mundane economic debate one possible exception was Koopman's (1965, p. 231) ultimate acknowledgement in the mini-*methodenstreit* between the Burns-Mitchell school of cyclical analysis and the econometricians who studied instability that the Burns-Mitchell approach, in the then state of knowledge, may not have been too inefficient a way to proceed. So viewed it is not surprising that monetarists are more impressed with the relationships they find between changes in the money supply and subsequent economic activity, while nonmonetarists are impressed with changes in economic activity and subsequent changes in the money supply. Neither can convincingly claim that it alone bases its findings on the empirical record.

I cannot claim to be surprised then that I conclude that economic theorists—in what they choose to study, in how they study it, and in the conclusions they come to—are very much influenced by factors that shaped them as scholars and as human beings and that their work hence reflects their own value system. It is no more surprising that rational-expectations adherents found a way to deny the interventionist implications of Keynesian analysis than it is that modern Keynesians found a way to come to interventionist conclusions in models that also managed at the same time to include rational expectations. The broader implication, of course, is, as we have previously asserted, that "positive" economic analysis is no more "value free" than normative economic analysis.

A far more critical question, therefore, for economists to ponder than whether, say, monetary changes or aggregate activity changes occur first is the overarching question, "Does work in economic theory color economists' overall attitude, or does overall attitude color work in economic theory?"

Clearly they influence each other, and clearly, too, Rogin was correct in his view of the effect of a system of values on economic research. In this connection, E.S. Phelps (19, p. 49) recently commented,

> The rational expectationists adopted ... the "island scenario" because, as is often suggested, they were by training more comfortable with market clearing than with job rationing ... but also, and much more importantly I suspect, because a heavy part of their training and interests lay in econometrics, in which the convention of the period—in fact, the year and the quarter-year—had become ingrained. Had the econometrics of the 1960s routinely used daily and weekly data interspersed with lower frequency data, as many econometricians are beginning to do now, the postulate that in each "period," hence in each day, all prices and wages are reestablished, would have been seen to be the absurdity that it is, and the entire New Classical school might never have had so long a run.

The implications of what Phelps is saying are not surprising to an institutionalist. Despite adherence to the scientific method, the biggest mistake an economist (or any other scientist) can make is to fail to remember that scientific analysis is never value-free. Not only is the tradition of (mostly static) equilibrium analysis thoroughly established in the training of most economists, but their methodological predisposition proceeds often by convention. This is particularly noteworthy in recent work in economic theory. New classical theory has the great appeal that it enabled economists who were uncomfortable with the implications of Keynesian analysis to restore a crucial part of the methodological world that Keynes had destroyed. Whether that destruction proves a temporary diversion or something more permanent is part of the contemporary debate.

It is thus clear that each economist who has contributed to this volume continues to find vindication of his chosen approach in ongoing research. This is neither new nor surprising. What have we learned about the role of economic theory? I think we must conclude that many economists continue to insist that the basic role of theory is derived from its role as critical base of improving public policy. (There are economists who make this link less direct. Muth is certainly one.) A critical role for theory is to help devise the most effective policy for achieving whatever economic goals societal consensus pushes into the forefront. But beyond this there are other roles for theory that cannot be gainsayed. A number of roles involve work that is less directly related to policy but is indirectly or ultimately linked to improved policy.

In the final analysis, therefore, economic theory also plays a role or roles more sociological in character and related to some of the matters Warren Samuels discussed in the first essay. Economic theory, and more particularly economic methodology, appears to play a part in bonding individual economists to schools of economic thought. There are complex relations between the evidence economists look at and the training they have received with which to do the looking. That training, in turn, reflects the surrounding contemporary culture in subtle and complex ways. Such an atmosphere in which to conduct the most scholarly and dispassionate research is unavoidable. It needs most essentially only to be recognized and factored into the process by which economists derive their conclusions.

This conclusion will be disturbing only to those who regard economists as somehow disconnected from society—as Olympian analysts examining evidence dispassionately and, of course, with absolute objectivity. As we have noted earlier, there is nothing in the conventional pursuit of economic analysis by means of the scientific method that precludes recognizing the influence of surrounding culture and values on myriad aspects of what economists do. As the essays in this collection attest, a major predisposing factor is not necessarily whether or not scholars look at "reality" for confirmation of a tentative hypothesis, but on what part of reality they choose to place the emphasis. Rather than deny it, the prudent scientist faces this directly and takes it into account in his or her analyses.

The Role of Economic Theory: A Summing Up

Inquiry in any field is purposive. The basic question to be faced in judging theory is, "Whose purpose should be served?" It seems to me that even those in this volume who argue that a basic role for theory is to increase understanding but not necessarily to develop public policy are being careful to move themselves beyond the charge sometimes leveled at mainstream theorizing by heterodox economists—that theory is simply an exercise in intellectual gymnastics and is therefore its own reward. Whether the charge is justified can be determined insofar as the contributors to this volume are concerned. If we classify the contributors broadly into interventionists and noninterventionists, we can say that Samuels, Klein, Sherman, Boitani and Salanti, and Tool are all clearly interventionists and would (and do) in the end, whatever else they say, assert that a principal function of theory is to help improve public policy by advancing the theory from which it is derived. What of the noninterventionists? Buchanan, the most noninterventionist of the contributors, is careful to distinguish his view of economic theory from the familiar (and quintessentially noninterventionist) theory of Lionel Robbins. For Buchanan the role of theory is to explain individual

exchange relationships—how, in fact, allocation works. Although he carefully eschews any attempt to use theory for micromanagement, there is
nonetheless throughout the notion that we do not yet understand all we
should about these exchange relationships. There is a place for "improving"
economic science. (It would scarcely need improving if our understanding
were perfect and the operation of the economy correspondingly perfect.)
Many economists would disagree with Buchanan's denigration of Keynes
and Keynesians (in his view they were given "quasi-scientific status").
Buchanan presumably finds their contributions small because they made
incorrect assumptions. Basically the economy is not "broke" and so doesn't
need their fixing. Buchanan finds the major role for economic theory to lie
in convincing the community that market principals do work. In the end,
this will require demonstration based on a viable definition of what
"working" means.

Mayer concentrates on an appraisal of modern monetarism, but from
his assessment it is clear that he agrees that the role of economic theory
is found ultimately in the answer to "how useful it prove[s] in advancing
our evolving understanding." He underscores this point by considering the
effect of monetarist theory on the understanding of nonmonetarists concerning the operation of the economy. Mayer goes further in acknowledging
that all theories are part ideology. He is thus in the camp of those who
agree that theory is rarely value free. He includes Keynesian and classical
theories as well as monetarism in this characterization.

Muth is easier to characterize. Despite his rejection of much that is
common to interventionists, he, too, judges economic theory by its contribution to "the well-being of an economy." Clearly "well-being" has a
distinctly normative ring to it, although its precise formulation can be in
dispute. Is it Buchanan's market system as opposed to "socialism" or Klein's
full employment as opposed to unacceptable unemployment and recurring
recession that is to be faced and ameliorated? In any case, by suggesting
that all that is required for public policy is "empirical laws" derived,
presumably, from the empirical record, Muth suggests that public policy
should derive directly from what Vining would call the "hypothesis seeking" stage rather than from the "hypothesis testing" stage of economic
analysis.

Maskin argues that much economic theory is neither normative nor
positive but what he calls "conceptual" economic theory. As such he belongs
with the majority of contributors in this volume who argue that the role of
economic theory is to help understand the economy better. Beyond this,
however, it is not entirely clear whether, in his view, economic theory is
merely to understand the economy or to improve the economy. He offers

a clue, however. His illustrations concerning the role of economic theory involve two from modern theory that he terms "prominent"—signaling and perfect equilibrium. These topics may be contrasted with the combination of social, political, and economic issues—income distribution, racism, sexism, concentrated economic power, widespread unemployment and inflation, and so on, which are the subjects toward which economic theory is directed in a number of the other essays. Maskin would argue no doubt that he is not suggesting that the latter are unimportant but that "abstract theory" is one step removed from these applications. Whether this means that the methodological approach taken by any given economist is merely a matter of preference or reflects one's personal views about whether intervention is a necessary implicit focus for economic theory is thus a question to be addressed. (That is, Maskin's essay raises legitimate questions about how far removed "basic research" can be from policy questions and still be labeled "relevant." It is perhaps significant, in this connection, that the word "policy" never appears in Maskin's essay.

There is some evidence that economists, as scholars in many fields, often talk past each other rather than to each other. Nonetheless, the contributors have offered much food for thought in the diverse ways in which they have tackled the basic assignment.

In the end, Buchanan and Sherman, perhaps as close to polar opposites as we have in this group, would agree that the role of economic theory is "to understand the economy we in fact have." The difference is that Sherman would add "in order to change it" and Buchanan would add "in order mostly to appreciate it."

References

Koopmans, Tjalling. 1965. "Additional Comment." In R.A. Gordon and L.R. Klein, *Readings in Business Cycles*, Vol. 10. Homewood, Ill.: Irwin.

Moore, Geoffrey H. 1983. *Business Cycles, Inflation, and Forecasting* (2nd ed.). National Bureau of Economic Research, Studies in Business Cycles, No. 24. Cambridge, Mass.: Ballinger.

Phelps, E.S. 19.

Rogin, Leo. 1956. *The Meaning and Validity of Economic Theory*. New York: Harper.

About the Authors

Andrea Boitani studied economics at the Universities of Roma and Cambridge. He has been assistant professor of economics at the Catholic University of Milan and is now associate professor at the University of Perugia. He is author of articles on post-Keynesian and New Keynesian economics, privatization policy, and the economics of innovation. He is presently working on a book on the New Keynesian research program.

James M. Buchanan was born October 3, 1919, in Murfreesboro, Tennessee. He currently holds the positions of advisory general director, Center for Study of Public Choice, and Harris University Professor, George Mason University, Fairfax, Virginia and is the holder of the Nobel Prize in Economic Science, 1986. Professor Buchanan received his B.A. from Middle Tennessee State College in 1940, his M.S. from the University of Tennessee in 1941, and his Ph.D. from the University of Chicago in 1948. Along with Gordon Tullock, Professor Buchanan is generally recognized as a cofounder of the public-choice (or perhaps, Virginia) school of economic thought. The following is a short list of his most well-known major works: *Explorations into Constitutional Economics* (1989); *Economics: Between Predictive Science and Moral Philosophy* (1987); *The Reason of Rules* (with Geoffrey Brennan, 1985); *Freedom in Constitutional Contract* (1978); *The Limits of Liberty* (1975); *The Calculus of Consent* (1962).

Lawrence R. Klein is the Benjamin Franklin Professor of Economics at the University of Pennsylvania, was the founder of Wharton Econometric Forecasting Associates, and is a former chairman of their Scientific Advisory Board. He is also principal investigator of Project LINK, an international research group for the statistical study of world trade and payments.

249

Professor Klein is the author of many articles and books in economics, specializing in econometrics. He is past president of the American Economic Association, the Eastern Economic Association, and the Econometric Society. He is a member of the American Academy of Arts and Sciences, the American Philosophical Society, and the National Academy of Sciences. He has often been an adviser to the U.S. government and many international organizations. He is the holder of several honorary degrees from universities around the world and in 1980 was awarded the Alfred Nobel Memorial Prize in economic sciences.

Philip A. Klein is professor of economics at the Pennsylvania State University. He obtained his B.A. and M.A. from the University of Texas and his doctorate from the University of California at Berkeley. He has taught in a number of colleges and universities both in the United States and abroad. He was for many years on the staff of the National Bureau of Economic Research and, at the present time, is research associate at the Center for International Business Cycle Research at Columbia University. He is an adjunct scholar at the American Enterprise Institute and several times has been an academic visitor at the London School of Economics. He has consulted for a number of international organizations and has received three Fulbright faculty fellowships over the years. He has worked with Geoffrey H. Moore for more than thirty years, and they have published widely together. Klein has also written extensively on institutional economics and is a past president of the Association for Evolutionary Economics. He is currently an associate editor of the *International Journal of Forecasting*.

Eric S. Maskin has been professor of economics at Harvard University since 1985. He taught at MIT from 1977 to 1984. He was educated at Harvard and was a postdoctoral fellow at Cambridge University. He was also on two separate occasions a visiting fellow at Cambridge.

Thomas Mayer is professor emeritus of economics at the University of California, Davis. Previously he taught at Michigan State University, Notre Dame University, and as a visitor at the University of California, Berkeley, and West Virginia University. His main fields are monetary policy, applied macroeconomics, and methodology. His publications include *Truth Versus Precision in Economics, Money Banking and the Economy* (with J. Duesenberry and R. Aliber), *Monetarism and Macroeconomic Policy, The Structure of Monetarism, Permanent Income, Wealth and Consumption, Intermediate Macroeconomics* (with D. Rowan), *Monetary Policy in the*

United States, and articles in professional journals. He edited *The Political Economy of American Monetary Policy*.

John F. Muth teaches production management in the School of Business at Indiana University, Bloomington. He studied industrial engineering at Washington University (St. Louis) and economics at Carnegie-Mellon University.

His books include *Planning Production, Inventories, and Work Force*, with C.C. Holt, F. Modigliani, and H.A. Simon, and *Operations Management: Analysis for Decisions* with G.K. Groff. He is the author of "Optimal Properties of Exponentially Weighted Forecasts" (*Journal of the American Statistical Association*, 1960) and "Rational Expectations and the Theory of Price Movements" (*Econometrica*, 1961). Recent work is concerned with the learning curve (*Management Science*, 1986) and a theory of the production function. A monograph about this stream of research is in preparation. Other recent research is in automatic programming of numerically controlled machine tools, group technology, and networks of deterministic queues.

Andrea Salanti graduated from the Catholic University of Milan in 1977. Since 1978 he has been assistant professor and is now associate professor at the University of Bergamo. He is author of recent articles on economic methodology in *Kyklos, HOPE, Economic Notes* and *Economics and Philosophy*. He is currently working on a book on the past and current debates in economic methodology.

Warren J. Samuels is professor of economics at Michigan State University. He specializes in the history of economic thought and methodology, law and economics, and public expenditure theory. He is the author of *The Classical Theory of Economic Policy* and *Pareto on Policy*, as well as numerous articles, and the editor of *Research in the History of Economic Thought and Methodology*. Five volumes of his collected papers were published in 1992 by Macmillan Press Ltd. His current research is principally on the concept of the invisible hand.

Howard J. Sherman is professor of economics at University of California, Riverside. His approach may be described as radical or critical Marxian political economy. He has written a number of books and articles in macroeconomic theory, culminating in *The Business Cycle: Growth and Crisis under Capitalism* (Princeton University Press, 1991). He has written two books and a number of articles in comparative economic analysis, the most recent being a coauthored book, *Comparing Economic Systems* (Harcourt-Brace-Jovanovich, 1989, 2nd ed.). He has also written two books and a number of articles on radical or Marxian economic theory, the most recent being *Foundations of Radical Political Economy* (M.E. Sharpe, 1987).

Marc R. Tool is professor emeritus of economics at California State University, Sacramento and editor emeritus of the *Journal of Economic Issues* (1981–1991). He is past president of the Association for Evolutionary Economics (AFEE). He is the author of *The Discretionary Economy* (1979, 1985), *Essays in Social Value Theory* (1986), and of several articles for collected volumes. He is the editor of *An Institutionalist Guide to Economics and Public Policy* (1984), *Evolutionary Economics, I & II* (1988), and coeditor of *A Handbook on Institutional and evolutionary Economics* (forthcoming). He was the recipient of the AFEE Veblen-Commons Award in 1988.

Index

AD-AS macro models, 135
AFL-CIO, 83
Africa, 73
African-Americans, 84, 234
aggregate demand
  in Brunner-Meltzer monetarism, 174, 179
  in new Keynesian economics, 13, 136, 139, 145
  in post-Keynesian economics, 133–4
aggregate supply, 13, 136, 145
allocative efficiency, 218
allocative inefficiency, 103
American Revolution, 85
analytical tools, 29, 33
antitrust laws, 209, 241
as if methodology, 123, 128–9, 135, 163
aspiration level model, 104
assumptions, 28
asymmetric information, 13, 137, 141, 143–6
attention, concentration of, 3, 34, 40
Australia, 73
Austrian economics, 32, 59
axiomatic theory, 220

balance-of-payments analysis, 7, 72
behavioral cost analysis, 198
blacks, *see* African-Americans

bounded rationality, 198
Boyle's law, 110
Brunner-Meltzer monetarism, 14, 159, 160, 161, 171–5, 181n.14, 181–2n.15, 239
  monetary policy in, 176, 178–9
  rhetoric of, 172–3
  theory of income determination in, 173–5
business-cycle analysis
  in Keynesian economics, 139–40, 143, 144
  in macroeconomics, 62
  in monetarism, 162, 163

California, 83
Canada, 73
capital expansion, 64
capital flows, 72
capital formation, 64
capital gains taxes, 82, 85
capitalism
  in critical Marxian economics, 8, 82–4, 86, 93, 234
  in institutionalism, 209
  in neoclassical economics, 78
  in post-Keynesian economics, 129, 132, 133
capital marginal efficiency, 6, 64
capital markets, 13, 143–6
cardinal utility theory, 208

catallaxy, 52, 56, 59
Cauchy-Pareto output distribution,
    11
central banks, 14, 161, 162, 169, 177,
    182n.20
Central Europe, 58
ceteris paribus assumptions, 3, 34,
    128
Chicago monetarism, see quantity
    theory
China, 73, 78
Chrysler Corporation, 83
class conflicts, 8, 9, 78, 79, 81, 86–7,
    234
  economic, 77, 81, 82–3
  ideological, 77, 81, 85
  social-political, 77, 81, 83–5
classical economics, 124 see also
    neoclassical economics
  Keynesian economics compared
    with, 65–6
  new Keynesian economics
    compared with, 135, 139
  post-Keynesian economics
    compared with, 126, 127, 131–2
  postrevolutionary movement and,
    48, 53, 54, 57
  quantity theory compared with,
    163, 165
class relations, 9, 81, 86
Coase theorum, 44n.11
Cobb-Douglas production function,
    11, 112
collective bargaining, 82
commercial trade flow analysis, 7, 72
commodity prices, 72
common paradigms, 25
communism, 50–1
Communist Party, 86
competition, 124, see also imperfect
    competition; perfect competition
concepts, 3, 23
conceptual economic theory, 15–6,
    187–94, 239–40, 247–8
  perfect equilibrium in, 15–6, 188,
    191–4, 247
  signaling in, 15, 188–91, 247
confirmed hypotheses, 31
consistent expectations, 71–2

constitutional economics, 56, 59
constitutional framework, 48, 52–3,
    58
consumption
  propensity to, 6, 64, 100–1, 167–8
  stable, 165
contestable market theory, 209, 221
convergence, 102
coordination failures, 129, 137–9,
    140
cost-benefit analysis, 221
credit markets, 13, 143–6
critical Marxian economics, 8–9,
    77–94, 233–4
  empiricism and, 78, 87–8
  historical approach in, 78, 86–7
  materialism and, 87–8
  rationalism and, 78, 87–8
  relational (holistic) approach in, 8,
    78, 79–81
  scientific determinism and, 8, 9,
    78, 89–92
  theory and ethics in, 92–3
  types of conflicts in, 81
criticism, 3, 35, 36
Czechoslovakia, 58

data envelopment analysis, 103
deductive reasoning, 3, 25, 34
  in institutionalism, 16, 202–3,
    207–8, 216, 217
deficits
  Brunner-Meltzer monetarism on,
    174
  quantity theory on, 166–7, 170–1
demand-side functions
  in institutionalism, 208
  in Keynesian economics, 64, 65–6,
    145
democracy, 83–4
deregulation, 70
description, 29, 30, 35
desirability, 3, 24
determinism, 26–7, 108–9
  scientific, 8, 9, 78, 89–92
Dewey, John, 16, 17, 88, 197,
    199–207, 217, 222, 241
diffusion of information, 113, 114

discretionary monetary policy, 14,
    176–9, 239
discursive roles, 33–4
discussion, frameworks for, 3, 33, 35,
    40, 41
Duhem-Quine thesis, 148

Eastern Europe, 58, 89, 232
econometric models, 7, 69, 101, 172
economic class conflicts, 77, 81, 82–3
economic expectations, 98–100
economic models, 104–5
economic order, 32, 40
*Economics of Imperfect Competition,
    The*, 131, 133
economic structure, 8, 79–80, 81
education/salary correlation, 188–9
effective demand, 65, 124, 125, 126,
    132–5, 137
efficiency wages, 141–2, 143–4,
    150n.28
empirical laws, 101, 115, 235, 247
empirical regularities, 100–1, 235–6
empiricism
    in Brunner-Meltzer monetarism,
        172
    in critical Marxian economics, 78,
        87–8
    logical, 28
    in neoclassical economics, 78
    in quantity theory, 164, 165, 169
employment, *see also* unemployment
    full, 13, 133, 139
    monetarism and, 161
    post-Keynesian economics and,
        129, 130, 133
endowment theory, 198
environmental conflicts, 8, 81, 85
environmental issues, 7, 74
epistemology, 34
equilibrium
    in conceptual economic theory,
        189–91
    in institutionalism, 219–20
    in post-Keynesian economics, 12,
        129–31
equity bases, 143–4
equity rationing, 144

error-learning expectations models,
    165–6
errors in variables models, 102,
    103
ethics
    in critical Marxian economics,
        92–3
    in institutionalism, 220
exchange relationships, 5, 52
expectancy theory, 10, 104, 106–7
expectations, 97, 98–103
    consistent, 71–2
    economic, 98–100
    implicit, 102
    rational, *see* rational expectations
        model
experimental economics, 59
explanation, 29, 30, 35
exponentially weighted moving
    averages, 99
externalities, 137–9
extrinsic rewards, 106–7

facts, 24–5
    stylized, 20, 30, 129
    theory-laden, 30
fatalism, 89–90
Federal Reserve, 14, 169–70, 171,
    176–9, 180
firm, theory of the, 10, 107–8, 110,
    115
Fisher effect, 134
flow-of-funds accounting (F/F), 7, 72,
    73
foreign-exchange markets, 72
free will, 8, 77, 78, 89–92
French Revolution, 85
Friedman, Milton, 14, 89, 99, 101,
    123, 129, 135, 207, *see also*
    quantity theory
full employment, 13, 133, 139
fundamental psychological law, 100
futures data, 7, 72, 129

game theory, 2
    new Keynesian economics and,
        137, 142

postrevolutionary movement and,
     55–6, 59–60
GDP, 167, 176–7, 179
gender conflicts, 8, 79, 81, 84–5, 86,
     87
general equilibrium theory, 12, 28,
     59
     Keynesian economics and, 128–9,
          136, 137, 138
*General Theory of Employment,
     Interest, and Money, The*, 61, 62,
     66, 122, 130, 131, 132, 133, 244
Germany, 6, 63
GNP, 70
Gorbachev, Mikhail, 84
government, 26, *see also* deficits;
     interventionism;
     noninterventionism
     public-interest theory of, 162, 163
government bonds, 144
Granger causality tests, 170
Great Britain, 54
Great Depression, 242–3
     Keynesian economics and, 5, 6, 55,
          63, 64, 231
     monetarism and, 178
     quantity theory and, 168
"green" macroeconomic theory, 7, 74
Greenwald-Stiglitz model, 140, 141

hegemonic paradigms, 25
heuristic role of theory, 29, 32, 33–4,
     37
household, theory of the, 115
hypotheses, 30–1
     confirmed, 31
     in institutionalism, 16
     in social inquiry, 203

idealism, 54–5, 87
idea systematizing, 33, 40
ideological class conflicts, 77, 81, 85
ideology, 4, 18, 27, 29, 36, 40, 41
immigration, 72
imperfect competition
     in new Keynesian economics, 13,
          137–40, 145

in post-Keynesian economics,
     12–3, 131–5
imperfect information, 102
implicit expectations models, 102
income determination, theory of,
     161, 173–5
increasing returns, 137–8, 142,
     149n.22, 150n.23
indexation, 142, 150n.31
India, 73
inductive reasoning, 3, 16, 25,
     202–3
inefficiency, 97–8, 103–7
     allocative, 103
     in rational expectations model,
          9–10, 11
     technical, 103
inequity theory, 10, 104, 105
inflation
     in Keynesian economics, 67, 68–9,
          73
     in monetarism, 14, 161, 176
innovations, adoption of, 113–4
input
     inequity theory and, 105
     Keynesian economics and, 123,
          143
     production functions and,
          112–3
input-output analysis, 5, 59, 73
input pricing, 54, 55
inside information, 189–90
insiders-outsiders models, 142
institutionalism, 2, 9, 16–7, 78,
     197–224, 231, 233, 240–2, 245
     character of inquiry in, 214–7
     critical Marxian economics
          compared with, 78, 82, 86, 89
     economic order in, 32
     human focus and context of
          inquiry in, 210–12
     liberal, 78, 82
     monetarism compared with, 163
     outcomes of inquiry in, 217–21
     purposes of inquiry in, 207–10
     radical, 78
     scope of inquiry in, 212–4
     social inquiry in, 197, 199–207
instrumental-value theory, 206

interest rates, 101
  foreign, 72–3
  in Keynesian economics, 72–3, 144
  in macroeconomics, 62
  in monetarism, 162, 179
  in post-Keynesian economics, 130
  in quantity theory, 167–8, 170
international trade, 64, 66, 72–3
intertemporal coordination failures, 129
interventionism, 2, 5, 8, 20, 232–3, 246, *see also* noninterventionism
  beliefs in, 243–4
  institutionalism on, 209
  in Keynesian economics, 12, 122
  in rational expectations model, 234–5, 236
intrinsic rewards, 106–7
inverse elasticity rule, 214
invisible hand concept, 62
involuntary unemployment, 131, 132, 139, 141–2
IS-LM model, 100, 165, 174

Japan, 73
job search theory, 109, 114

Kaldor-Hicks extension/revision, 218
Kaleckian economics, 13, 124, 132, 133–4, 147
Kant, Immanuel, 22
Keynesian economics, 2, 5–6, 7, 8, 9, 12–3, 19, 61–74, 121–51, 231–2, 237–9, 243, 244, 245, 247
  Brunner-Meltzer monetarism compared with, 172, 174, 175
  conceptual theory compared with, 240
  critical Marxism compared with, 78, 233
  evolution of, 64–5
  future development of, 70–4
  Great Depression and, 5, 6, 55, 63, 64, 231
  mercantilism and, 51
  monetarism compared with, 14, 65, 70, 74, 160, 161, 176, 177, 179

  new, 13, 121, 132, 135–43, 145, 147
  post, *see* post-Keynesian economics
  quantity theory compared with, 163, 164–5, 166–7, 168, 170, 171
  return to, 74
  theory/policy correspondence in, 63–4
  underemployment equilibrium in, 6, 65–70, 139
Keynesian-neoclassical synthesis, 7, 69–70, 71–4, 137

labor demand, 6–7, 64, 67, 101, 143–4
labor market segmentation, 132
labor productivity, 133, 218
labor supply, 6–7, 64, 66–7, 101
laissez-faire
  institutionalism and, 208–9
  Keynesian economics and, 12, 122
  postrevolutionary movement and, 53, 55
leading economic indicators, 10, 99–100, 235, 236
learning curves, 11, 108–10, 115
legitimation, 3, 35, 36, 40, 44n.14
liberal institutionalism, 78, 82
libertarian anarchists, 53
liquid assets, 170, 171
liquidity preference theory, 6, 64, 65, 73
logic, 34
Logic: The Theory of Inquiry, 16, 199
logical empiricism, 28

macrodistribution of income, 133
macroeconomic externalities, 138
macroeconomics, 1, 2, 13, 18, 101, 115, 129, 135
  contemporary, 162–3
  evolution of, 61–2
  Great Depression and, 5, 231

Keynesian, *see* Keynesian
    economics
  in mid-1950s, 13–4, 161–2
  monetarism and, 13–4, 159–60
  postrevolutionary movement and,
    51, 55–6
  quantity theory and, 165
magic of the market, *see* miracle of
    the market
manageability, 3, 34
marginal efficiency of capital, 6, 64
marginal efficiency of investment,
    166–7
marginalist revolution, 54, 55
marginal labor productivity, 218
marginal propensity to consume,
    100–1
market coordination theory, 55,
    see also coordination failures
market exchange, 53
market structure, 131–2
Marshallian theory, 4, 14, 34, 39, 56,
    237
  in Brunner-Meltzer monetarism,
    173
  in new Keynesian economics,
    136
  in post-Keynesian economics, 12,
    124, 128–9, 131, 133, 147
Marxism
  critical, *see* critical Marxian
    economics
  economic order in, 32
  official, 8, 77, 78, 79, 91
  postrevolutionary movement and,
    48, 54–5
materialism, 87–8
mathematization
  institutionalism and, 214–7
  postrevolutionary movement and,
    55–6
maximization paradigm, 4, 47, 49,
    55–6
medieval Europe, 87
menu costs approach, 140–2
mercantilism, 51, 55, 57, 242
"Methodology of Positive
    Economics", 129
Michigan model, 7, 70, 71

microeconomics, 2, 107–8, 115
  Great Depression and, 5, 231
  new Keynesian economics and,
    135
  post-Keynesian economics and,
    129
migration, 73
minor movements, 169–70
miracle of the market, 56–9, 74
modeling techniques, 10, 235
models, 3, 23
monetarism, 2, 7, 13–5, 19–20,
    159–83, 239, 244, 247, *see also*
    Brunner-Meltzer monetarism;
    quantity theory
  economic order in, 32
  Keynesian economics compared
    with, 14, 65, 70, 74, 160, 161,
    176, 177, 179
  monetary policy in, 14, 162,
    175–9
  new Keynesian economics
    compared with, 136
*Monetary History of the United
    States*, 177, 178
monetary policies, 101
  in conceptual economic theory,
    191
  discretionary, 14, 176–9, 239
  in Keynesian economics, 63, 64,
    65, 144
  in monetarism, 14, 162, 175–9
monetary shocks, 145–6, 168, 175
money
  nominal, 136, 139
  in post-Keynesian economics,
    129–31
money demand, 173–4
money illusion, 6, 66–7, 68, 135, 136
money markets, 166, 174
money neutrality/nonneutrality, 139,
    140, 144, 145
money supply, 101
  in Brunner-Meltzer monetarism,
    174
  in Keynesian economics, 144, 161
  in monetarism, 161, 179, 239, 244
  in new Keynesian economics, 139
  in quantity theory, 167, 168–9

monopolies
  in conceptual economic theory,
    189
  in institutionalism, 209
  in post-Keynesian economics,
    133–4
moving averages, 10, 98–100, 235
multiple equilibria, 102
multiplier effects, 138, 139, 174
multiplier principle, 63
M–1 velocity, 178, 179, 180
M–2 velocity, 170, 180

Nash equilibrium, 137, 138–9, 191,
    192–4
national income and product
    accounts (NIPA), 72, 73
nationality conflicts, 81, 86
natural equilibrium, 127
natural laws, 127–8, 210
natural prices, 125
natural-rate hypothesis, 175–6
neoclassical economics, 2, 4, 40, 41,
    43n.4, 163, *see also* Keynesian-
    neoclassical synthesis
  Brunner-Meltzer monetarism
    compared with, 172
  consequences of dependence on,
    221–3
  critical Marxian economics
    compared with, 8, 77, 78, 79, 82,
    83, 93, 94
  determinism and, 26
  economic order in, 32
  institutionalism compared with,
    16–7, 197, 198, 199, 200, 207–23
  Keynesian economics compared
    with, 122, 123, 245
  post-Keynesian economics
    compared with, 130, 132
  postrevolutionary movement and,
    48
neo-Ricardian economics, 130–1,
    148n.2
neo-Walrasian approach, 125
new institutional economics, 59
new Keynesian economics, 13, 121,
    132, 135–43, 145, 147

nominal income determination,
    theory of, 161
nominal money, 136, 139
nominal prices, 65
nominal rigidities, 13, 139–43, 145–6
nominal shocks, 140, 141, 142
nominal wage rates, 66, 133–4
noninterventionism, 2, 5, 7, 9, 18, 19,
    230–1, 232–3, 246, *see also*
    interventionism
  beliefs in, 243–4
  in conceptual theory, 240
  Keynesian economics and, 74
non-Walrasian theory, 128, 135
normal cost pricing hypothesis, 134
normative-positive dualism, 2, 3, 36,
    239
  conceptual economic theory and,
    15, 20, 187–8, 190, 239–40,
    247–8
  critical Marxian economics and, 9
  institutionalism and, 17, 205–6,
    213, 233, 240, 241
normative theory, 24, 35

official Marxian economics, 8, 77, 78,
    79, 91
oligopolies, 133, 134, 198, 209
optimal control theory, 59
optimal growth theory, 59
optimal taxation, 59
Optimum Quantity of Money, The,
    163
ordinal utility theory, 208
organization theory, 198
organizing principles, 3, 33–4
output
  Cauchy-Pareto distribution of, 11
  Keynesian economics and, 143–4
  post-Keynesian economics and,
    130, 133
  production functions in, 110–13
output pricing, 54

paradigms, 3, 4, 25, 77–8, 89, *see
    also* specific paradigms
  defined, 77

Pareto efficient, 187
Pareto-efficiency full-employment
  equilibrium, 13, 139
Pareto inefficiency, 138
Pareto-inferior underemployment
  equilibrium, 139
Pareto-inferior unemployment
  equilibrium, 13
Pareto optimality, 207, 217–9
pattern models, 27
perfect competition
  in new Keynesian economics, 13,
    137–8, 139–40
  in post-Keynesian economics,
    131–2
perfect equilibrium, 15–6, 188,
  191–4, 247
  subgame, 16, 192–4
Phillips curve, 7, 65, 68–9, 100, 101
Pigouvian economics, 136
pleasure-pain calculus, 211
political class conflicts, see
  social-political class conflicts
Popperian epistemology, 22
portfolio analysis, 7, 72
positive reinforcement, 104
positive theory, 24, see also
    normative-positive dualism
  critical Marxian economics and,
    77, 88
  prescriptive use of, 35
post-Keynesian economics, 12–3, 78,
  121, 123–4, 144–5, 148n.2, 198
  economic order in, 32
  effective demand in, 124, 125, 126,
    132–5
  financial requirements in, 132–5
  monetarism compared with, 163
  new Keynesian economics
    compared with, 135, 137
  radical, 78
  strand 1 of, 12, 123, 124–8
  strand 2 of, 12, 124, 128–32, 147
  strand 3 of, 12–3, 124, 128, 132–5,
    147
post-Marshall economics, 56
postrevolutionary movement, 47–60
  constitutional framework for, 48,
    52–3, 58
  miracle of the market in, 56–9

pragmatic instrumental inquiry,
    theory of, see social inquiry
predeterminism, 8, 77, 78, 89–92
prediction, 29, 30–1, 35, 231–2
prescription, 3, 35, 40
price rigidity
  Keynesian economics and,
    145–6
  new Keynesian economics and,
    135–6, 137
  post-Keynesian economics and,
    133–4
prices
  commodity, 72
  input, 54, 55
  institutionalism and, 208
  macroeconomics and, 62
  monetarism and, 162
  natural, 125
  new Keynesian economics and,
    139–41
  nominal, 65
  output, 54
  quantity theory on, 167, 168, 170
  Ramsey, 214
price staggering, 140
price stickiness, 169
price-theory model, 212–3, 221
pricing-cum-investment hypothesis,
    134
production functions, 108, 110–13,
    115, 123
  Cobb-Douglas, 11, 112
  Keynesian economics and, 64, 69
  rational expectations model and,
    11
profit maximizing, 208, 217
profits
  in critical Marxian economics, 82
  in institutionalism, 218
  in post-Keynesian economics, 133,
    134
  uniform rate of, 124, 125
projection, 4, 36–7, 40
propensity to consume, 6, 64, 100–1,
    167–8
property rights, 59, 84
protectionism, 63
psychic balm, 4, 29, 36, 37–8, 40,
    41

public-choice theory, 2, 4–5, 18, 55, 59, 177, 231
public-interest theory, 162, 163

quantity-adjustment costs, 141
quantity theory, 14, 40, 159, 160, 163–71, 180n.4, 180–1n.5, 181n.9, 239
  Brunner-Meltzer monetarism compared with, 172, 173, 174–5
  monetary policy in, 176, 177, 178
  rhetoric of, 164–6

racial conflicts, 8, 79, 81, 84–5, 86, 87
radical economics, 2, 82
radical indeterminacy, 37–8, 40
radical institutionalism, 78
radical post-Keynesian economics, 78
Ramsey pricing, 214
rational expectations model, 2, 9–11, 19, 100–1, 220–1, 234–7, 244
  Brunner-Meltzer monetarism and, 173, 175
  criticisms of, 101–3
  Keynesian economics and, 123
  new Keynesian economics and, 135, 136
  quantity theory and, 165–6
rationalism, 97–8
  in critical Marxian economics, 78, 87–8
Reagan administration, 84
real income distribution, 200
realism, 122–3, 124, 125, 132
reality
  definition of, 31–2, 35, 41
  social construction of, 3, 29, 35, 40
real rigidities, 13, 139–43
real wage rigidity, 141
real wages
  in institutionalism, 208, 218
  in Keynesian economics, 66, 67, 143–4
  in post-Keynesian economics, 133–4
recessions, 144, 179
reciprocal externalities, 137–8

regulatory theory, 198
religious conflicts, 86
reserves, 178, 179
resource allocation, 9, 18, 19, 49, 56
reverse causation, 169, 171
revolution, 9, 86, 87, 92
rewards, 106–7
rhetoric
  of Brunner-Meltzer monetarism, 172–3
  of quantity theory, 164–6
  roles of in theory, 3, 33–4
Ricardian theory, 54, 130–1, 148n.2, 171, 242
rigor, 28, 33, 43–4n.10
risk aversion, 140, 143, 144, 145
romanticism, 54–5

salary/education correlation, 188–9
Say's law, 44n.11, 129, 137, 208
science, economics as, 39–40
scientific determinism, 8, 9, 78, 89–92
self-employment, 137
self-interest, 18
  conceptual theory and, 16
  monetarism and, 162, 163, 177
  postrevolutionary movement and, 47–8, 51
semi-rule, 178
shocks, 144, 167–8
  monetary, 145–6, 168, 175
  nominal, 140, 141, 142
  supply-side, 69
signaling, 15, 188–91, 247
Smith, Adam, 5, 38, 51–2, 57, 61–2, 125, 242, 243
social choice theory, 59
social construction of reality, 3, 29, 35, 40
social control, 4, 18, 29, 35, 36, 37, 40, 41
social inquiry, 197, 199–207
socialism, 83, 209, see also Postrevolutionary movement
  failure of, 4–5, 18, 47–9
  miracle of the market and, 56–9
socialism in the large, 18, 60
socialism in the small, 18, 60

social-political class conflicts, 77, 81, 83–5
social structure, 8, 79–80, 81
Soviet revolution, 86
Soviet Union, 52, 78, 84, 89
speculation, 63, 162
spontaneous order paradigm, 5, 231
Sraffian economics, 123, 130
St. Louis equation, 160
stable consumption, 165
stable equilibrium, 191
stable velocity, 165
stagflation, 69
stagnation, theory of, 133
Stalinism, 9, 79, 88
statistical theory of reliability, 110
stochastic theories, 109
storytelling, 39, 40
strategic complementarity, 137–9, 140–1
strikes, 82
Studies in the Quantity Theory of Money, 161
stylized facts, 20, 30, 129
subgame-perfect equilibrium, 16, 192–4
substitution curves, 11, 108
supply-side functions, 7–8, 64, 65–6, 70, 74, 145
supply-side shocks, 69
surplus value theory, 54
symmetric information, 13, 137

tautology, 3, 27–8
taxation
    capital gains, 82, 85
    Keynesian macroeconomics and, 63, 64, 65, 74
    monetarism and, 162
    optimal, 59
technical inefficiency, 103
technology, 10–11, 12, 97–8, 107–14
tendency statements, 27
theoretical pluralism, 41, 42n.2
theory-laden facts, 30
Theory of Economic Dynamics, 133
theory of the firm, 10, 107–8, 110, 115

theory of the household, 115
time-series analysis, 98–9, 101
trade unions, *see* unions
transaction cost analysis, 198, 214
Treatise on Money, 244
Treaty of Versailles, 63
true uncertainty, 128
truth, 3, 16, 24
two-factor model, 104

uncertainty
    Keynesian economics and, 145
    new Keynesian economics and, 136
    post-Keynesian economics and, 128, 129–31
    true, 128
underemployment equilibrium, 6, 65–70, 139
understanding, 32, 35, 41
unemployment, 231, 233, 243, *see also* employment
    involuntary, *see* involuntary unemployment
    Keynesian economics and, 65–70
    monetarism and, 14, 176
    new Keynesian economics and, 137–9, 141–2
    post-Keynesian economics and, 133–4
unemployment benefits, 82
unemployment equilibrium, 13, 101
    new Keynesian economics and, 139–43
    post-Keynesian economics and, 126, 131, 132
uniform rate of profits, 124, 125
unions, 66, 82, 132, 142
United States, immigration to, 73
utilitarianism, 54–5
utility maximizing, 208, 211–2, 217

validity, 3, 24
velocity, 14, 167
    M-1, 178, 179, 180
    M-2, 170, 180
    stable, 165

voluntarism, 89–90
voting, 83, 84

wage-determination equation,
  67–9
wage rates, 65, 66–9
  nominal, 66, 133–4
wage rigidity, 135–6, 137, 141
  in post-Keynesian economics,
  132
  real, 141
wages, 104–5, 107
  in critical Marxian economics, 82
  efficiency, 141–2, 143–4, 150n.28
  in new Keynesian economics,
  140–2
  real, *see* real wages
wage staggering, 140
wage stickiness, 12, 66, 132

Walrasian economics, 125, 128, 131,
  135
  Brunner-Meltzer monetarism and,
  173
  new Keynesian economics and, 13,
  136, 137, 138, 139
warranted assertions, 17, 205, 206,
  217, 241
Wealth of Nations, The, 51–2
wealth variables, 173–4, 239
Weibull distributions, 110
Western countries, 59–60
Western Europe, 73
wishful thinking, 4, 18, 27, 36, 41
women's movement, 84–5, 234
workability, 3, 24
working class, 8, 82–3, 84, 86, 233–4

X-efficiency, 10, 103